The Seven Dwarfs
and the Age of the Mandarins
AUSTRALIAN GOVERNMENT ADMINISTRATION
IN THE POST-WAR RECONSTRUCTION ERA

The Seven Dwarfs
and the Age of the Mandarins
AUSTRALIAN GOVERNMENT ADMINISTRATION
IN THE POST-WAR RECONSTRUCTION ERA

EDITED BY SAMUEL FURPHY

PRESS

Published by ANU Press
The Australian National University
Acton ACT 2601, Australia
Email: anupress@anu.edu.au
This title is also available online at http://press.anu.edu.au

---

National Library of Australia Cataloguing-in-Publication entry

Title: The seven dwarfs and the age of the mandarins : Australian government administration in the post-war reconstruction era / editor Samuel Furphy.

ISBN: 9781925022322 (paperback) 9781925022339 (ebook)

Subjects: Government executives--Australia--Biography.
            Civil service--Australia--History.
            Public administration--Australia--History.
            Reconstruction (1939–1951)--Australia--History.
            Postwar reconstruction--Australia--History.
            Federal government--Australia--History.
            Australia--Officials and employees--Biography.
            Australia--Politics and government--1945– .

Other Creators/Contributors:
            Furphy, Samuel, editor.

Dewey Number: 352.30994

All rights reserved. No part of this publication may be reproduced, stored in a retrieval system or transmitted in any form or by any means, electronic, mechanical, photocopying or otherwise, without the prior permission of the publisher.

The ANU.Lives Series in Biography is an initiative of the National Centre of Biography at The Australian National University, http://ncb.anu.edu.au/.

Cover design by ANU Press

Layout by ANU Press

This edition © 2015 ANU Press

Contents

Illustrations vii
Contributors ix
Acknowledgements xiii
Preface xv
    J.R. Nethercote and Samuel Furphy

Part I

1. The Seven Dwarfs: A Team of Rivals 3
    Nicholas Brown

2. The Post-War Reconstruction Project 31
    Stuart Macintyre

3. Australia and the Keynesian Revolution 53
    Alex Millmow

4. An Age of the Mandarins? Government in
   New Zealand, 1940–51 81
    John R. Martin

Part II

5. Sir Frederick Shedden: The Forerunner 113
    David Horner

6. Sir Roland Wilson – *Primus Inter Pares* 125
    Selwyn Cornish

7. Coombs the Keynesian 143
    Tim Rowse

8. Sir John Crawford and Agriculture and Trade 169
    David Lee

9. Sir Allen Brown: An Exemplary Public Servant 183
    Sir Peter Lawler

10. Sir Frederick Wheeler: Public Servant 191
    Ian Hancock

11. Paul Hasluck with Dr Evatt at the United Nations 209
    Geoffrey Bolton

12. John Burton: Forgotten Mandarin? 219
    Adam Hughes Henry

13. Sir Arthur Tange: Departmental Reformer 233
    Peter Edwards

14. Sir James Plimsoll: Mandarin Abroad 241
    Jeremy Hearder

Illustrations

Sir Robert Garran, c1930	xvii
J.B. (Ben) Chifley, c1949	10
Robert Menzies, c1950	17
Sir Henry Bland, 1966	25
Sir Richard Randall, 1966	27
H.C. Coombs with Prime Minister Ben Chifley in London, 1946	35
John Dedman, 1941	37
Dr H.C. (Nugget) Coombs, 1942	41
Sir Douglas Berry Copland, 1951	54
Professor L.F. Giblin, portrait by Sir William Dobell, c1945	56
Peter Fraser, c1940	82
B.C. (Sir Bernard) Ashwin, c1955	86
Sir Frederick Shedden with Prime Minister John Curtin and Mrs Curtin, 1944	115
Sir Roland Wilson, 1965	134
Dr H.C. (Nugget) Coombs, 1950	146
Sir John Crawford, 1967	171
Sir Allen Brown, 1958	184
Frederick Wheeler, 1959	194
Paul Hasluck, 1954	211
Dr H.V. Evatt at the United Nations, 1949	215
Dr John Wear Burton, c1951	222
Sir Arthur Tange, 1965	237
Sir James Plimsoll, 1965	243

Contributors

Geoffrey Bolton is senior scholar in residence at Murdoch University (Chancellor 2002–06) and an emeritus professor at Edith Cowan University. He continues to research and write on Australian history, British Commonwealth history, and eighteenth and early nineteenth-century British and Irish history. His most recent book is *Paul Hasluck: A Life* (2014).

Nicholas Brown is a professor of history in the Research School of Social Sciences at The Australian National University. He is the author of several books including *Governing Prosperity: Social Analysis and Social Change in Australia in the 1950s* (1995) and *A History of Canberra* (2014). He is currently working on a collaborative study of Sir John Crawford with Stuart McIntyre, David Lee, Frank Bongiorno, and Dennis Blight.

Selwyn Cornish is an adjunct associate professor in the Research School of Economics at The Australian National University, and the official historian of the Reserve Bank of Australia. He is the author of *The Evolution of Central Banking in Australia* (2010), and (with William Coleman and Alf Hagger) *Giblin's Platoon: The Trials and Triumphs of the Economist in Australian Public Life* (2006).

Peter Edwards is an historian and biographer, who has published extensively on Australian and international history and politics. He is the author of *Arthur Tange: Last of the Mandarins* (2006), which won the Queensland Premier's Literary Award for history and the Western Australian Premier's Book Award for non-fiction.

Samuel Furphy is a research fellow in the National Centre of Biography at The Australian National University, where he has worked as a research editor for the *Australian Dictionary of Biography* since 2010. His most recent book is *Edward M. Curr and the Tide of History* (2013), based on his doctoral research at the University of Melbourne. He is currently the recipient of an Australian Research Council early career research award.

Ian Hancock is an historian and biographer and a former lecturer at Monash University and The Australian National University. A leading historian of the Liberal Party in Australia, he is the author of several political biographies and is currently completing a biography of a former Attorney General and leading barrister, Tom Hughes. He is also working with Nicholas Brown on a biography of Sir Frederick Wheeler.

Jeremy Hearder studied at Melbourne and Stanford universities before serving as an Australian diplomat for 38 years. His postings abroad were Vientiane, Dar es Salaam, Bangkok, Nairobi, Brussels, Harare (as High Commissioner), Suva (as High Commissioner), Chicago (as Consul General), and Wellington (as Deputy High Commissioner). He is the author of *Jim Plim Ambassador Extraordinary: A Biography of Sir James Plimsoll* (2015).

Adam Hughes Henry completed a PhD thesis in the School of History, Research School of Social Sciences, at The Australian National University in 2012. A book based on his thesis, *The Gatekeepers and Australian Foreign Policy*, will be published in 2015. He is currently a visiting fellow in the ANU College of Asia & the Pacific, and a research associate in the Faculty of Arts and Design at the University of Canberra.

David Horner is an emeritus professor in the Strategic and Defence Studies Centre at The Australian National University, where he has worked since 1990. Earlier he served for 25 years in the Australian Army. He is the author or editor of 32 books, including *Defence Supremo: Sir Frederick Shedden and the Making of Australian Defence Policy* (2000) and *The Spy Catchers: The Official History of ASIO, Volume I: 1949–1963* (2014).

Sir Peter Lawler joined the Department of Post-War Reconstruction in 1944 and transferred to the Prime Minister's Department in 1950. He was deputy secretary from 1964 before serving as secretary of the departments of the Special Minister of State (1972–75) then Administrative Services (1975–83). From 1983, until his retirement in 1986, he was Ambassador to the Republic of Ireland and Ambassador to the Holy See.

David Lee is director of the Historical Publications and Information Section of the Department of Foreign Affairs and Trade. He has published several books on the history of Australian foreign policy, international history, and the history of the British Empire and Commonwealth. He is currently writing a history of mining in Australia after 1960, and working on a collaborative study of Sir John Crawford.

Stuart Macintyre is an emeritus laureate professor of the University of Melbourne. He is the author of many books, including *The History Wars* (2003, with Anna Clark) and a co-editor (with Alison Bashford) of *The Cambridge History of Australia* (2013). His history of post-war reconstruction, *Australia's Boldest Experiment: War and Reconstruction*, will be published in 2015.

John R. Martin was a public servant for over 30 years in New Zealand, serving in the Department of Island Territories, the Treasury, the Department of Health, and the New Zealand Planning Council. He has also taught public policy at the School of Government at Victoria University of Wellington.

Alex Millmow is an associate professor of economics at Federation University, Ballarat, and a former officer of the Commonwealth Treasury. He has published extensively on Keynesian economics and is a founder and co-editor of the *Journal of Economic and Social Policy*.

J.R. Nethercote is an adjunct professor at the Australian Catholic University, Canberra Campus. At different times he worked for the Public Service Board, the Royal Commission on Australian Government Administration, the Public Service Commission of Canada, and the Senate Standing Committee on Finance and Public Administration. He edited the *Canberra Bulletin of Public Administration* for 20 years. Among the books he has edited or jointly edited are *Parliament and Bureaucracy* (1982), *The Menzies Era* (1995), *The House on Capital Hill* (1996) and *Liberalism and the Australian Federation* (2001).

Tim Rowse is a professorial fellow at the University of Western Sydney. He has worked mainly within the history discipline, but his formal training is in government, sociology and anthropology. He is the author or editor of many books, including two on H.C. Coombs: *Nugget Coombs: A Reforming Life* (2002) and *Obliged to be Difficult: Nugget Coombs' Legacy in Indigenous Affairs* (2000).

Acknowledgements

This book, and the conference that preceded it, was made possible by the generous support of several organisations, including the Public Policy Institute at the Australian Catholic University, the Australia and New Zealand School of Government, the Academy of Social Sciences in Australia, the Economic Society of Australia, and the Museum of Australian Democracy. Convened by the National Centre of Biography at The Australian National University, the conference received funding from the ANU College of Arts and Social Sciences, and the Research School of Social Sciences.

The editor wishes to thank several people for their contribution to the book. John Nethercote played a crucial role in assembling a group of talented speakers for the conference, and his expertise has shaped the book in various other ways. Christine Fernon and Karen Ciuffetelli, from the National Centre of Biography, contributed greatly to the successful organisation of the conference. I would like to thank the editorial board of the ANU.Lives Series and the three anonymous reviewers for their helpful suggestions regarding the draft manuscript. I am also indebted to Geoff Hunt for his precise copyediting, and to the team at ANU Press for design and production. Finally, I would like to thank the contributors, who have provided a diverse and fascinating range of informative and well-researched essays.

Preface

J.R. Nethercote and Samuel Furphy

One evening during the early 1980s the then speaker of the House of Representatives, Sir Billy Snedden, a former treasurer and leader of the Liberal Party, was in an expansive mood following a hearty dinner in the warm comfortable dining room of what is now called Old Parliament House. In the course of much reminiscence and anecdotage the topic of the 'Seven Dwarfs' came up – the formidable public service figures who rose to so much eminence in the Australian government during the Second World War and in the post-war reconstruction era. But who precisely were these dwarfs?[1]

Three names came readily to mind. First and foremost there was Sir Roland Wilson – Australian statistician; secretary of Labour and National Service (1940–46); economic adviser to the Treasury; secretary to the Treasury (1951–66); and thereafter chair of both the Commonwealth Bank and Qantas. There was Dr H.C. 'Nugget' Coombs – director-general, Post-War Reconstruction (1943–49); thence governor of the Commonwealth Bank and, following its establishment in 1960, the Reserve Bank of Australia; he was later chair of both the Arts Council (now the Australia Council) and the Council for Aboriginal Affairs. Later still, he headed the Royal Commission on Australian Government Administration (1974–76). And, always on any list, Sir John Crawford – foundation director of the Bureau of Agricultural Economics; secretary, Department of Commerce and Agriculture (1950–56), thence Trade (1956–60); followed by a succession of posts at The Australian National University culminating in the vice-chancellorship and, finally, in succession to Coombs, the chancellor.

Various other names were suggested: Sir Frederick Shedden, long-time head of Defence; Sir Kenneth Bailey, the solicitor-general and head of Attorney-General's, subsequently high commissioner to Canada; the statistician Stan Carver; Sir Allen Brown, Coombs' successor at Post-War Reconstruction, later head of Prime Minister's Department; Sir Henry Bland at Labour in Melbourne, later secretary, Department of Defence; and Sir Richard Randall, Wilson's successor at the Treasury.

But was there no definitive list? Sir Billy would find out from the experts. The Parliamentary Library was contacted and it went to work with a will.

---

1   The first part of this preface is largely based on an article published in 2010: J.R. Nethercote, 'Unearthing the Seven Dwarfs and the Age of the Mandarins', *Canberra Times*, 5 October 2010, 'Public Sector Informant', 26–7.

The Seven Dwarfs and the Age of the Mandarins

Not long afterwards, a very senior figure from the library personally provided the speaker with the answer to his question: Doc, Dopey, Sleepy, Sneezy, Happy, Bashful and Grumpy. The speaker was incandescent! – fortunately this was the era before performance bonuses. Next day the lofty figure from the library defended himself rhetorically – well, what would you have said?

Even to this day, the identity of the seven dwarfs remains a matter of dinner party conversation. As also is the identity of Snow White. Conventional wisdom usually sees Ben Chifley as Snow White. But was it Menzies? What is not in doubt is why the seven dwarfs and their generation were important. They were not simply present when the Australia of the middle years of the twentieth century took shape; they were, in many respects, the architects. Sparked by the Second World War, but continuing through the long post-war boom, the size of government and the range of its responsibilities grew. Central to this growth was the increasing ascendancy of the Commonwealth in the affairs of the federation. Government became more active and more interventionist. Extensive activity within Australia was reflected by comparable activity in numerous conferences abroad, to which Australia sent representatives, ranging from Bretton Woods where the international monetary system was established, to the creation of the United Nations itself, as well as the Food and Agriculture Organization, and the General Agreement on Tariffs and Trade. The policies being promoted were markedly Keynesian in character, especially in advocacy of full employment, and, in the welfare field, strongly influenced by the 1942 report by Sir William Beveridge.

This was the era of the first sustained endeavours by the Commonwealth to equip itself with substantial policy capacity. Hitherto, the Commonwealth, to the extent it recognised a need for strength in policy, relied on *ad hoc* arrangements, usually involving academics to fill the need. For example, several professors of economics had been on hand as the Commonwealth tried to deal with the Depression, including L.F. Giblin and Douglas Copland from the University of Melbourne, Edward Shann from Western Australia (later Adelaide), and Leslie Melville from Adelaide. The need for greater strength had been felt by S.M. Bruce, prime minister from 1923 until 1929, but not effectively addressed; the Depression revealed, however, serious weaknesses in the public service in terms of policy capacity.

An exception to this early rule was Sir Robert Garran, secretary of the Attorney-General's Department from the inception of the Commonwealth and solicitor-general from 1917. Garran was unquestionably a mandarin, a statesman in disguise. Relatively unusually for the time, he had university degrees, in arts and law. Prior to his Commonwealth career he was a barrister in Sydney. He did not work his way up through the ranks – he came in at the top. When he retired in 1932, however, he left a public service hostile to graduates except those with professional degrees, mainly law, engineering and medicine. It was also a public service in which the road to the top largely began at the bottom.

Sir Robert Garran, c1930

Source: National Library of Australia, nla.pic-an23435998

An important and necessary step forward was taken in 1935 when the Lyons Government secured an amendment to the public service legislation authorising direct recruitment of graduates to administrative posts, albeit on very restrictive terms. It is doubtful that even this modest move would have eventuated had its principal advocate not been General Sir John Monash. His interest at least neutralised opposition from returned servicemen who then dominated the general administrative ranks of the public service, and the applicable unions. But the strength of union opposition, indeed, hostility, to any special appointments was very evident a few years later when Roland Wilson was recruited to the then Bureau of Census and Statistics (now the ABS), and shortly afterwards elevated to the post of statistician. The then Department of External Affairs (now Foreign Affairs and Trade) commenced recruitment of graduates in 1937; early recruits included Keith Waller, subsequently a secretary of the department; and Peter Heydon who, as secretary to the Department of Immigration during the 1960s, played an influential role in overturning the White Australia policy.

The Treasury organised its first search for graduates in 1939. Frederick Wheeler, who had already come to Canberra with Copland, was the first recruit; he would later head the department. Wheeler had previously worked for the State Savings Bank of Victoria whilst completing a degree in commerce at the University of Melbourne. The banks were a major source of quality personnel for the Commonwealth public service. Coombs came from the Commonwealth Bank, to which he returned as a board member in 1943 and as governor in 1949. The Bank of New South Wales, now Westpac, was especially significant. Alfred Davidson, the general manager, had systematically developed the bank's capacities in economics since the 1930s. Under the guidance of Edward Shann, an Economics Department was built up. Among its alumni who eventually found their way into government were Arthur Tange (who also attended the Bretton Woods meetings), James Plimsoll, John Crawford, Walter Ives, and Ron Mendelsohn.

Other famous names came directly to government from university. John Burton, secretary at External Affairs from 1947 to 1950, secured the first public service postgraduate scholarship for doctoral research at the London School of Economics. L.F. 'Fin' Crisp joined the Department of Labour on return from Oxford where he had been studying on a Rhodes scholarship. He later shifted to Post-War Reconstruction and was director-general when the department was abolished in 1950. Among the early graduate recruits, economists predominated. In those days, economics had a breadth that it has largely lost in later more specialist times. More interestingly, many of these graduates had studied Keynes' *General Theory* first hand, directly from proof copies of the book sent to economics professors around the Empire. But other disciplines were not unrepresented – there were some lawyers and even some graduates in arts.

From the beginning there were differences of opinion among this new elite, in the first instance over the relative roles of tax and loans in financing the war effort. With the passage of time, and as the focus increasingly moved from fighting the war to preparing for peace, argument grew around the relative merits of government activity and intervention versus market-based methods. There were likewise contests between those for whom the primary purpose was growth and those with an eye to distribution. These battles continued for several decades and their ghosts are still present today. In institutional terms they centred around the Treasury, apostle of growth and sceptical of intervention, and the Department of Trade, especially keen on government activism, particularly in its guise from 1963 as the Department of Trade and Industry.

Other countries took a similar path to Australia, with certain national variations. In New Zealand, for example, the minister of finance, Gordon Coates, established a 'brains trust' of economists and civil servants to advise him in the mid-1930s. In Whitehall, the influx of new people occasioned by the war included a number of women; not very long afterwards the Attlee Government removed the prohibition on permanent employment of married women. At the administrative level, women hardly figure in the Australian story. One who did was Wilmot Debenham, wife of Jock Phillips, Coombs' successor as governor of the Reserve Bank. Having worked as an assistant to Leslie Melville at the Commonwealth Bank in the 1930s, Debenham joined the Commonwealth Rationing Commission during the Second World War. Coombs wrote that she 'was in many ways the mainstay of the team which devised the clothes rationing "scale"'.[2] She was subsequently secretary (1943–44) to the Commonwealth Housing Commission, for which she co-authored an influential report. In the Department of Labour and National Service, two other women are notable: the welfare activist Constance Duncan produced a report in 1944 on the children of working mothers; while the teacher and author Flora Eldershaw gave advice on women's legal rights, working conditions, and equal pay. The contribution of women to the Australian public service was limited, however, by both prevailing attitudes to gender roles and a prohibition on the permanent employment of married women, which was not lifted until 1966.

By a quirk, a number of the most able of those coming into the Commonwealth public service in this period, especially after the outbreak of war in 1939, were conspicuous for their diminutive height as well as for their intellectual qualities. All the 'dwarfs', whether the long list or the shorter more definitive list, became departmental or agency heads, and many of their generation rose to the top of the public service in succeeding decades. Their careers were unusual. Many of them dealt only with people at the top – ministers or department heads; because of the circumstances of the war and post-war reconstruction they had a much broader canvas on which to work than did later generations of officialdom. It was a fascinating period of government and in society. The dwarfs and their peers give the period character, colour, personality and vitality, which the story might otherwise lack.

The impetus for this volume, and the 2010 conference upon which it is based, was a realisation that the 'Seven Dwarfs' and their colleague mandarins had

---

2   H.C. Coombs, *Trial Balance* (South Melbourne: Macmillan, 1981), 18.

begun to appear in the pages of the *Australian Dictionary of Biography (ADB)*, notably in volumes 17 and 18, and in the lists of names for volumes currently in preparation. While all were granted longer than usual entries, the biographical chapters in this book provide a fuller portrait than is possible in the *ADB*, which is primarily a work of reference. A further aim of this book is to place these important lives in context – to conceive of them as a discernible group representing a highly significant period in the history of the Australian public service. The book is divided into two parts: the first contains four thematic chapters; the second is composed of 10 biographical chapters. The 14 chapter authors represent a variety of disciplinary backgrounds, including history, political science, sociology, and economics. The biographical chapters are varied in style and intent. Some are the distilled conclusions of academic research; others are lively recollections of senior public servants with extensive personal experience of their subjects. Some offer a conventional narrative-style sketch; some are impressionistic; while others focus on a specific theme or event in the life of their subject. This rich combination of academic disciplines and biographical styles is deliberate, adding greatly to the depth of the book. Several of the seven men most commonly considered to be the 'Seven Dwarfs' are featured in this book. The omission of others, and the inclusion of taller but otherwise similar contemporaries, is a product of the expertise available at the conference in 2010.

In Chapter 1, the first of the thematic chapters, Nicholas Brown provides a detailed assessment of the possible identities of the 'Seven Dwarfs', but more importantly considers the usefulness of the phrase (and the related term, 'Mandarin') as a means of understanding a significant era in the history of the Australian public service. This is followed by Stuart Macintyre's account of the Department of Post-War Reconstruction and its importance in the era of the public service mandarin; not only did three of the seven dwarfs play key roles in the department, but it was a training ground for a large number of future department heads. In Chapter 3, Alex Millmow explores the impact in Australia of the revolution in economic theory sparked by John Maynard Keynes, noting the significant influence of Keynesian thought on many of the key public service figures in the post-war period. John Martin's Chapter 4 then provides a valuable point of comparison, exploring the history of New Zealand's public service during and immediately after the Second World War.

In the first of the biographical chapters, David Horner draws on his biography of Sir Frederick Shedden to paint a more concise portrait; Shedden is often counted one of the seven dwarfs, but differed from his colleagues in significant ways, not least because he rose to the top during the 1930s after two decades in the ranks. In Chapter 6, Selwyn Cornish assesses the life and influence of Sir Roland Wilson, whom he credits with transforming the Treasury into a department whose key role was the provision of economic advice to government. In Chapter 7,

Tim Rowse provides not a biographical sketch of 'Nugget' Coombs, but a detailed analysis of his engagement with Keynesian economics immediately prior to the Second World War. In Chapter 8, David Lee focuses particularly on Sir John Crawford's 10 years as a public service head, during which time he was instrumental in reshaping Australia's trade policy. This is followed by Sir Peter Lawler's engaging recollections of Sir Allen Brown, Coombs' successor at Post-War Reconstruction before heading a reinforced Prime Minister's Department. In Chapter 10, Ian Hancock charts the four-decade career of Sir Frederick Wheeler, which included more than 10 years as chairman of the Public Service Board and seven years as secretary of the Treasury, during which time he had to cope with what has become known as the Loans Affair.

The book then shifts focus to four leading figures in the Department of External Affairs, Paul Hasluck, John Burton, Arthur Tange, and James Plimsoll. In Chapter 11, Geoffrey Bolton, author of a recent biography of Hasluck, assesses Sir Paul's pre-political career, notably his attendance with Dr H.V. Evatt at the San Francisco Conference that founded the United Nations. Adam Henry reappraises the career of Dr John Burton, secretary of External Affairs (1947–50), who left the public service for an academic career in international relations, and peace and conflict studies. Peter Edwards, author of a full-length biography of Sir Arthur Tange, considers Tange's earlier career in External Affairs rather than his later role as secretary of the Department of Defence. In the final chapter, Jeremy Hearder provides an impressionistic account of the career diplomat Sir James Plimsoll, complementing his recently published biography of Plimsoll, and his entry in volume 18 of the *Australian Dictionary of Biography*.

Part I

1

The Seven Dwarfs: A Team of Rivals

Nicholas Brown

The persistence of the idea of the 'seven dwarfs' in the fairly thin soil of Commonwealth Public Service (CPS) history testifies to its usefulness – although just as the actual composition of the group remains a matter for debate, so does the question of their significance continue to prompt varied interpretations. In a general sense, the term is well enough understood. The expression, 'seven dwarfs', refers to the careers and characteristics of a group of men who secured great influence and authority within and around the CPS from the 1940s until, in some cases, well into the 1980s. They represented a marked expansion in the reach, standing and professionalism of public policy in Australia. They are also a neat encapsulation of 'the new mandarins' – a wider company of senior bureaucrats – who rose to prominence in that period, and were associated with a distinct ethic of independence and authority.

As a descriptor, then, the term is fairly settled. But the explanations it embodies are less agreed. Not only the individuals concerned but also the starting point for their ascendancy varies in accounts, depending on the emphasis given to internal factors within the CPS (recruitment, mentorship, opportunity), external factors (the role of elected governments, the impact of major events such as the Great Depression and the Second World War, or of ideas such as Keynesianism), and the interplay between them. More important, perhaps – although a good deal less discussed – is how to mark the end of their 'period'. At what point can the distinctive combination of factors they reflected – the 'age' of these mandarins – be said to have 'passed'?

It is notable, for example, that in the surge of CPS 'reformism' that commenced in the early 1980s, the scrutiny of an allegedly pervasive inefficiency, rigidity and insularity reached back usually within a 20-year span of memory or political purchase. As the prime minister, Bob Hawke, declared in 1986:

> The Public Service has, in many ways, reflected the easy-going, 'she'll-be-right-mate' management and work style of the lucky Australia of the 1960s and 1970s. We can afford this no longer.[1]

---

1 R.J.L. Hawke, *Commonwealth Parliamentary Debates*, House of Representatives, 25 September 1986, 1448.

Before that, and perhaps untouchable in terms of collective or institutional memory, or deemed irrelevant to political bargaining over the reach and repercussions of government from the 1960s onwards, was the land of the seven dwarfs. How are we to understand the transition both in to, and out of, that land? From this perspective, the endurance, and usefulness, of the dwarfs' story is not just the CPS folklore it is sometimes seen to be. It also raises questions about how we are to understand the changing relations between government, politics and society in Australia.

Most contributors to this collection engage with these questions in ways arising from a close study of individuals who were either likely members of the company of dwarfs, or who presided as mandarins – figures who acquired high bureaucratic office on the basis of exactingly examined merit – over that transformation within the CPS. Stuart Macintyre, in the next essay, considers how formative the context of wartime management and especially post-war reconstruction was for this cohort. My task is to set a different kind of context. What was the nature of the networks in which these figures became so prominent, and how might the relationships between them help us understand their significance as a group? In particular, I want to outline what came to be understood and expected of the figure of the senior public servant in those years: the range of roles, skills, behaviours and attitudes associated with that figure, as exemplified by the dwarfs. Rivalry, as my title suggests, was as much a characteristic of those relationships as cohesion, and underscored the extent to which these individuals were *making* their context on the basis of highly personalised resources and recognition rather than simply finding roles within established institutions.

From this perspective, it is important also to consider the character of the community and institutions within which these figures worked – the Canberra that suddenly, if austerely and incompletely, acquired the status and functions that might at last be said to be appropriate for a national capital; and the institutions that were charged with the functions of an equally sudden, austere and incomplete new vision of national government. This was the dwarfs' landscape, and one in which we might begin to understand their historical significance, even in the larger pursuit of that endemic Australian 'blood sport' (so it seemed to the 1983 Review of Commonwealth Administration) of rubbishing the CPS.[2]

Just to remind ourselves that there is nothing new to this sport, in April 1945 the *Sydney Morning Herald* unkindly quipped that:

> If V-2's had completely obliterated London, surviving Londoners could have built elsewhere a city that in tradition and spirit would again be

---

2   Review of Commonwealth Administration, *Report* (Canberra: AGPS, 1983), x.

London. If similar disaster overcame Canberra, surviving Canberrans would emerge as a flock of homeless people without real ties of common interest other than nationality and community in distress.[3]

A good deal of what has been invested in the 'seven dwarfs' and their period hinges on an attempt to rebut such an assessment. As an idea, the dwarfs assert that the Canberra, and the CPS, that emerged from the Second World War had undergone a qualitative as well as a quantitative change, and acquired a marked competence, if not quite a 'tradition and spirit'. Commentators in the early 1940s lamented that Australia had been forced to cobble together an 'all in' war effort in 'the absence of an effective Federal seat of government' due to the long-term 'passive resistance' of many interests to all that Canberra might be.[4] Towards the decade's end it was argued instead that improvements in the capacity and quality of Australian government 'may be expected as [it] … becomes more diversified [and] firmly rooted in an alert Canberra community'.[5] Self-serving that last assessment might be – it came from Dr P.W.E. Curtin, an official who benefitted from being a part of that emerging community. But this transition nonetheless suggests some of the ways in which we might assess the collective significance of the individuals studied elsewhere in this book, and – from my particular perspective – how we might characterise (in Tim Rowse's formulation) the 'competitive collegiate' ethic they established in government.[6]

There is, however, a fundamental question to be addressed first. Who *were* the seven dwarfs? At one level, to pose this question is to risk being drawn back into CPS nostalgia. As John Nethercote has observed, debate over the names to be included in their ranks has long been standard fare at national capital dinner-party conversations, the pre-occupation of Canberra aficionados and tragics. So, too, has been the question of when the term itself was first coined. Responses to the announcement of the conference on which this book is based proved that these issues still cause a measure of perturbation. Reputations and legacies are in the balance, especially in a city in which even street addresses were, not too long ago, read as rankings of CPS seniority. And, perhaps more fundamentally, up for grabs in finalising the cast are characterisations of the inner circles, and the core functions and ideas, of government during a period of pronounced change.

The enumeration of the company in itself influences how we are to account for its significance – for its nexus between the talents, personalities and commitments of individuals, and a context punctured by major events: depression, war, and not least the change of government in 1949. At one end of the spectrum, there was a depth of personal experience common to most of the contenders. They

---

3   *Sydney Morning Herald*, 14 April 1945, 8.
4   F.A. Bland, 'Public Administration in Wartime', *Australian Quarterly*, 14, no. 4 (1942), 52.
5   P.W.E. Curtin, 'Politics and Administration II', *Public Administration*, 8, no. 1 (1949), 18.
6   T. Rowse, *Nugget Coombs: A Reforming Life* (Port Melbourne, VIC: Cambridge University Press, 2001), 154.

came from relatively modest backgrounds, scholarship educations, and were products, as John Crawford (one undisputed member of the group) put it, of 'the thirties when our minds were beset by problems of the depression, of social misery and of threatening events on the world scene'.[7] Bright, direct, defiant in insisting (as Roland Wilson, another certain member, stated) on never ignoring 'the voice of the people' in dealing with the cautions or ambitions of politicians, they worked with an expansion of public policy into new areas of economic and social management, and geared towards ensuring that such crises did not return.[8]

The stamp of the 'Keynesian Crusade' – H.C. Coombs' term (he is also a sure bet for a place) – was to some extent on them all, if worn over time with varying levels of comfort.[9] That crusade – going well beyond questions of economic management to images of social progress – defined the frontiers they often broached as individuals, not only in policy but in new ways of behaving in often unprecedented contexts. If they were products, as mandarins should be, of merit-based education systems, those systems in themselves were far from entrenched at the time of their ascendancy. Each of the figures discussed in this book benefitted from initiatives taken by schools and universities, and in newly consolidating academic disciplines such as economics, to redress a paucity of knowledge and skill amid the crises of the time. And such training still stood in a rather equivocal relation to established structures of government, which were only overcome under the pressure of extreme circumstances. The image of the 'seven dwarfs' is often, in retrospect, one of mature men, advanced, secure, wise and worn in their careers. They rose, however, on the wave of a desperate search – in the aftermath of the First World War – by teachers, academics and then official mentors to find in a younger generation some redress to the heavy hand of the old.[10]

Balanced against this emphasis on personal experience and commitment is a characterisation of the bureaucratic systems that the dwarfs came to exemplify. In moving from nine years of wartime and reconstruction mainly under Labor into an unprecedented 23 years under the Coalition parties, the dwarfs were associated with a paradigm of public service neutrality and impartiality. For figures who, in several cases especially, were closely associated with Labor's post-war agenda, their acceptance by a new government, with an explicitly contrasting free enterprise ideology, was testimony to another set of qualities. Navigating this transition after 1949 itself made a priority of strict professionalism. Into the post-war decades, over and above their individual attributes, they were

---

7   J. Crawford, *University and Government* (Canberra: Royal Institute of Public Administration, A.C.T. Group, 1969), 2.
8   R. Wilson, quoted in S. Cornish, *Sir Roland Wilson: A Biographical Essay* (Canberra: Sir Roland Wilson Foundation, ANU, 2005), 30.
9   H.C. Coombs, *Trial Balance* (Melbourne: Macmillan, 1981).
10 See N. Brown, *Richard Downing: Economics, Advocacy and Social Reform in Australia* (Carlton South, VIC: Melbourne University Press, 2001), 42–43.

increasingly seen to have embodied the concept and responsibilities of the 'permanent head' of government departments. And they invested this position with its own pragmatism and power. The role of the permanent head might have demanded (as Frederick Wheeler, a central mandarin but not a dwarf, dryly noted) 'an onerous career involving much self-denial'. But its performance was also the stuff of the legend surrounding these figures, of the power of 'Canberra' and the authority of government associated with them at its pinnacle.[11]

In this interplay of personalities and processes, as well as between internal CPS and external intellectual and political influences, the identity of the dwarfs has been debated for years, and related back to tensions in the group itself. Were there contests between – to take an example flagged by Nethercote – those for whom the primary purpose of public policy was to generate growth as a reward for enterprise, and those with an eye to the more equitable distribution of the gains from that growth? Or – anticipating later debates about the representativeness of the CPS – over the insularity of 'Canberra', and the dominance of influences such as a 'Treasury line' in the making and implementation of policy? Or more simply about the competition for resouces – including for people, and in turn for influence – in the very constrained environment that was Canberra until at least the 1960s. For a group identified collectively with a transformation of the CPS in general, they have also gone down in history and myth individually as 'great haters', deeply resentful of the claims each other made for their specific terrain.[12] Is it possible to bring any resolution to these tensions and questions?

Early in the 1990s, Geoffrey Bolton instigated a poll on the question of who were the seven dwarfs at a time when more of those with some first-hand acquaintance with the phenomenon were still able to contribute. Yet even then, it would seem from an extensive correspondence between Bolton and many others, to some extent mediated by the *Australian Dictionary of Biography*, no clear contingent emerged.[13]

The names that were canvassed in this exchange are familiar enough, although some shoot quicker across the sky than other more constant stars. A consolidated list of contenders includes Coombs, Wilson, Crawford, Wheeler, Richard Randall, Allen Brown, Henry Bland, Frederick Shedden, Trevor Swan, Frank Strahan, Kenneth Bailey, William Dunk, Jock Weeden and Stan Carver. In itself, this is an interesting field, indicating areas of government identified as potentially fitting within the matrix of factors associated with the dwarfs. Many, however, can be set aside fairly quickly – again, in a process of elimination that is revealing of the boundaries set for the dwarfs and their significance.

---

11   F.H. Wheeler, 'The Professional Career Public Service: Some Reflections of a Practitioner', *Australian Journal of Public Administration*, 39, no. 2 (1980), 165.
12   R. Beale, quoted by P. Shergold, *Once was Camelot in Canberra? Reflections on Public Service Leadership*, Sir Roland Wilson Foundation Lecture, 2004 (Canberra: The Australian National University, 2005), 3.
13   The following draws on a file of correspondence and clippings, kept by Bolton and in possession of the *ADB*.

Strahan, head of the Prime Minister's Department until 1949, and a confidante of several prime ministers, had few backers in Bolton's poll; he described himself as 'just a clerk', and cannot be associated with the transition from Labor to the Coalition in power, which is central to the collective identity of the 'dwarfs'. So he can be scratched fairly quickly. So can Bailey. Secretary of the Attorney-General's Department (1946–64) and solicitor-general (1946–65), he was a significant figure in advising government on the legality of the powers sought in the expanding domain of Commonwealth legislation. But – in addition to being judged too tall by Robert Parker, an ANU political scientist who knew the field well – Bailey did not have the instrumental engagement with policy that came with dwarfdom.

Dunk, briefly secretary of External Affairs (1945–47), then chairman of the Public Service Board (1947–60), was also too tall and mostly outside direct engagement with the high policy, if not the intrigue, of Canberra. Dunk's mantra, 'civilisation is management', expressed his commitment to the rejuvenation of a 'run-down' post-war CPS, but a good deal of his time was spent in managing both the political and industrial strains of seeking such improvement rather than with the processes of policy reform itself.[14] Weeden, who guided the Commonwealth's move into education, was deemed to lack the highly desirable qualification in economics that characterised most of the dwarfs, but also to work in a field that was not sufficiently central to the core policy priorities of the time. Swan, while undeniably an influential economist closely in touch with those priorities, moved to the fledgling Australian National University in 1950 with the hope that some research–government fusion might develop, but this never happened. Whatever the extent of his back-door or 'brown bag' advice to government through the 1950s, he stood on one side of the divide between academic analysis and policy professionalism that was increasingly deeply scored in Canberra through those years. Swan was nominated by Sir Harold White, who was an ambitious advocate for his own bastion, the Parliamentary and National libraries. Certainly canny, White has also sometimes been mentioned as a possible dwarf – but he at least did us the service of declining inclusion in the corps.

Confounded by such a list of contenders, Parker suggested that the play of the concept was perhaps more important than a settled company. Even so, such a first cut gets a good deal closer to a manageable list of names and claims. Building on such possibilities, and spurred by Bolton's inquiry, the *Canberra Times* confidently declared in 1992 that the team was:

- Crawford: Post-War Reconstruction, then secretary of both Commerce and Agriculture (1950–56) and Trade (1956–60)

---

14   N. Brown, 'Dunk, Sir William Ernest (1897–1984)', *Australian Dictionary of Biography*, 17 (Melbourne: Melbourne University Press, 2007), 345–6.

- Bland: director-general of Manpower then secretary of Labour and National Service (1952–67)
- Wilson: secretary of Labour and National Service (1940–46), then Commonwealth statistician (1946–51) and secretary to the Treasury (1951–66)
- Randall: Treasury, succeeding Wilson as secretary (1966–71)
- Coombs: director-general of Post-War Reconstruction, then governor of the Commonwealth Bank (1949–59) and Reserve Bank (1960–68)
- Carver: Commonwealth statistician (1951–62)
- Brown: Post-War Reconstruction, then secretary of Prime Minister's Department (1949–58).

Yet, averaging out the 'hits' in Bolton's poll, the most preferred company is:
- Coombs
- Wilson
- Crawford
- Brown
- Bland
- Randall
- Shedden: secretary, Department of Defence (1937–56).

In one of the few instances of a contender actually associating himself with the company, Bland gave Crawford, Randall, Wilson, Coombs, Brown, Carver and himself as the definitive list, citing as the formative context a working party established in 1947 to serve the Investment and Employment Committee, with Chifley as chairman, and a brief to get to grips with the reality of post-war government.[15] But the exclusion of Shedden from Bland's account is problematic, and Carver does not rate a place in more recent 'official' guides.[16] In a sign of how contested the last seat on the bench could be, the *ADB* itself questioned Carver's standing as a possible 'dwarf' by describing him as 'essentially a statistician'.[17] Equally, while Shedden rather than Carver figured in a profile of 'The Biggest Little Men in Australia' published in the *Financial Review* in 1965, that profile also noted that his 'inclusion is usually regarded as being mainly coincidental in that he was a department head and happened to be about the same physical size as the other six'.[18]

---

15   *Australian*, 21 January 1967, 9; Sir Henry Bland, interviewed by Mel Pratt, 8–10 January 1975, National Library of Australia (NLA) TRC 121, 60.
16   J. Adams and C. Oates, *Serving the Nation: 100 Years of Public Service* (Canberra: Public Service and Merit Protection Commission, 2001), 146–7.
17   M. Kerley, 'Carver, Sir Stanley Roy (1897-1967)', *Australian Dictionary of Biography*, 13 (Melbourne: Melbourne University Press, 1993), 93.
18   *Financial Review*, 12 November 1965, 2–3.

J.B. (Ben) Chifley, c1949

Source: National Archives of Australia, A462, 778/03 PART 2

The various permutations of this list perhaps in themselves reflect rivalries among candidates – and no doubt the debate will continue, spurred once again by this collection of essays. But, drawing this particular auction to a close – however provisionally – the most likely seven are (in a rough order of certainty): Coombs, Wilson, Crawford, Brown, Bland, Randall, and Shedden.

Likely – but perhaps not all equally deserving. In one of the clear signs of competition for recognition, or just plain bitchiness, David Horner quotes Arthur Tange – secretary of the Department of External Affairs (1954–65), certainly a mandarin but not a dwarf – saying of Shedden that he fulfilled the dictionary definition of 'bureaucrat': 'an official who works by fixed meetings without exercising intelligent judgement'.[19] That might have been the insider's perspective, and reflective of the tensions developing between an External Affairs department self-consciously preening its intellectual ascendancy and a Defence establishment a good deal more 'grounded' in its business. It is also worth noting in passing a more populist perspective of 1964, which praised Carver as the only public servant who at least had a tangible output, being the 'figure-juggling juggernaut' in charge of an agency that could tell the nation something useful about itself. Carver's command of the facts of population, productivity and prosperity was then contrasted by journalist Frank Clune to higher-minded public servants who were consumed in a 'vast amount of political and social manoeuvring and rumours': 'If you want to see the Australian ruling class', Clune concluded, 'go to Canberra. The air of life here is superannuation.'[20]

Already, these variations on the list of dwarfs suggests something of what was at stake in being included. One qualification is indisputable: the *Financial Review* gave the height range for its selection as running from Wilson at 5 feet (152.4 cm) and 9 stone (57 kg) to Coombs at 5 feet 3 inches (160 cm) and 10 stone (63.5 kg) – roughly the height of the average Spanish man of the 1950s. But, beyond shared stature, what does such a list suggest?

As argued already, what rides on the shoulders of this group is a characterisation of a – if not the – major period in the consolidation of the CPS. And, as also already noted, there are two central elements to this consolidation – personal attributes and experience, and professional role – that do not necessarily sit easily together. The groupings offer one way into figuring out how the tensions between these elements were managed at the time, and might be evaluated in retrospect.

Turning to that first element: personal experience and commitment. The seven dwarfs symbolise the transformation of government under the pressures of the

---

19 Tange, quoted in D. Horner, *Defence Supremo: Sir Frederick Shedden and the Making of Australian Defence Policy* (Sydney: Allen & Unwin, 2000), 7.
20 F. Clune, *Journey to Kosciusko* (Sydney: Angus and Robertson, 1964), 245–6.

Second World War, both in the rapidly centralised functions and expanding reach of what in 1939 was termed the Federal Government but by 1945 was the Commonwealth, and in the recruitment of specifically identified expertise to manage these processes.[21] This element is exemplified by the Keynesian paradigm: government transformed by young, university-trained, and theoretically informed reformers. These figures sought to translate a broad domain of civic concern formed in contexts of depression and unemployment into careers spent dealing with pressures first of wartime mobilisation and reconstruction, then of inflation and full employment, and with the expanding role of public investment in general. These iterations developed their own tensions as well as ideals. As Weller, Scott and Stevens put it, 'peace and prosperity engendered expectations and hope among public servants that they could improve conditions for the community'.[22] But in the process, some aspects of that paradigm in themselves came under strain. Not least among these aspects were the judgments made in attributing relative weightings to the virtues practised in public and private spending and saving, work and enterprise, to the old solidarities of labour and class, the new claims of enterprise and welfare, or the ideals of citizenship and security. These weightings went beyond calculations of economic growth or national income in determining the merits or impact of policies on a society in itself posing new issues for government. In responding to these issues, the post-war mandarins were learning and testing themselves and their convictions as they went.

These men were emphatically not the economic rationalists of the 1980s, with their deference to the discipline of the market. They were instead conscious – as Coombs would put it – of using 'other people's money' to achieve a range of social outcomes within the context of a tight bargain between stability and growth, prosperity and regulation, the respective roles and responsibilities of the government and the people.[23] Crawford is recalled for 'the restrained bitterness with which he spoke of those bureaucrats to whom the poor and the unemployed were not persons but simply component figures in a statistical index'.[24] That tension was implicit within their shared professionalism: how was it best to evoke the society over which they exercised influence?

As Harold Perkin has argued, public service professionalism through the twentieth century developed in an unsteady bargain between 'an old loyalty to class-based politics', embodied in ideas of 'service', and a rising ethic of

---

21 See F. Brennan, *Canberra in Crisis* (Canberra: Dalton, 1971), 150.
22 P. Weller, J. Scott and B. Stevens, *From Postbox to Powerhouse: A Centenary History of the Department of Prime Minister and Cabinet* (Sydney: Allen & Unwin, 2011), 48–9.
23 H.C. Coombs, *Other People's Money: Economic Essays* (Canberra: Australian National University Press, 1971).
24 O. Spate, 'Sir John Crawford (1910–1984)', Obituaries Australia, National Centre of Biography, The Australian National University, oa.anu.edu.au/obituary/crawford-sir-john-grenfell-jack-1391/text1390, accessed 13 September 2011.

'equality of opportunity', relating more to formations of the 'public' to be served, or represented.[25] The post-war social contract was informed by an increased negotiation of these values, albeit with its own Australian inflections. One of its leading exponents, R.I. Downing, who had his own place in the 'official family' of advisers that grew around the Labor Government in Canberra in the 1940s, and in the 'Keynesian crusade', phrased it from his Melbourne academic vantage in 1956 in these terms:

> This is precisely what we are trained for – to identify what it is we have to give up, and how much, in order to get a little more of something else we want; to present the facts to the people; and to leave them to choose what they want.[26]

The dwarfs presided over a model of government framed by that sense of responsibility, that idea of managing the needs and demands arising from a pluralistic if regulated society: to 'present the facts' if not persuade on 'the wants', and to mark out an appropriate domain of 'choice'.

Equally, in that same address to a Canberra audience, Downing could not resist the parting shot: 'In my strictly personal platform for economic policy, in fact, my main plank is the abolition of Canberra. You all ought to come back and live with us'. That aside touches on the second element of the dwarfs' landscape: the entrenching of concepts of public service professionalism into the practices of policy development, ministerial advice and public responsiveness in the context of a marked expansion of central government.

Patrick Weller has offered a neat summary of this professionalism from the time of the dwarfs: 'the official adviser, buoyed with expertise and knowledge, bolstered by a monopoly of access, dominating many of the ministers'.[27] This was the domain of the 'mandarin' – the figure who not only exercised a considerable element of control over what was 'left' to 'the people' to choose, but also over what went to the minister to decide. And this practice permeated deeply into departmental cultures, with a range of effects.

After 1939, telegraph boys were increasingly unlikely to rise to the top of the public service, but scholarships boys – so the dwarfs showed – had a better chance, and steadily, if slowly, so did university graduates in general. From the margins of dwarfdom, a figure such as Dunk recognised this as he lobbied for public service reform through the 1950s. Without a university degree himself, he conceded that his generation of managers must effectively ensure their own

---

25 H. Perkin, *The Rise of Professional Society: England Since 1880* (London: Routledge, 2001), 517.
26 R.I. Downing, 'Is an Economic Policy Possible?', *Australian Journal of Public Administration*, 15, no. 4 (1956), 273–4, 281.
27 P. Weller, *Australia's Mandarins: The Frank and the Fearless* (Sydney: Allen & Unwin, 2001), 9.

obsolence given the demand for new policy skills. In the first stages of this process, however, a distinct, perhaps more innately competitive ethic characterised Commonwealth departments at the forefront of policy development.

Always conscious, in their inter-war educations, of insecurity in the lives around them, and of the rare opportunities extended to them, the dwarfs imbibed certain precepts about the work of government. They understood both its powers (which were not to be exploited in ways that – as the 1930s showed – could fail, resulting in waste and unrest) and its privileges (from which they benefitted, but which were not to be assumed or exploited). Even in the resistances they faced in bringing their expertise into systems still largely defined by seniority and its tribalisms, they realised that the structures of government were to be worked with (or at least *within*), not challenged. As Wheeler – who would savour these processes more than most – reflected in 1980, the senior 'professional, career public servant' (each of those terms mattering exactly to him) was 'richly rewarded by the fascination of being associated with the political while not being of it'.[28] For all their conspicuous markers of higher education, the dwarfs would often make their way with a reflex rejection of ideology and abstraction. Their role was to ensure the system worked as efficiently and effectively as possible: they were its creatures, not the other way around. They were also its custodians, and gatekeepers.

Even so, there was a qualification, or a twist, to this relationship. Paul Hasluck – not a dwarf, but potentially a mandarin until his own turn to politics in that climactic election of 1949 – observed what he took to be a distinctly Australian phenomenon of the immediate post-war decades. Well-educated public servants, he argued, now found themselves dealing with politicians who had risen to ministerial rank but tended to lack an education 'comparable to that of their advisers'.[29] Such a disjunction was new, and enhanced the power of the dwarfs. The structures of government within which they worked were not seen as theirs by right, but theirs to influence, guide and protect. Again, as Hasluck noted of the connection between the public servant and politics, with his own slant on the fascination observed by Wheeler, 'one has to recognize that a policy decision does not freeze politics [to the extent it must be taken into account by the public servant], but only turns political energy into the chosen direction', which it then became the public servant's responsibility to pursue.[30] The domain of the senior public servant was newly energised by these responsibilities in the expanding compass of post-war government.

---

28   Wheeler, 'The Professional Career Public Servant', 165.
29   P. Hasluck, *The Public Servant and Politics* (Canberra: Royal Institute of Public Administration, A.C.T. Group, 1968), 15.
30   Ibid., 3.

Importantly, these distinctions were not just learnt on the job; they were part of the education that an inter-war generation tested as they journeyed forward. 'A bureaucracy', Henry Bland's father, Professor F.A. Bland, wrote in a 1923 Workers' Education Association textbook on government in Australia (a book itself addressing the scarcity of any local work reflecting on these issues), 'is mainly distinguishable by its irresponsiveness to the public will'. To that extent, for those schooled on Bland's textbook and the larger British and American literature on which it drew, 'bureaucracy' was to be unfavourably distinguished from the more plain-spoken, plain-acting concept of 'public administration', dealing more directly with matters of policy implementation, not policy formation. Bland further cautioned that:

> The development of an expert official class, the multiplicity of departments, their imperfect coordination, the impossibility of adequate ministerial supervision, the unwillingness of Parliament to adapt its procedure to modern economic and social needs, all tend to widen the gulf between expert officialdom and the public.[31]

Dealing with that 'gulf' – even if implicitly rejecting it as anachronistic – required careful footwork. When Roland Wilson (with two doctorates in economics) was appointed secretary to the Treasury in 1951, the move was seen as 'the first Australian experiment of this kind' – a perception that Wilson moderated by offering the assurance that he would 'never be guilty of ignoring the voice of the people'. He also undertook 'to subject my thinking to the supervision of my political masters', a discipline necessary to correct for the tendency of 'some of our public service administrators … [to become] too much infatuated with their own crack-pot ideas'.[32] But, from the late 1940s and into the 1950s, each side of this bargain – the 'people' and the 'masters' – were often far from stable entities. 'Frank and fearless advice' was itself premised on an expertise that transcended the flux of opinion and politics. The transition of 1949 highlighted this – new Liberal ministers reportedly finding themselves 'completely incapable of coping with the voluminous duties' that represented the changed dimensions of policy through the 1940s, and equally wary of advice from those who had served the previous government, and on questions that saw divergent options on those issues of enterprise or equity, distribution or growth.[33] None of the dwarfs is remembered for doing what they were told by ministers still finding their feet. They are, instead, remembered for the innovation, the consolidation and the character they brought to the tasks of and demands on government as it weathered such transformations.

---

31 F.A. Bland, *Shadows and Realities of Government* (Sydney: WEA, 1923), 5.
32 Wilson, quoted in S. Cornish, *Sir Roland Wilson: A Biographical Essay* (Canberra: The Sir Roland Wilson Foundation, 2002), 30.
33 *Inside Canberra*, 12 January 1950, 8 June 1950, 26 October 1950.

Each of the individuals studied in this book draws out specific aspects of these elements in transition. Some are intangible. Wheeler, for example, emphasised the concept of 'style' — manner more than matter — when he came to reflect on what defined the most effective senior officials in his experience.[34] And — if not quite style in itself — a certain brusque efficiency and impatience seems to have characterised many of the dwarfs in their personality, and their determination that the work of government take place in a domain clearly demarcated from the flux of mere opinion or politics, and in departments that they ruled closely. Overwork was no doubt part of the explanation for that terseness — and the demands of their jobs were never far from candid exchanges among them. But such a demeanour was also cultivated as an expression of the responsibility they carried, and the terms in which they carried it. Allen Brown — one of the two lawyers among the dwarfs (the other was Bland) — was noted by the *Australian* in 1971 as having the reputation as 'a ruthless, abrupt administrator'. The London *Times* was a little softer, welcoming him in 1959 as Deputy High Commissioner in Australia House at end of his time at the Prime Minister's Department:

> Wiry and normally placid, and neither hearty nor arty, he is a much more than fair sample of highly professional civil servants developed in Canberra.[35]

If part of the success of the dwarfs was that — as John Bunting (Brown's successor in Canberra) put it — they were 'companions' to Sir Robert Menzies as an equally shrewd, enduring prime minister (and presumably their Snow White — he himself was heard to claim this role), it was also the case that each carved out a formidable authority of their own.[36] 'Neither hearty nor arty' reflects something of that careful cultivation — perhaps in that particular instance filtered through a British search for a way of comprehending this new kind of Australian on the Strand. Not all were as 'naturally taciturn' as Brown, but the *Times*' sense of a type is revealing. All faced the challenge of securing support for the business of national government that was often under scrutiny for its partiality, its extravagance, and its distance from the 'reality' of the rest of the nation.

---

34 Wheeler, 'The Professional Career Public Servant', 162.
35 *Australian*, 28 September 1971; *Times*, 3 January 1959.
36 H.W. Arndt to G. Bolton, 27 February 1992; Bunting, quoted in Adams and Oates, *Serving the Nation*, 146; Weller, Scott and Stevens, *Postbox to Powerhouse*, 52.

1. The Seven Dwarfs: A Team of Rivals

Robert Menzies, c1950

Source: National Library of Australia, nla.pic-an12265907

The Department of Post-War Reconstruction, which bulked large in many careers as an emblem of the new reach of government, became in itself an object of planned obsolescence in this process, even under a Labor government as concerned about trimming the costs of a 'multiplicity of departments' as it was about containing perceptions of its addiction to 'planning'. With solid foundations still in industrial unionism and an ethic of egalitarianism, Labor had no necessary affiliation with big government. In 1946, it gave the task of trimming a wartime accretion of some 60,000 temporary CPS officers to J.T. Pinner, who was renowned for holding building contractors to account by counting the number of empty cement bags around Canberra's new Administrative Building.[37] Especially in the wake of the failure of the 1944 referendum on Commonwealth powers, the government itself was in no mood for allegations of excess or inefficiency. And with each post-war budget being rumoured, well into the 1950s, as being called to bring, or actually bringing, cuts to the public service, part of the skill of a mandarin was to preserve their domain under such scrutiny. Again, as Wilson made clear to Tange:

> What mattered for public servants was how their department was faring in a constant battle for influence. A truly successful public servant was one who led a department that was at or near the top of an imaginary league table. Standing in this table depended on perceptions of the department's strength and influence, particularly in the eyes of senior ministers and other departmental heads.[38]

At a basic level, as the post-war structures of government settled down, there was that inherent rivalry among the company – and it was transacted at the most basic levels of differentials in salary and opportunities for initiative. The announcement of an increase in salary to Allen Brown in 1954, for example, was enough to prompt Crawford to voice candid reservations to his minister, John McEwen, about his future in a service that seemed not to equally value his skills or commitment, and for McEwen to suggest that Menzies as prime minister needed to take note of such disquiet spreading among other largely indispensable permanent heads. As McEwen insisted, the matter was not simply one of ego, it was one of 'dignity'.[39]

Beyond such delicate dealings, however, was the more fundamental question of what would define the figure of the public servant through such transitions. In 1923, F.A. Bland had identified the pressing need to attend to the appropriate training of a public servant if the dangers of bureaucracy were to be avoided. His counsel then was that an administrator needed a general,

---

37 G.E. Pettit, 'John Thomas Pinner', *Australian Dictionary of Biography*, 16 (Melbourne: Melbourne University Press, 2002), 5–6.
38 Wilson, quoted in P. Edwards, *Arthur Tange: The Last of the Mandarins* (Sydney: Allen & Unwin, 2006), 83.
39 McEwen to Menzies, 3 March 1954, NAA M2576/1.

liberal university education as both 'a protection against the disillusionment which accompanies life's inevitable routine' but also as a way of recognising the social transformation impelled by the First World War. Bland cited the perception of J.A. Hobson in 1921:

> Rude, unformed, wasteful energy counted more heavily in the rough and tumble of the world that has passed away. Now, conscious, calculated policies are demanded in all those departments of life in which the struggle for survival and success is carried on.

'Conscious, calculated policies' were not so much matters of expertise, but of reflection and sound judgment, seasoned by a perspective that encompassed a necessary understanding of the strained nature of social cohesion as well as of the endurance of 'disillusionment'. Into the 1930s, the service the dwarfs and their cohorts entered was slowly edging towards benefitting from the kind of scholarship and part-time study provision Bland encouraged.[40] Such provision would, he hoped (this time quoting the Macdonnell Commission on the British Civil Service of 1915), enable 'the clever sons of poor parents to benefit by University training and thereby enter the Civil Service', so that 'the interests of democracy and of the Public Service can and ought to be reconciled'.[41]

And so a few of these Australian 'clever sons' were finding their way up the ladder of an education system that was highly competitive, working through a curriculum that was strong on a meritocratic 'impulse to select and differentiate', to identify the boys who wanted to 'get on', and to cultivate – in the introduction of uniforms, houses and badges – an ethic of loyalty and good citizenship.[42] Their secondary schooling might have culminated in a leaving certificate that – at least in New South Wales – was characterised as having 'a halo around it as big as a bale of hay and worth about as much', but at least that was some recognition of an educational ideal.[43] Once through that process, they might proceed to universities – where the dwarfs mostly studied part-time, and for several with interruptions demanded by family or personal economic circumstances – which had also begun to urge bright students to see the public service as a worthwhile career. What was sought was a fusion (again in Macdonnell's formulation, endorsed by Bland) of 'Civil Service' and 'Public Service'. But still this did not necessarily translate into ready opportunities. It was only when senior university economists – such as L.F. Giblin and D.B. Copland – were called to advise on the urgent demands of 'total war'

---

40 See R.D. Scott and R.L. Wetherell, 'Public Administration as a Teaching and Research Field', *Australian Journal of Public Administration*, 29, no. 3-4 (1980): 480–1.
41 Bland, *Shadows and Realities*, 17, 30, 34.
42 See C. Campbell and G. Sherrington, *Comprehensive Public High School: Historical Perspectives* (London: Palgrave, 2006), 30–3.
43 A. Barcan, *Two Centuries of Education in New South Wales* (Kensington: UNSW Press, 1988), 249.

mobilisation that they could follow through on acts of patronage for their best students. That mentorship shaped several early careers for dwarfs and mandarins, but perhaps also further conditioned a sense of debt, duty, and deference; responsibilities to be bestowed and honoured, continuing in the spirit of the educations they had gained so far. These young men were disciplined and clever, but not encouraged to be simply smart.

In 1939, to take one example, Fred Wheeler was among those select few drawn into the wartime 'kindergarten' of junior officers in Canberra. Copland borrowed Wheeler, whom he had taught as a part-time commerce student, from the State Savings Bank of Victoria – where his placement in the loans arrears department offered its own exposure to the lingering hardship of the 1930s – to work with him as wartime Prices Commissioner, an office established early to contain the black-marketing and distortions of the First World War. Clearly able, Wheeler soon moved to a position as assistant research officer in Treasury. In a Christmas card to Wheeler's wife, Copland reassured her – the gesture itself indicating the depth of personal patronage – that in moving to the Treasury 'Fred has made an excellent impression in the office with the regular men in the Service'. That phrase, 'regular men', suggests something of the ranks into which a figure such as Wheeler, with (as Copland noted) his 'economic training', needed to fit. Copland continued:

> If he stays in Treasury he must expect to move slowly in advancement at first, and the atmosphere can't be quite the same as in Price Fixing, nor will the work be quite as exciting or as exacting. I have no doubts as to his ultimate success, but you must always remember that the glittering prizes seem remote at first, and are in fact remote.[44]

These emphases are revealing. Such tactical patience no doubt bred its own instincts of competition and of protecting turf. What was understood, however, was that a career in government might eventually offer its own 'glittering prizes' in recognition and seniority for those who at once 'fitted in' and slowly rose above.

A transformation, of sorts, had clearly begun in framing the ideal of the public servant, recognising the need for the kind of skills and expertise associated with a university education, but also for the balances to be struck in translating that education into practice. Care went into framing who the new, post-war public servant ought to be. The first post-1945 annual report of the Public Service Board noted a 'distinct change' in the functions of government during the Second World War. This change was characterised as a move from 'regulation' to the emerging 'positive and constructive responsibilities' of government. Further,

---

44 D.B. Copland to P. Wheeler, 22 December 1939, Wheeler Papers, NLA MS 8096, Box 2.

the imperative was to explain these new responsibilities to a public that was, as a whole, increasingly implicated in its business, from welfare to health, from saving to spending. In 1947, the Board presented its new identikit for the type of officer appropriate to these demands:

> men must have an opportunity of executive practice and … to make mistakes before the age of 30 if they are ever to reach the ranks of successful executives. Delay in giving this experience often means that an officer is called on to take an important executive post at a time when he has lost the mental resilience which would make him fully effective.[45]

While much of this formulation was borrowed from early British advocacy (the threshold of 30 came from W.H. Beveridge in 1920 and was quoted by Bland), the emphases were distinct. The capacity to endure inter-war boredom became the post-war challenge of individual responsibility, to muster 'mental resilience'. The test of democracy was now a more specifically defined task of framing policies which could secure popular consent. Equally marked was an implicit break from the established Australian model of public service security as a reward for military service. Gavin Long has calculated that the average age of enlisted men in 1940 was 27, and even allowing for the impact of conscription in 1942, the new, rising public servant was clearly not intended to build on the ranks of such men.[46] The public service was to make a generational and attitudinal leap with an ethic embellished in the 1948 Public Service Board report:

> He (the ideal public servant) is intelligent but with a full share of earthiness. He thrives on the gross air of everyday affairs. He has the common touch … he is a well-rounded, well-balanced man, broadbacked, with a certain simplicity of nature and the sense of proportion that goes with a sense of humour.

The profile went on, concluding with 'we are looking for the sort of youngster who, with right handling, great care and great patience, will turn out sometime in his thirties or forties to be that sort of man'.[47]

This culture of carefully cultivated generalist professionalism sought a balance between qualities of personality and capacities of management. It envisaged officers who would back-fill the paths forged by the dwarfs and their like, and build a service that matched the changes they represented. This is one reason why the 'seven dwarfs' mattered so much in the dinner party conversations among those who were of their age, and defined themselves through what this select, and selected, company stood for. And in this process of consolidation, other resistances

---

45 Public Service Board, *Twenty-Third Annual Report* (Canberra: AGPS, 1947), 7.
46 G. Long, *To Benghazi* (Canberra: Australian War Memorial, 1952), 58.
47 Public Service Board, *Twenty-Fourth Annual Report* (Canberra: AGPS, 1948), 5–6.

relaxed. As H.F. Whitlam noted in the first Garran Memorial Oration in 1959 – a lecture series in itself indicating a CPS keen to reflect on its own evolution – the rising currency of the word 'bureaucracy' was becoming less the 'continental nuisance' Carlyle (and Bland) had dismissed. Its increasing currency indicated 'a public consciousness that more and more government power is concentrated in the public service'. The tasks of effectively handling those 'positive and constructive' interventions in the widening and interdependent fields of social and economic policy had become more generic public service attributes as post-war prosperity settled into its own orchestrated balances and disciplines. Just as the 'public administration' Bland had taught in the inter-war years became the 'political science' of the post-war years – an older instrumentalism giving way to a new amalgam of social, economic and political pressures to be mastered – so did the public servant settle into more sophisticated practices of (in Hasluck's formulation) training 'political energy into the chosen direction'.[48]

In the expansion of the post-war CPS – even despite Pinner's stringency – from 12 departments in 1939 to twice that number and nearly 160,000 under the Public Service Act in 1957, the time available for 'right handling' was both scarce and frugally bestowed.[49] The truth of Wilson's advice to Tange on the necessity of inter-departmental rivalry was hammered home in a tight control of staffing, let alone innovation, however much the actual composition of the service might have become steadily younger, better paid and better educated. But something of its goals can be glimpsed in the foundation of the Australian Administrative Staff College in 1957, by then expressing a concept of professional administration that united both public and private sector officers in new tasks of what was termed 'statecraft'. Aspiring officials were to be assessed on their capacity to take 'maximum responsibility' as individuals called upon to judge and act, to delegate and manage the spread of talents beneath them, and to apply the precepts of vocational guidance and aptitude testing in acheiving a more subtle mix of task and personality in the service.[50]

A similar framework informed the hearings conducted in the late 1950s by the Committee of Inquiry into Public Service Recruitment, chaired by Sir Richard Boyer, as it tackled the task of developing a senior 'administrative civil service' appropriate for the times, while also noting that the prejudices against such a stratum had scarcely altered since the war. Boyer's report made a strong case for recognition of a 'liberal education' alongside the dominance of economics as a suitable training for a 'second division' of administrative officers. 'Equality of opportunity', the report argued, could no longer be simply addressed by

---

48 Scott and Wettenhall, 'Public Administration as a Teaching and Research Field', 461.
49 These figures are taken from the *Report* of the Committee of Inquiry into Public Service Recruitment (Canberra: APGS, 1959), 9.
50 D.B. Copland, *Administrative Staff Training: A New Frontier in Education* (Melbourne: Cheshire, 1957), 20, 22.

recruitment 'from below' in a society in which access to education was greatly expanding. The opportunities that could be safely bestowed on the 'clever sons of workers' now had to be spread across a citizenry created by prosperity and its wise government.[51] And the responsibilities of such government equally centred on economic stability and all that was associated with a 'full employment goal and reality' – the promise of prosperity (and its challenges to recruitment for what was still an often disparaged public service) on the one hand; the prospect of inflationary and growth-induced pressures (and their associated demands on public policy) on the other.[52]

Both the interests and pressures encompassed in Boyer's consultations and final report exemplified the Keynesian contract in operation into the 1950s and later. That contract, clearly, had its strengths – and Boyer's call for the more systematic recognition of education and talent was one element of the commitment to public sector reform it hoped to support. But the report and its reception also reflected the boundaries within which that reform might occur. A course at the Staff College went to only a few, and several of Boyer's recommendations – including to end the marriage bar for women – were largely dismissed as 'overly theoretical', and likely to upset the fragile balance of roles and responsibilities in the labour market as well as in government. The spirit of Boyer's inquiry was only 'slowly and unspectacularly' implemented by the Public Service Board, largely under Wheeler's influence, through the 1960s.[53]

Each dwarf – and each mandarin – had their own perspectives on such challenges. As secretary of the Department of Labour and National Service, for example, Bland (the younger) was – as Tom Sheridan notes – interventionist in everything from executive government and the secret surveillance of industrial activists through to the determination of wage awards and trade union governance.[54] Bland is perhaps the least frequently mentioned/remembered of the dwarfs, in part because of his very equivocal relationship to Canberra – which he found 'incestuous', and prone to make a 'song and dance' about policy – and because of his predisposition to step outside the world of the bureaucrat, believing that 'an awful lot can be achieved by having quiet lunches with people, going for walks in gardens and not telling the world what one is doing until the time is right'.[55] In another perspective on the terms of rivalry, it is revealing that when Wheeler and Bland were under close consideration to succeed Dunk at the Public Service Board, Bland was dismissed as too combative and lacking

---

51   Committee of Inquiry into Public Service Recruitment, *Report*, 10.
52   Ibid., 9.
53   See G. Caiden, 'Administrative Reform', *Australian Journal of Public Administration*, 29, no. 3–4 (1980), 441.
54   T. Sheridan, 'Regulator Par Excellence: Sir Henry Bland and Industrial Relations 1950–1967', *Journal of Industrial Relations*, 41, no. 2 (1999), 228–55.
55   J. Farquarson, 'Sir Henry Bland (1909–1997)', *Canberra Times*, 13 November 1997, 11.

in 'the intellectual integrity which is the prime quality required'.[56] Held in this balance were those elements of personal style, of the specific structures of government and policy networks, and of the politics of bargaining in general, which clearly shaped the work of the dwarfs and gave them distinct Australian inflections. Bland had close relations with his first minister, Harold Holt, with the National Civic Council of right-wing Catholic trade unionists, and with the then president of the Australian Council of Trade Unions, Albert Monk, but less so with Holt's successor, William McMahon, and the more fractured, public, controversialist style of politics that characterised the second half of the 1960s. He was, like each of the dwarfs in their own ways, of a time that was passing.

It is important to note again – as with Perkin's sense of the political alignments of public sector professionalism – that the Australian aproach to cultivating these generalised skills of oversight and management reflected wider patterns. In his study of Whitehall, for example, Peter Hennessy observes similar processes in Britain. Hennessy's account suggests that while the UK Home Civil Service had a jump on its Australian counterpart in thinking of the 'higher bureaucracy ... as a distinctive career' in the inter-war years, similar ideals, constraints and reservations were prevalent as it adjusted to post-war circumstances. Between the wars, Sir Warren Fisher, permanent secretary of the Treasury, still held to the view that taking bright young things fresh from civil service exams was no way to build real bureaucratic leadership: 'if you do that they will then get to work and take their little pens in their infant hands and will write away little criticisms of every sort and kind, very clever ones no doubt, but there is no training for constructive work'. It was only under the pressure of the Second World War, Hennessy argues, that Whitehall – like Canberra – became of necessity 'an adventure playground for all the talents'. Given the interconnections of British elites, and perhaps the immediacy of the threat, Britain benefitted from a more systematic recruitment of experts than occurred in Australia.

Yet it was still the case that a range of factors saw the gains in 'fluid, capable and managerial' capacity in government won during the war sacrificed in the post-war years. The 'type' of public servant to be preferred in post-war Britain, whether under Labour or the Conservatives, was not – Hennessy insists – a figure of specialisation or expertise, of the kind that had found a place during the pressures of total war mobilisation. They were instead those who assumed a largely manufactured mantle of general professionalism, capable of containing processes of adjustment to post-1945 circumstances that ranged from anxieties over upward class mobility to concerns over the expanding welfare state. Overall, Hennessy argues, the result in discarding specific expertise was 'probably the greatest lost opportunity in the history of British public administration'.[57]

---

56   Dunk to Crawford, 31 August 1959, Crawford Papers, NLA MS 4514, Box 81, folder headed 'Staffing Wheeler F'.
57   P. Hennessy, *Whitehall* (London: Secker and Warburg, 1989), 54, 120, 156.

1. The Seven Dwarfs: A Team of Rivals

Sir Henry Bland, 1966

Source: National Archives of Australia, A1200, L58484

Does this judgment apply to Australia? Is it part of the legend, and the legacy, of the 'seven dwarfs'? In this survey, I have attempted only to suggest some themes that might be borne in mind in seeing a pattern in the more detailed accounts of careers and contributions that follow. Certainly, as noted at the outset, the land of the dwarfs was to be comprehensively challenged by the 1980s, and was already under siege by the 1970s. It was threatened by a range of pressures, to some extent coalescing around another crucial change of government in 1972. Labor returned to power in that year with its own suspicions of officials still captive to 23 years under the Coalition, and with its own aspirations for a more socially representative bureaucracy, extending beyond the 'well-balanced, broadbacked man' to a figure, or figures, more attuned to the diversity then increasingly characterising Australian society. The 'impartiality' of a permanent head began to seem less than an asset in managing this transition, or in being accountable to governments embracing a more explicit mandate for change. Again, however, the question of balancing factors internal and external to the CPS should be taken into account in making sense of these pressures.

The dwarfs, while path-breakers in many ways, were also well-matched to the tasks their times gave them – to that balance of judgment, attitude and influence required to regulate that restless beast, the fully employed Australian economy. Bland faced industrial issues associated with those pressures very directly, if discretely, as did Coombs, adjusting monetary mechanisms as governor of the Commonwealth (later the Reserve) Bank in Sydney. In Canberra, the Treasury was at it all the time. Sir Richard Randall's triumph, as its secretary, was said to be a campaign to cut income tax, and his responsibility for the phrasing of budget speeches that got the fiscal messages of admonition and exhortation right for a restless electorate.[58] External Affairs wrestled with an attempt to boost its own standing in the ruck of public service recruiting, but its cultivation of a diplomatic intake in a highly competitive employment market never quite achieved the balance sought between generalist skills, the right 'type', and a representative range in backgrounds to diffuse easy jibes at elitism. Across the board, it remained the case, as Ruth Atkins observed, that, in the rapidly expanding national capital, the concept of 'the public' morphed seamlessly into that of the 'public servant' as a custodian, a safe pair of hands, a continuity to be balanced against the more uncertain commodity of 'the private', whether in politics, pressure groups or policy. Increasingly becoming the home for central agencies, and for the deals within government, the city itself boomed, acquired sophistication, and exemplified a tendency for debates over priorities and values to be cast in terms of disputes between departments rather than in society or the economy beyond them.[59] As critics were to note into the 1960s – confirming Downing's alarm – Canberra seemed locked in a spiral of 'few industries and too much industry', becoming more insular, and insulated, in this growth.[60]

---

58 *Bulletin*, 14 November 1970; see generally G. Whitwell, *The Treasury Line* (Sydney: Allen and Unwin, 1986).
59 R. Atkins, *The Government of the Australian Capital Territory* (St Lucia: University of Queensland Press, 1978), 8.
60 *Bulletin* (Sydney), 24 April 1957, 6.

1. The Seven Dwarfs: A Team of Rivals

Sir Richard Randall, 1966

Source: National Archives of Australia, A1200, L57983

Rivalries remained intense. Bastions such as the Commonwealth Club grew to accommodate, diffuse and civilise the jostling of many of the mandarins engaged in these processes (Crawford, Dunk, Brown and Tange were among its earliest members in 1955, although it remained more a roost for External

Affairs officials – perhaps self-consciously a 'flock of homeless people' – than for other departments well into the 1960s). And it was perhaps from the vantage of this select club that Wheeler (a member since 1960) observed that 'the attitude, behaviour and standards of the corps of Permanent Heads is of far greater importance in determining the tone and ethos of higher Public Service than all the rules and regulations'.[61] Style, again, mattered – by now, it was a badge of acceptance.

There were, however, increasing signs of fracture within this landscape. Boyer's unaddressed recommendations nagged – how should the public service of the late 1940s and 1950s adjust to the changing world of the 1960s? An increasingly analytical academic and journalistic perspective on the CPS and on policy development more generally began wondering whether the business of government, as it increasingly intersected with a diversification of social aspirations and attitudes, was perhaps no longer best served only by the priorities of economic management, but needed to take advice from other fields.[62]

Even within the domain of economics there was pressure. Crawford, for example, sought, through his participation in the Committee of Economic Enquiry – established by the Menzies Government in 1963 under the chairmanship of industrial executive (Sir) James Vernon – to expand the capacity of economic policy to engage with the intersecting dynamics of demographic trends, educational opportunities, public health, physical infrastructure constraints, natural resource possibilities, and industrial productivity in Australia. Released in 1965, the Vernon Report espoused a concept of 'growth' which, beyond its material benefits, 'endows the community with a sense of vigor and social purpose'. 'Growth' was the concept that, the committee argued, 'will make it easier for the community to exercise an even more fundamental kind of choice' about the conduct of their lives.[63] But it also required a more concerted program of planning, and this was the core recommendation from Vernon that the government and the Treasury in particular rejected. In this stand-off came perhaps the most public display of the rivalries and tensions that had always nagged away at the company of dwarfs, but now became public, and fed into public questioning.

It was the 'mauling' of the Vernon Report – despite it being, as Crawford noted, only 'mildly critical' of the government's record in economic management – that prompted the *Financial Review* in 1965 to bring the idea of the seven dwarfs

---

61   Wheeler, 'The Professional Career Public Servant', 173.
62   See B. Juddery, *At the Centre: The Australian Bureaucracy in the 1970s* (Melbourne: Cheshire, 1974), 77; also D. Glover, 'National Complacency? Australia in the Later Menzies Years: The Evidence of *Prospect*, *The Observer* and *The Bulletin*, 1958–1964', *Journal of Australian Studies*, 54/55 (1997): 176–87.
63   Committee of Economic Enquiry, *Report of the Committee of Economic Enquiry*, Vol. 1 (Canberra: AGPS, 1965), 29.

back into the spotlight. The Report was not asking for much in terms of an independent group of economic policy advisers. It was trying, perhaps, to achieve what Allen Brown had hoped to secure in the early 1950s, in salvaging the best of Post-War Reconstruction's experts for the Prime Minister's Department before they were scattered to other departments. Yet even in this tussle over the Vernon Report, the *Financial Review* concluded, 'the seven dwarfs ... have proven to be a most unradical group with a decided bias towards conservatism'. As individuals, in their internalised and externalised stances of (in Wheeler's term) 'self-denial', they had not sought to recast the structures of government. Nor in 1965 would they enter too far into public debate — that was not their role.[64] They tended, instead, to hold tight to the established places.

In the mid-1960s, then, the tensions that had — as Nethercote suggests — been with the dwarfs from the start, in their backgrounds and their dispositions, remained salient. But where once those tensions had been contained within a series of assumptions about the fit between the role and figure of the public servant and the settings of public policy, they now were steadily exposed by changes in those settings. Individual careers were far from over, but they were diversifying. Crawford was at ANU, building the research culture on big issues he had long sought within government; Brown spent a decade in diplomacy; Wilson became chairman of the Commonwealth Bank and QANTAS; Bland retired to corporate directorships, though he found time to conduct several government reviews and, briefly, to chair, and cut, the ABC. Coombs left the Reserve Bank in 1968 and became closely associated with several dimensions of the social and cultural questioning in Australia over the following years — in the arts, over the environment, and most particularly in Aboriginal affairs. Wheeler, securing at last the 'glittering prize' of becoming secretary of the Treasury in 1971, would confront a prime minister whom he judged to be breaking with the proprieties that underpinned accountable government. Around Whitlam, as Wheeler despaired, there had clustered an 'ebullient community ... in which groups claim the right to push and act on the basis of self-interest, often using whatever power is to hand regardless of the consequence to others'.[65] This was no way to behave; it was a fracture in all that the age of the seven dwarfs had represented — or a loss of control over the forces they had always feared.

In 1958, Sir Robert Garran assured readers of his memoirs that the national capital had long passed the point where its petty insularity could be evoked by the motto, 'by their incomes you shall know them'.[66] But with the passing of the dwarfs it was not just the austere and unimpeachable authority of a few wise and feared permanent heads that was slowly, at first imperceptibly,

---

64 *Financial Review*, 12 November 1965, 3.
65 Wheeler, 'The Professional Career Public Servant', 179.
66 R. Garran, *Prosper the Commonwealth* (Sydney: Angus and Robertson, 1958), 286.

being consigned to history. It was also a way of characterising a contract of government, and a figure to embody it, which set a distinct stamp on formative processes of post-war national development. It is hard to imagine the dwarfs enduring the charge of presiding over a '"she'll-be-right-mate" management and work style' in the 1980s. It is equally hard to imagine that such a charge would ever have been made against them in their time; Wheeler, as Ian Hancock notes in his chapter, stared down parliamentary scrutiny of his actions. That parliament would presume to push even further into the actions of officers at much lower levels within departments was inconceivable – then. Yet, if the 'age' of such figures now seems discontinuous with much that has followed, it is worth checking such nostalgia, or such dismissal, to ask instead what rose and fell with them in the work of government, and created the space in which such change was possible. The biographically informed chapters that follow go a long way in teasing out the extent to which the seven dwarfs were not simply a settled company in a faraway land, but a group characterised by tensions, rivalries, and 'styles' that were a part of transitions with long-term significance.

2

The Post-War Reconstruction Project

Stuart Macintyre

Yet out of evil cometh good.
— John Dedman, tabling the White Paper
on Full Employment[1]

Post-War Reconstruction is a term with a distinct Australian resonance. All of the participants in the Second World War had aims that informed their planning of arrangements for the end of hostilities. Among the Allies these goals found expression in the Atlantic Charter of August 1941, whereby Churchill and Roosevelt affirmed the principles on which their countries based 'their hopes for a better future for the world'. The principles included the assurance that 'all the men in all the lands may live out their lives in freedom from fear and want'. The two freedoms were drawn from President Roosevelt's State of the Union address at the beginning of 1941, and he took the other two freedoms it enunciated, freedom of speech and freedom of worship, as implicit in the Charter.[2]

For the first year of his premiership, Churchill had resisted any statement of Britain's objectives; he said later that the planners of the post-war order should not overlook the recipe given in a cookery book for jugged hare, which began 'First catch your hare'.[3] But Roosevelt's State of the Union address was intended to reconcile the American public to the Lend-Lease scheme and therefore included a provision for free trade, which inevitably drew the Allies into protracted negotiations over the post-war economic order.

In any case, there were insistent pressures in wartime Britain for a post-war commitment, especially after the Labour Party entered the government and the Beveridge Report identified freedom from want as one of 'the five giants on the road of reconstruction', the others being 'disease, ignorance, squalor and

---

1   *Digest of Decisions and Announcements*, 103 (26 May – 14 June 1945), 11.
2   W.L. Langer and S.E. Gleason, *The World Crisis and American Foreign Policy: The Undeclared War* (London: Royal Institute of International Affairs, 1953), chs 9, 21.
3   D. Reynolds, 'The Atlantic "Flop": British Foreign Policy and the Churchill–Roosevelt Meeting of August 1941', in D. Brinkley and D.R. Facey-Crowther, eds, *The Atlantic Charter* (New York: St Martin's Press, 1994), 129–50.

idleness'.⁴ Duff Cooper, the minister of information, persuaded the War Cabinet in August 1940 to establish a sub-committee on war aims, and Labour's Arthur Greenwood assumed ministerial responsibility for the Reconstruction Committee in January 1941; his colleague, William Jowitt, was appointed minister in charge of reconstruction in February 1942. Other ministers began planning post-war projects and numerous non-government organisations contributed their own blueprints. It was the same in Canada, where the president of McGill University chaired an Advisory Committee on Reconstruction from 1941 to 1943, and then C.D. Howe, a senior member of Mackenzie King's Cabinet, was appointed minister of reconstruction.⁵ New Zealand followed a similar course of consultation and planning.

There was a marked similarity also in the range of activities that the Allies envisaged. An immediate task would be demobilisation, repatriation and rehabilitation of members of the armed forces, along with generous schemes of education and training. Then there was the conversion of the wartime economy to civilian production, including disposal of assets and redeployment of munitions workers. All the Allies embraced full employment as an official objective and issued statements that explained how government would manage the economy to sustain growth. Making good the backlog of housing was another priority, along with restoration of investment in industry and public utilities. While New Zealand and the United States had introduced measures of social welfare during the 1930s, they joined the other Allies in extending income support and increasing provision for health and education. Population policy was a common concern, joined to ambitious schemes of immigration. Town planning and community development were also prominent.

All these initiatives made for an expansion of government and an enlargement of citizenship, but it was only in Australia that they were comprehended under the rubric of post-war reconstruction. That term had restricted currency in the United States, which emerged from the war as the dominant world power. Its Gross Domestic Product doubled between 1939 and 1945, providing both guns and butter, and a Gallup poll early in 1945 found that only 36 per cent of respondents believed they had made any real sacrifice for the war.⁶ While the United States took on new international responsibilities after the war, it did not see any need to plan new domestic arrangements; on the contrary, the task was to return the country to normality as quickly as possible. Canada enjoyed a good war for it too served as an arsenal for the Allied forces.⁷ When Douglas

---

4   P. Addison, *The Road to 1945: British Politics and the Second World War* (London: Jonathon Cape, 1975; rev. edn, London: Pimlico, 1994), 17.
5   R. Bothwell and W. Kilbourn, *C.D. Howe: A Biography* (Toronto: McClelland and Stewart, 1979), ch. 12.
6   J. Gilbert, *Another Chance: Postwar America, 1945-1968* (Philadelphia: Temple University Press, 1981), 8.
7   *The World Economy: Volume 1: A Millennial Perspective; Volume 2: Historical Statistics* (Paris: OECD, 2006), 462.

Copland, the Australian Prices Commissioner, visited Canada early in 1945, he was struck by the country's prosperity – industry was booming, most goods were in ample supply and, when he asked what was happening in the Ministry of Reconstruction, he found that it was principally concerned with the disposal of government-owned plant and equipment.[8]

The United Kingdom, on the other hand, emerged from the war exhausted and impoverished. Reconstruction was undoubtedly necessary to make good the effects of the blitz, yet the Attlee Government embarked on an economic and social program of heroic proportions while struggling to preserve the country's status as a world power. The Labour Party's electoral program in 1945 was entitled, *Let Us Face the Future*, but those who set about doing so coined far grander phrases: they were creating 'The New Order', building a 'New Jerusalem' that would support all citizens 'From Cradle to Grave'.[9] Talk of reconstruction, so common in early wartime discussion, fell into disuse, partly because it reminded many Britons of the conspicuous failure of an earlier ministry of that name created during the First World War to redeem David Lloyd George's pledge of 'A Land Fit for Heroes'. For that matter, the associations in the United States were equally unattractive. The Reconstruction that followed the Civil War (which seems to be where the term originated) had only compounded the rancour of the former Confederate states.

Rehabilitation and reconstruction were included in the functions of the Department of Labour and National Service created in October 1940; a Reconstruction Division was established in that department at the end of the year, and in February 1941 an interdepartmental committee was formed to coordinate the planning. The new Labor Government attached the term to a variety of initiatives taken during the critical phase of the war against Japan. In opening the Constitutional Convention in November 1942, John Curtin explained that extensive new powers were required for 'the vital task of post-war reconstruction'. Following the undertaking by the states that they would transfer these powers to the Commonwealth, he formed the Department of Post-War Reconstruction.[10]

By this time reconstruction had taken on an enlarged meaning. When Roland Wilson, who as head of the Department of Labour and National Service guided the initial work of the Reconstruction Division, appeared before the Parliamentary Committee on Social Services to explain progress, he conceded that the word could mean constructing again or constructing anew, but suggested that reconstruction should be distinguished from restoration. Its usage, he noted,

---

8 'Notes on 1944-45 Trip', 9 February 1945, Copland Papers, National Library of Australia (NLA) MS 3800, Box 152.
9 P. Clarke, *The Last Thousand Days of the British Empire* (London: Allen Lane, 2007), 309.
10 *Digest of Decisions and Announcements*, 46 (12 November – 6 December 1942), 22.

stretched from the 'severely practical and rather humdrum tasks' of beating swords into ploughshares to the 'aspirations of a people to build Jerusalem in Australia's brown and pleasant land'.[11]

It was the work of the Department of Post-War Reconstruction that gave the term its expanded Australian valency. New Zealand provides an instructive contrast for there was a marked similarity between the two countries in the scale of their war effort and the methods they employed to sustain it, as well as a close correspondence of their post-war aspirations. But New Zealand chose to pursue them through a Cabinet sub-committee of senior ministers and an executive committee of the departmental heads, coordinating activity by means of an Organisation for National Development located within the Prime Minister's Department and generating a host of national and regional planning committees. This unwieldy structure was impractical and soon abandoned.[12] Canada briefly used a Department of Reconstruction, but C.D. Howe preferred to work through his major portfolio of Munitions and Supply, and was unsympathetic to the expansive schemes devised by the earlier Committee on Reconstruction.[13] Similarly, the British Ministry remained small and devoid of substantial responsibilities. Accordingly the appellation fell into disuse. Few Australians remarked on its persistence here, and Australian historians took it over as a shorthand term for an epoch and an ethos.

The Department of Post-War Reconstruction contained three of the seven dwarfs – Dr H.C. Coombs, J.G. Crawford and Allen Brown. It emerged out of another department headed by a fourth dwarf, Dr Roland Wilson, and nurtured a remarkable number of future departmental heads – Harold Breen, John Bunting, Lenox Hewitt, John Knott, Cecil (Eske) Lambert, Peter Lawler, Charles McFadyen, William McLaren, Arthur Tange and Geoffrey Yeend. All three heads of the Prime Minister's Department between 1949 and 1971 were former officers of Post-War Reconstruction. Established at a time when Prime Minister's was little more than a secretariat and Treasury a budget office, the new department was able to initiate policy. It had powerful ministers in Chifley and Dedman. A new creation, it recruited extensively from outside the ranks of the pre-war public service and thus escaped the overhang of ageing ex-AIF functionaries. The leading officers were young university graduates who flourished as the Commonwealth Public Service (CPS) took on a new professionalism.

---

11   'Research on Internal Subjects, Economic and Social – Evidence Submitted to the Social Security Committee', 20 June 1942, National Archives of Australia (NAA) A9816, 1943/413.
12   J.V.T. Baker, *The New Zealand People at War: War Economy* (Wellington: Historical Publications Branch, Department of Internal Affairs, 1965), 527–30.
13   R. Bothwell, I. Drummond and J. English, *Canada since 1945: Power, Politics and Provincialism* (Toronto: University of Toronto Press, 1981), 65–9.

2. The Post-War Reconstruction Project

H.C. Coombs with Prime Minister Ben Chifley in London, 1946

Source: National Archives of Australia, M2153, 6/2

Yet the department was also a product of wartime improvisation, a somewhat belated device to bring together a number of disparate ventures. Initially, it was not intended to undertake administrative activities; rather, it would support and coordinate the work of commissions of inquiry on rural reconstruction, housing, public works and secondary industry (and for this reason it was initially designated as a ministry), and then plan their implementation by other departments (so that it was represented in a very wide range of interdepartmental committees). It soon embarked on additional activities – such as immigration, regional planning and community development – that were usually suggested by Coombs as director-general to Chifley as minister and justified by their relevance to the declared goals of national development, full employment and rising living standards. Some of the proposed commissions, such as one on public works, fell victim to obstruction by the states; others, such as education and Aboriginals, were rejected by Chifley, who enjoyed close relations with Coombs but remained instinctively cautious. The department also acquired administrative functions, some of them taken over from the Department of War Organisation of Industry when that department was absorbed in 1945, and then hived off to other departments before its abolition at the end of the decade. In 1945 it had a staff complement of just under 1,000.[14]

The results were uneven. Coombs' energetic leadership was interrupted by long periods abroad and some of the divisional heads lacked his political acumen. The failure of the Commonwealth to obtain the additional powers sought by referendum in 1944 necessitated reliance on the cooperation of the often uncooperative states; among the casualties were the housing program and the scheme for technical training. The abrupt conclusion of the Pacific War threw plans for an orderly transition into disarray. So, too, the immediate cessation of the Lend-Lease program, the dollar shortage and deteriorating industrial relations imposed severe constraints on the plans for industrial development. With the onset of the Cold War, a deteriorating political climate diminished the public support on which post-war reconstruction was premised.

Most of all, the project was seriously handicapped by its association with wartime austerity. A country that was weary of manpower direction, regulation and rationing, expected peace to bring relief from state control. It did not help that Coombs had been director of Rationing and Dedman was remembered as the man who cancelled Christmas.

---

14   First Report of the Committee of Review of Civil Staffing of Wartime Activities, 27 July 1945, NAA M448, 105.

2. The Post-War Reconstruction Project

John Dedman, 1941

Source: Australian War Memorial, 010015

Closely linked to this mood of disenchantment was a suspicion of the planner. Joanne Pemberton has noted how the idea of planning was born out of the misery and chaos of the inter-war years. The wartime emergency brought intellectuals confident of their capacity to build a new order on the ruins of the old into new positions of influence, and planning achieved a 'rhetorical dominance'.[15] But their participation in a Labor government steeped in ancestral memories of class conflict meant that planning lost its earlier connotations of science and social progress. As demonstrated in the all-too-frequent paeans to planning delivered by Lloyd Ross, the director of Public Relations in the Department of Post-War Reconstruction, it had become a political creed.[16]

Paul Hasluck writes in the second volume of his war history that '[i]n the public service, and on the fringes of the public service, in various agencies created for the purpose, there grew up towards the end of the war a group of persons who might best be described as the planners'. But Hasluck was himself an early planner, the joint secretary of the Inter-Departmental Committee on External Relations established in 1941, and head of the post-war section of the Department of External Affairs created in April 1942. He goes on to suggest that:

> The planners were a new phenomenon in Australian government and the administrative arrangements made for post-war reconstruction gave them unusual opportunities. They were a new and devout group who had believed in the planned state and had communed about it when they were only a devout few in the political catacombs, and now the Emperor himself had embraced their religion.[17]

Ronald Walker takes a different perspective. An early adviser to government on post-war reconstruction, and then deputy director-general of the Department of War Organisation of Industry, he was better placed to assess the transformation of the public service. In his subsequent account of *The Australian Economy in War and Reconstruction*, he noted how the sudden expansion of wartime administration spawned many new departments and directorates, with overlapping functions, inconsistent reporting lines and a maze of interdepartmental committees and councils to coordinate their efforts. Generally speaking, he observed, federal ministers took a less active part in the administration of their departments than their state counterparts and permanent heads carried a heavier burden of

---

15   J. Pemberton, 'The Middle Way: The Discourse of Planning in Britain, Australia and the League in the Interwar Years', *Australian Journal of Politics and History*, 52, no. 1 (2006), 48–63; '"O Brave New Social Order": The Controversy Over Planning in Australia and Britain in the 1940s', *Journal of Australian Studies*, 83 (2004), 35–47.
16   L. Ross, 'A New Social Order', in D.A.S. Campbell, ed., *Post-War Reconstruction in Australia* (Sydney: Australian Publishing Company in conjunction with the Australian Institute of Political Science, 1944), 183–237.
17   P. Hasluck, *The Government and the People 1942–1945* (Canberra: Australian War Memorial, 1970), 445.

responsibility. The absence of a senior administrative class, as in Britain or the United States, made it necessary to recruit from business, the universities and the legal profession.[18]

In Walker's opinion, businessmen often found it difficult to adapt to different methods and expectations, though they quickly acquired 'the civil-service custom of appraising the status of an officer by the number of drawers in his desk'. The lawyers, with their familiarity with paperwork and orderly minds, were more easily absorbed. Academics brought a certain literary facility and an ability to master large bodies of information, and Walker judged them to be readier than businessmen to appreciate the professional qualities of the regular public servant. He singled out his own profession: 'the building of the war-time administrative machine fell very largely to economists'.[19]

Walker might be thought here to be indulging in self-service, though he acknowledged that the economists who acquired executive duties were not always viewed favourably by members of the permanent public service or the public, which expected them to advise on policy rather than execute it. 'If the Australian public service were nearer the British in quality', he added, 'economists would not have figured so prominently in war administration' and could have made a greater contribution as expert advisers.[20] L.F. Giblin, the father figure of the economics profession, who exercised considerable influence from the chair of the advisory Financial and Economic Committee, judged that Australian economists possessed 'an acute political sense'. They were frequently 'more practical and realistic than the business men' and thus given responsibility for some of the 'most acutely practical' administrative tasks such as price control, rationing and labour allocation. 'The word of complaint or abuse is "academic"; but in truth they are the least academic of God's creatures.'[21]

There were indeed complaints of impractical academics invading the public service. The director of the Associated Chamber of Manufacturers denounced the 'economists, ranging in hue from full pink to deep red mostly deep red' who had descended upon Canberra to impose their schemes on the nation.[22] Arthur Fadden, the leader of the Opposition, criticised the Curtin Government's reliance upon 'men who had little or no experience of business and industrial life'.[23] His Country Party colleague, Larry Anthony, decried the 'itch to interfere on the part of professors, economists and other cap-and-gown gentlemen'.[24]

---

18   E.R. Walker, *The Australian Economy in War and Reconstruction* (New York: Oxford University Press, 1947), ch. 5.
19   Ibid., 126–8.
20   Ibid., 128.
21   L.F. Giblin, 'Reconstruction in Australia', *Agenda: A Quarterly Journal of Reconstruction*, 2, no. 3 (1943), 216.
22   'Pink and Red Economists Find Sanctuary in ACT', *Canberra Times*, 14 April 1943.
23   'Mr Fadden Attacks New Department', *Sydney Morning Herald*, 18 August 1943.
24   *Commonwealth Parliamentary Debates*, 173 (3 February 1943), 245.

We should remember also the advice given by Copland when the head of the Prime Minister's Department asked why his assistant was occupying a bench in the parliamentary gardens: 'Mr Downing does his best work in a rose garden'. There was also the occasion when Dick Downing, resplendent in the purple scarf of his Cambridge college, entered a room in Parliament House in search of Copland. Seeing that he was interrupting a meeting chaired by the prime minister, Downing withdrew. 'Tell me', asked John Curtin, 'who was that very distinguished-looking gentleman with a bath-towel round his neck?' Informed that it was the assistant economic consultant to the prime minister, his only comment was 'Oh, indeed'.[25]

These observations have particular relevance for the dwarfs and other senior public servants whose careers progressed through the Department of Post-War Reconstruction. Many of them were economists seconded to government duty in an advisory role, sometimes from universities and sometimes – like Coombs, Crawford and Tange – from banks. They soon became administrators and were caught up in the tangled web of wartime decision-making. Some returned subsequently to academic posts, while others stayed on to put their stamp on public policy over the following decades. And perforce their duties in the Department of Post-War Reconstruction meant that they were all planners.

In the space that is available to me I shall trace out these patterns in the formative wartime years. I suggest there were two phases. The first lasted from late 1940 to the end of 1942, when the planning of post-war reconstruction was neglected and ineffective. The second begins with the advent of Coombs as director-general of the new department, when planning became an urgent necessity.

The Menzies Government made provision for planning reconstruction as a result of its political difficulties. Following the election in September 1940, the Coalition lacked a majority in the House of Representatives. After protracted negotiations with Labor failed to secure a wartime National government, Menzies acceded to the conditions that Curtin attached to his support of the war effort – that there should be an Advisory War Council and that a start should be made on reconstruction planning. Hence a Reconstruction Division was included in the newly formed Department of Labour and National Service. At the beginning of 1941, Menzies formally requested Harold Holt, the minister, to investigate the tasks of post-war reconstruction and especially the re-employment of servicemen and war workers. Holt explained that the investigation would need to be coordinated with other federal departments and the Cabinet approved establishment of an Inter-Departmental Advisory Committee on Reconstruction.[26]

---

25   N. Brown, '"Mr Downing Does His Best Work in a Rose Garden": An Economist in Canberra in the 1940s', *Canberra Bulletin of Public Administration*, 80 (September 1996): 33–45; G. Firth to H. Arndt, 4 June 1976, Firth Papers, NLA Acc. 01/273, Box 9A.
26   Minister for Labour and National Service, 'Co-ordination of Reconstruction Planning', 7 February 1941, NAA A9816/3, 1943/550; see also Holt in *Commonwealth Parliamentary Debates*, 165 (4 December 1940), 438.

2. The Post-War Reconstruction Project

Dr H.C. (Nugget) Coombs, 1942

Source: Australian War Memorial, 136412

Ronald Wilson accordingly invited representatives of the service departments, Postmaster-General's, Supply and Development, Trade and Customs, the Treasury, the Tariff Board, the Prices Commissioner, the Coordinator-General of Works, the Repatriation Commission, the Financial and Economic Committee and the Council for Scientific and Industrial Research (CSIR) to a first meeting. The committee that assembled in Canberra on 14 March 1941 is more aptly described as a conference. It was chaired by Holt, with Herbert Evatt – the former justice of the High Court who had recently arrived in the House of Representatives and was impatient for office – accepting appointment as director of research and serving as the deputy chair. After noting some dimensions of the task, the participants decided that specialist sub-committees should pursue them.[27]

This was the first and last meeting of the Advisory Committee. In its aftermath a number of departmental heads submitted statements amplifying the views they had expressed at the meeting and suggesting how the sub-committees might proceed. Several were anxious to volunteer their services (so the Tariff Board took charge of investigating the post-war prospects for industry) and others warned the Advisory Committee from trespassing (hence the secretary of the Department of the Interior insisted that the committee should not concern itself with migration, and Wilson had to remind him that his department had joined its deliberations at the express request of his minister).[28] Giblin, as the chair of the Financial and Economic Committee, and Copland, as Prices Commissioner, provided perceptive comments about economic aspects of reconstruction, while David Rivett, as head of the CSIR, offered the mordant observation that 'the only completely satisfactory manner of dealing with unemployment' seemed to be war. He also remarked on the paradox of reconstruction in its Australian usage: 'Reconstruction implies prior destruction. So far there has not been much destruction here ... We can therefore to an extent determine our immediate "destruction" for war purposes, with an eye to reconstruction.'[29]

Six sub-committees were constituted, and the one that made most substantial progress was the Inter-Departmental Committee on External Relations, which worked with Treasury, External Affairs and the Financial and Economic Committee on the implications of Article VII of the Lend-Lease scheme, which pledged Australia and other beneficiaries of American assistance to liberalise trade restrictions. The states agreed to begin their own post-war planning, but a mid-year meeting of their liaison officers in Canberra revealed a low level of activity.

---

27   'Report of the First Meeting of the Inter-Departmental Committee on Reconstruction', NAA A9816/3, 1943/553.
28   Statement by Tariff Board, 22 April 1941, NAA A9816/3, 1943/555; J.A. Carrodus, Secretary of the Department of the Interior, to R. Wilson, 2 October 1941, and Wilson to Carrodus, 24 November 1941, NAA A9816/3, 1943/441.
29   D. Rivett, 'Notes', NAA A9816/3, 1943/555.

The universities were enlisted to undertake investigation of aspects of reconstruction, using a Commonwealth grant for social science research that Roland Wilson established, but this too was of limited utility.

These activities were coordinated by the Reconstruction Division of the department, which was also responsible for gathering and disseminating information. The Division consisted of a small group of research officers recently recruited to the public service: P.W.E. ('Pike') Curtin, a contemporary of Coombs who had studied at the London School of Economics; P.R.H. ('Perce') Judd, formerly economics teacher at Adelaide High; L.F. ('Fin') Crisp, who studied economics at Oxford as a Rhodes scholar until the outbreak of war; G.G. (Gerald) Firth, an Englishman who had come to Australia as a research fellow in the economics department of the University of Melbourne; and A.H. (Arthur) Tange, an economics graduate of the University of Western Australia who had worked for the Bank of New South Wales. Curtin and Judd were in their early thirties, the others still in their twenties. Their location in the Old Hospital Building in Canberra separated them from the rest of the department in Melbourne, though they were encouraged and assisted by E.R. Richard ('Dick') Hayward, formerly personal assistant to Wilson and now assistant-director of the Industrial Welfare Division, and K.C.O. ('Mick') Shann, Wilson's current assistant. They dealt principally with young and rising officers of the public service in Canberra, notably Fred Wheeler in the Treasury and John Burton, who had moved from Labour and National Service to External Affairs in the previous year. The Division's other function, encouraging the study of reconstruction throughout the community, was hampered by the reluctance of the Cabinet to authorise publication of the literature it prepared.[30]

The change of government in October 1941 brought no greater urgency. Eddie Ward, the new minister, showed a conspicuous lack of interest in this part of his portfolio and had to be prodded by Chifley to revive the Inter-Departmental Committee on External Relations so that Australia could establish its position on Article VII for imminent negotiations.[31] Ward also allowed the Tariff Board to retain responsibility for advising on the post-war conversion of wartime industries, a task for which it was ill equipped.[32] Chifley showed increasing interest in reconstruction during 1942, as did the Joint Parliamentary Committee on Social Security. Its fifth report, presented in October 1942, stressed the need for a comprehensive plan, criticised the Inter-Departmental Committee as too

---

30 Weekly reports of Division's activities, August–November 1941, NAA A9861/3, 1943/743.
31 Chifley to Ward, 18 March 1942, NAA A9816/3, 1943/441.
32 Ward, Cabinet submission, 5 May 1942, NAA M4481, 109.

unwieldy to direct and coordinate such planning, and recommended a minister be given responsibility with the assistance of a new National Planning and Coordination Committee.[33]

Throughout 1942 the officers of the Reconstruction Division chafed at the restrictions they encountered. Arthur Tange, who joined it in February 1942, later recalled that 'I more than once wondered just what was expected of us and what purpose I was serving'. There was almost no direction from above – the Cabinet was preoccupied with the war crisis, Wilson was more than fully occupied, and if anyone had stopped a minister or senior officer in a corridor and said he wanted to talk about post-war housing, rural reconstruction or other such matter, 'he was probably in peril of his life'.[34]

Gerald Firth, who shared the feeling of futility, sought solace from Giblin and Copland, his former colleagues at the University of Melbourne. With Giblin's encouragement, he hit upon the idea of 'handing the whole show' over to Coombs, who was at that time adviser to the Treasury. Firth could see one impediment to such an arrangement, the unlikelihood that the head of Treasury, Stuart McFarlane, would accept responsibility for reconstruction. He did not see another, the fact that Coombs was about to become director of Rationing. Nevertheless, early in April 1942, he approached Coombs, who suggested that it might be possible to resolve the problem 'by getting Chifley to take on Reconstruction more or less as a separate portfolio – Coombs being responsible in regard to reconstruction'.[35] Firth assumed that Coombs' appointment a week later nullified the scheme but, from this point, Chifley assumed greater responsibility for reconstruction. In May, he took a submission prepared by the Reconstruction Division for the creation of a Rural Reconstruction Commission to Cabinet, and in August he was appointed to the chair of a new Cabinet sub-committee to coordinate and direct reconstruction planning.[36]

The only remaining obstacle to creation of a department was the prime minister. Throughout 1942 John Curtin was preoccupied by the threat of invasion and wanted no distraction from the urgent tasks of national mobilisation. As late as September 1942, he insisted that the government had no intention of establishing a ministry of reconstruction.[37] If backbenchers such as Arthur Calwell were prepared to challenge Curtin – and Calwell claimed credit for the

---

33   T.H. Kewley, *Social Security in Australia 1900–1972* (2nd edn, Sydney: Sydney University Press, 1973), 176–9.
34   Arthur Tange, interviewed by J.D.B Miller, 1–23 April 1981, NLA TRC 1023; and see his memo to Coombs, 8 February 1942, Crisp Papers, NLA MS 5243/12/2.
35   Firth diary, 9–10 April 1942, NLA, Acc. 01/273.
36   Cabinet submission on 'Rural Reconstruction', NAA M448/1, 109; *Digest of Decisions and Announcements*, 36 (26 July – 10 August 1942), 14.
37   *Digest of Decisions and Announcements*, 43 (17–28 September 1942), 19.

2. The Post-War Reconstruction Project

resolution calling for a department of post-war reconstruction carried at the federal conference of the Labor Party in November 1942 – Chifley would not gainsay the leader he served so faithfully.[38]

It would seem that Roland Wilson played a decisive role. This most diminutive of the seven dwarfs, aptly described by Gerald Firth as a 'redoubtable little bastard', could see that his minister was wholly unsympathetic to the work of the Reconstruction Division.[39] Eddie Ward, the minister for Labour and National Service, was preoccupied with industrial relations, frequently clashing with Cabinet colleagues as he sought to strengthen the position of trade unions. Ward had little time for economists, whom he blamed for their part in designing the Premiers' Plan during the Depression, and he was suspicious of grandiose talk of a new social order. 'There is only one new order acceptable to the workers', he said in the House of Representatives during discussion of the Atlantic Charter, and 'that is the social ownership and control of production, distribution and exchange'.[40] Despairing of the inaction, Wilson met with Curtin sometime in the spring of 1942 and advised him that reconstruction should be taken out of Labour and National Service and put into a new department with Coombs as its director. Curtin accepted the proposal and advised Wilson to see Chifley and talk him into accepting responsibility for it.[41] It is clear that Chifley was predisposed to agree and, on 22 December 1942, he was appointed minister for Post-War Reconstruction.[42]

Two months earlier, Chifley had asked Coombs for advice about how the new entity might operate. The two men had already devised the Rural Reconstruction Commission as a mechanism for consultation, investigation and planning; a commission could be established under the national security regulations, gather evidence in a manner that allowed interested parties to put their case, yet operate with a level of autonomy that would protect it from capture by vested interests. Coombs envisaged additional commissions on secondary industries, housing, public works, education and Aboriginal policy. In providing these commissions with technical and research support, officers of the department would guide and direct them; collectively they would comprise a 'central reconstruction secretariat' that would ensure coherence. The problem exercising Coombs was implementation. It would be necessary to ensure the cooperation of other departments responsible for activities involved in reconstruction, and he

---

38 A. Calwell in *Commonwealth Parliamentary Debates*, 170 (6 May 1942), 913–14; and letter to Coombs, 19 January 1942, NAA M448/1, 39.
39 Firth diary, 11 November 1940.
40 *Commonwealth Parliamentary Debates*, 168 (21 August 1941), 99.
41 This account was given by Wilson in discussion at the 1981 Conference on Post-War Reconstruction; NLA TRC 1096.
42 *Digest of Decisions and Announcements*, 46 (12 November – 6 December 1942), 21–9; 48 (8–18 December 1942), 17.

thought this was best pursued through 'joint projects'. But the body responsible for reconstruction could not be simply 'another Commonwealth department', and should report directly to the treasurer.[43]

To emphasise that it was not another department, Post-War Reconstruction began as a ministry, that title encompassing the link between the commissions of inquiry and the research and administrative apparatus that served them. But as the commissions completed their work, they were replaced by departmental divisions (hence the Rural Division and the Secondary Industries Division) so that Post-War Reconstruction became a department, albeit one that was intended from the outset to have a finite existence. Its functions encompassed the preparation of plans for the transition from a wartime to a peacetime economy, along with a collaborative role in re-establishment of members of the services and war workers; the disposal of wartime buildings, plant and equipment; the maintenance and expansion of employment and the national income; the prevention of want and attainment of social security; and the development and conservation of the country's resources.

Coombs canvassed his ideas among colleagues and knowledge of his new role spread well in advance of its announcement. Ronald Walker wrote to Chifley early in November 1942 to welcome the Government's new resolve and endorse the combination of commissions and a 'central reconstruction secretariat'. While acknowledging the prior reluctance to embark on post-war reconstruction planning for fear of provoking domestic disunity, he warned that 'business men are already busy with their own plans to better their position in the post-war period', and stressed the urgency of mobilising public support for a genuine reconstruction.[44]

Coombs needed no such persuasion of the importance of public support. As Tim Rowse has explained, he paid particular attention to this aspect of the work of the Rationing Commission,[45] and had already advised Chifley that the reconstruction organisation would need 'to provide a channel through which public and sectional desire for reconstruction can flow and canalise this political energy into effective channels and prevent the development of a sense of frustration'. At this formative stage he took advice from Brian Fitzpatrick, then working as industrial liaison and research officer for the Rationing Commission, who reinforced the importance of stiffening morale.[46] He seems also to have been briefly impressed by the enigmatic Alf Conlon, who, in May 1942, had persuaded

---

43 Coombs, memorandum to Chifley, 22 October 1942, NAA M448/1, 109.
44 Walker to Chifley, 6 November 1942, NAA A9816/3, 1943/787.
45 T. Rowse, *Nugget Coombs: A Reforming Life* (Cambridge: Cambridge University Press, 2002), 92–9.
46 B. Fitzpatrick, 'Notes for Submission to the Honourable the Treasurer on Post-War Reconstruction Planning Organisation', n.d. [October 1941], NAA M481/1, 109; see also letters to Coombs, 27 September, 13 October 1942, Fitzpatrick Papers, NLA MS 4965/6/1-7.

2. The Post-War Reconstruction Project

Curtin to establish a Committee on National Morale 'responsible directly to the prime minister and consisting only of distinguished and disinterested minds' – though the prime minister's confidence in these experts was dispelled by their overblown proposal at the end of the year for a 'National Public Relations Service' with an annual budget of more than £1,000,000.[47] The new department embarked on a range of activities to publicise its work – publications, broadcasts, service education – and established a substantial network of discussion groups.

The central office of the department was in Canberra, along with a policy and research division, but most of the commissions and the divisions that carried out the work were based in Melbourne and Sydney. First came the Rural Reconstruction Commission, announced on New Year's Day; the Reconstruction Training Committee was formed in March 1943, the Housing Commission in April, the National Works Council in July and the Secondary Industries Commission in October 1943. The department also inherited some initiatives, such as the Universities Commission, which was incorporated into an Office of Education in 1945. In the same year it absorbed the Department of War Organisation of Industry.

Other components of reconstruction were undertaken elsewhere. Hence the department played little part in the expansion of social services, which began with child endowment under the Menzies Government and extended to widows' pensions, the National Welfare fund, unemployment and sickness benefits, free medicine and hospital care. It was given responsibility for preparation of the White Paper on Full Employment, which lagged behind similar statements in Britain, the United States and Canada; and Coombs failed to carry one of his most ambitions proposals, a Department of Economic Planning.

No attempt will be made here to assess the work of these agencies.[48] Rather, I shall venture some observations about the way the department worked that have implications for the era of the seven dwarfs.

My first observation is that Australia came late to the task of planning reconstruction. Coombs had scarcely begun his appointment as director-general before he was sent abroad to advise Evatt on negotiations in London, Washington and Hot Springs on post-war economic proposals, leaving Leslie Melville of the

---

47   'Report of Committee on Civilian Morale', n.d. [April 1942], and 'Plan for National Public Relations Service', n.d. [January 1943], NAA A5954, 328/21.
48   See H. Gallagher, *We Got A Fair Go: A History of the Commonwealth Reconstruction Training Scheme, 1945-1952* (Melbourne: H. Gallagher, c. 2003); E. Jones, 'Post-World War Two Industry Policy: Opportunities and Constraints', *Australian Economic History Review*, 42, no. 3 (November 2002), 312–33; T. Whitford and D. Boadle, 'Australia's Rural Reconstruction Commission, 1943–46: A Reassessment', *Australian Journal of Politics and History*, 54, no. 4 (December 2008), 525–44; A.W. Martin and J. Penny, 'The Rural Reconstruction Commission, 1943-1947', *Australian Journal of Politics and History*, 29, no. 2 (1983), and other papers presented at the 1981 Conference on Post-War Reconstruction.

Commonwealth Bank in charge of the new ministry. It was here that Coombs first expounded his 'positive approach' to Article VII of the Mutual Aid agreement, which linked domestic policies of full employment to the reduction of trade barriers, and he also found time to investigate the organisation of reconstruction planning in Britain. Reporting the failure of Jowitt's 'reconstruction secretariat' to exert any influence over the separate endeavours of various departments, he advised Chifley in July 1943 that '[t]his experience throws a lot of light on the problems which lie ahead of us'. But it would be some months before he could tackle them.[49]

The original idea was that the 'central reconstruction secretariat' would operate in tandem with the commissions, but in practice it lagged behind their investigations while they in turn were late in submitting the reports that were needed to set administrative arrangements in train. Coombs took care with his appointments – he sought out economics graduates such as Trevor Swan and Noel Butlin, and fought hard to secure the services of Flora Eldershaw – but sometimes had to make do with what he could get. One key appointment, that of Lloyd Ross as director of Public Relations, was imposed on him by the prime minister.

The recruitment of John Crawford revealed the flaws in the ministry's design. Crawford was working for the Rural Bank of New South Wales, and advising the Department of War Organisation of Industry, when Coombs invited him to become executive officer of the Rural Reconstruction Commission in January 1943. Crawford was wary of the ambiguities in this role, quickly fell out with members of the commission (whom he accused of 'preconceived and stupid prejudices') and within two months was threatening to resign. Coombs arranged for Crawford to become director of the Research Division, and his de facto deputy.[50] When this dwarf left to become director of the Bureau of Agricultural Economics in 1945, his replacement was Allen Brown, an equally redoubtable bureaucratic infighter. Crawford and Brown honed their skills in the maze of interdepartmental committees – the department was represented on a score of them by 1945 – but other divisional heads with more specialist expertise struggled.

The director-general was absent for long periods after the war, representing Australia in international negotiations over finance and trade, but he alone was able to resolve the frequent disputes with other departments. 'You must remember', Firth advised a scholar investigating the history of post-war reconstruction, 'that in his prime Coombs was able to charm birds out of trees'.[51] Tange recalled Coombs as idealistic and rather romantic, but 'one of the most persuasive men that I have ever met'.[52] Alan Renouf, who accompanied Coombs

---

49 Coombs to Chifley, 12 July 1943, NAA M448/1, 109.
50 Correspondence between Crawford and Coombs, 21 January – 30 March 1943, NAA M448/1, 39.
51 G. Firth to M. Howard, 14 February 1975, NLA MS Acc. 01/273, Box 9A.
52 A. Tange, interviewed by J.D.B. Miller, March 1981, NLA TRC 1023.

at the Havana Trade Conference, knew of no other Australian who exercised the same measure of intelligence, charm and persuasion.[53] His special relationship with Chifley enabled him to overcome Treasury resistance to some of the programs prepared by Post-War Reconstruction, but not all of them – his proposals for community centres and special assistance to women with family responsibilities were among the casualties. After 1945, when Chifley passed the portfolio to Dedman but kept the Treasury, he was increasingly inclined to follow its advice. R.H. Tawney's comment on the British experience after the First World War – 'For five years the Treasury had led a forlorn life. Now it crept from its corner making mournful noises' – had special force in Australia from 1945.[54]

A further difficulty was the uncertainty about the Commonwealth's powers for post-war reconstruction. At the Constitutional Convention in November 1942 the states undertook to transfer a wide range of powers, but in February 1943 the South Australian Parliament amended the enabling bill and it soon became apparent that other methods would be required. With an election due before the end of the year, however, Curtin was anxious to allay accusations that these powers would be used to impose socialism by stealth. Speaking at the Fremantle Town Hall on 29 April 1943, he declared that 'we have not socialised Australia and we don't intend to do so'.[55] Moreover, he was still adamant that invasion remained a real threat. Launching the third Liberty Loan on 28 March 1943, the prime minister said:

> I am not interested in the kind of world we are to have when the war is over. I have given thought to it, but I do not delude myself. You need not worry about the Beveridge plan … or Mr Chifley in his important task of reconstruction unless Japan is beaten.[56]

By June, Curtin was ready to concede that the imminent danger had passed, and in the subsequent election campaign he made much of Labor's plans for a new peacetime order. Yet it was not until August 1944 that the government sought the transfer of powers by referendum. That Curtin allowed Evatt to draft the terms of the referendum (especially the provision that all 14 powers should stand or fall together) and conduct the campaign remains a mystery.

The defeat of the referendum left the government reliant on wartime powers due to expire six months after the end of hostilities. This limitation bedevilled almost every field of reconstruction but its hampering effects were apparent long before the plebiscite. Many arrangements had to be determined during 1943

---

53   A. Renouf, *The Champagne Trail: Experiences of a Diplomat* (Melbourne: Sun Books, 1980), 37.
54   R.H. Tawney, 'The Abolition of Economic Controls', *Economic History Review*, 13, no. 1–2 (1943), 1–30.
55   *Digest of Decisions and Announcements*, 58 (12 April – 13 May 1943), 29.
56   Ibid., 56 (4 March – 1 April 1943), 43.

and the first half of 1944 at meetings with the state premiers, and necessitated a series of debilitating compromises. The failure to catch the wartime enthusiasm for reconstruction at its flood was costly.

The problem was compounded by ministerial rivalries. Dedman, who hoped in 1942 that he would be given responsibility for reconstruction, maintained a millenarian fervour that contrasted with Chifley's more restrained advocacy. Coombs suggested that his minister make an early statement of the broad objectives, and provided a draft. 'There is a danger', it warned, 'that reconstruction will become a magic word and create dreams that cannot be realised'.[57] The minister became more expansive after the 1943 election removed these constraints, though tight controls were maintained on statements from departmental staff.

The machinations of Evatt were far more damaging. His interest in post-war reconstruction fluctuated after his initial appointment in 1941 as director of research, which was conspicuously unproductive. Through John Burton, he kept up an interest during 1942 in the Inter-Departmental Committee on External Relations. As attorney-general, he was responsible for preparing the Constitutional Convention and summoned Crisp and Firth to join a team of public servants in Melbourne who prepared a lengthy *Case for Greater Commonwealth Powers*.[58] Evatt came late to an appreciation of the 'positive approach' to international economic arrangements, but took it up as part of his endeavour to assert an Australian influence in world affairs. To this end he had Tange transferred to the Department of External Affairs as a liaison officer early in 1944.[59]

Evatt's ally, J.A. Beasley, represented Australia at the International Labour Organization conference at Philadelphia in April 1944; against the advice of the economists, Beasley pursued an explicit commitment to full employment so ham-fistedly that the Americans withdrew their support for a broader endorsement. When the Australians did not get their way at the United Nations Monetary and Financial Conference at Bretton Woods in July 1944, Evatt instructed the delegation led by Leslie Melville not to sign the final record. It was fortunate that Roland Wilson accompanied Evatt and Frank Forde, the deputy prime minister, to the founding meeting of the United Nations at San Francisco in 1945, for Wilson was conspicuously immune to browbeating, but Evatt persisted nevertheless in inserting a weak provision for full employment into the United

---

57   Coombs to Chifley, 'Draft Policy Broadcast', 20 April 1943, NAA M448/1, 109; Chifley's use of these words is recorded in the transcript of his broadcast on 17 May 1943, Dedman Papers, NLA MS 987/1/508.
58   H.V. Evatt, *Post-War Reconstruction: A Case for Greater Commonwealth Powers Prepared for the Constitutional Convention at Canberra* (Melbourne: Government Printer, 1942); the minutes of the editorial committee are in the Fitzpatrick Papers, NLA MS 4965/6/86-92.
59   Tange to Crawford, 'Liaison Work in External Affairs', NAA M448/1, 110.

Nations Charter that lacked any machinery for its realisation.[60] Evatt was a constant vexation to Curtin; the normally imperturbable Chifley referred to him as 'my learned and no doubt very able friend down the passage'.[61]

The rise of the seven dwarfs brought economists into senior administrative posts, but they remained answerable to their ministers and the Cabinet, and it was their skill in managing this relationship that enabled them to prosper. There is an instructive contrast with James Brigden, the secretary of the Department of Munitions, who was dismissed after he clashed with his minister. Brigden (born in 1887), along with Copland (1894), Giblin (1872) and Richard Mills (1886), was one of the cohort of older economists who occupied important posts in the wartime government; but they came late to public service and did not aspire to build careers in it. They did nurture the careers of younger economists such as Coombs (born 1906), Crawford (1910) and Wilson (1904), who rose to prominence during the war and who by 1945 had overtaken their mentors in rank and influence. Giblin accepted this transformation readily; hence his recommendation of Coombs to Keynes as 'a good fellow, solid, no frills, no disturbing ego, very reasonable, though there is ground where I – Wilson also – cannot follow him'.[62] Copland found the supersession more difficult.

Those economists, younger still, who began their public service careers in the Department of Post-War Reconstruction encountered a particular challenge. As Tange would recall, 'We in PWR were seen as inexperienced new boys wearing fancy academic dress, theorising without the benefit of ever having negotiated a tariff agreement or a bulk commodity arrangement'.[63] Some reverted to academic dress – hence Firth, Butlin, Swan and Crisp, the last head of the department before its abolition in 1950. Others stayed on to apply their newly acquired skills to departmental administration. At the outbreak of war the Commonwealth Public Service consisted of 47,000 persons; by the last years of the war it had doubled in size and in the post-war period it continued to grow. In the course of the war 17 new departments were created as the Commonwealth began a lasting involvement in banking, employment, primary and secondary industries, shipping and transport, power, irrigation, health and social services. To direct these activities a new cadre of senior public servants was required, skilled in policy, administration and the exercise of power. This was the setting for the seven dwarfs.

---

60 The fullest account is S.R. Turnell, 'Monetary Reformers, Amateur Idealists and Keynesian Crusaders: Australian Economists' International Advocacy 1925–50', PhD thesis, Macquarie University, 1999.
61 As reported by E.H. Cox, 1 November 1946, Cox Papers, NLA MS 4554.
62 Quoted in W. Coleman, S. Cornish and A. Hagger, *Giblin's Platoon: The Trials and Triumph of the Economist in Australian Public Life* (Canberra: ANU E Press, 2006), 178, n. 9.
63 A. Tange, 'Plans for the World Economy: Hopes and Realities in Wartime Canberra', *Australian Journal of International Affairs*, 50, no. 3 (November 1996), 261.

3

Australia and the Keynesian Revolution

Alex Millmow

When the Nobel prize-winning economist Joe Stiglitz visited Australia in 2010 he commended the Rudd Government's policy response to the Global Financial Crisis as a proper and effective pre-emptive measure. The stimulus, which staved off any creeping sign of recession, bore a considerable Treasury imprint; and it could be said that the official family of economic advisers, that is, the Treasury and the Reserve Bank of Australia, were in their concerted action never so Keynesian in practice. It is appropriate then to visit the Keynesian revolution in post-war Australia recalling that three of the mandarins, Roland Wilson, John Crawford and H.C. 'Nugget' Coombs, were professionally trained economists. Moreover, as J.K. Galbraith reminds us, the Keynesian revolution was really a 'mandarin revolution', that is, an intellectually powered one.

The romanticist and rationalist account usually attributes the arrival of the Keynesian revolution in Australia to the outbreak of the Second World War and the enforced mobilisation of resources. While Keynes wanted America to be the laboratory where his new doctrines could be tested, it is a little known fact that it was Australia that proved the true testing ground. Australian economists were ahead of their counterparts elsewhere in adopting Keynes' insights into demand management, not just to prosecute the war but also to avoid any reoccurrence of depression. It was in November 1939, though, that a Keynesian revolution in economic policy may be said to have 'arrived' in this country. Like all revolutions it was to become compromised and sidetracked by political exigencies. One figure who saw this process was the New Zealand-born economist Douglas Copland, whose dissenting views on post-war economic management punctuate the second half of this chapter.

Usually the so-called 'golden age' of Keynesian economic management is associated with the years 1945 to 1973, after which the Keynesian consensus became unstuck as the anchors underpinning it came loose. However, as Selwyn Cornish has pointed out, even the first seven years of that period were pockmarked by policy error, aberrations and a reluctance to use market-friendly policies.¹ This chapter adopts Cornish's approach and extends it to the 1960 credit squeeze and beyond, showing how acceptance of Keynesian economic management always came second to politics.

Sir Douglas Berry Copland, 1951

Source: National Library of Australia, nla.pic-vn3942118

---

1 S. Cornish, 'The Keynesian Revolution in Australia: Fact or Fiction', *Australian Economic History Review*, 33, no. 2 (1993).

This chapter is divided into four parts. The first provides a little detail on the small Australian economics community that spearheaded the acceptance of Keynes' doctrine on national income determination. The second part concerns how economists received Keynes and sought to impart change in the policy settings up to the early stages of the Second World War. It briefly describes the mobilisation of economic expertise into the Australian war effort – a mobilisation of economics expertise far ahead of Britain and America at the time. The third and fourth parts address post-war economic issues using and examining, for instance, the debate about full employment but from the view of Copland who had, since war's end, been largely excluded from policy making circles. The last part of the chapter offers a retrospective about the revolution in economic practice.

The inter-war Australian economics community

The leading economists of the inter-war period were an extraordinary bunch of men. The two most significant figures, Douglas Copland and L.F. Giblin, were larger than life. Giblin was described as having the body of a prizefighter and being a natural leader of men. There have, in the last few years, been two monographs celebrating their contribution. One, *Giblin's Platoon*, celebrates the rise of the Australian economics profession through the lens and activities of Giblin.[2]

The other monograph, *The Power of Economic Ideas*, delves into the origins of macroeconomic management largely through the lens of Copland who was Foundation Dean of the Faculty of Commerce at the University of Melbourne.[3] Only he had formal, systematic training in economics.[4] Copland noted how his contemporaries were free of academic reserve and willing to enter into the fray of public debate. He would later remark that the post-Second World War generation of economists did not have the same gusto to enter into the fray of policy making.[5] This was partly because the Commonwealth Government had established its own pool of economic expertise after 1945.[6]

---

[2] W. Coleman, S. Cornish and A. Hagger, *Giblin's Platoon: The Trials and Triumph of the Economist in Australian Public Life* (Canberra: ANU E Press, 2006).
[3] A.J. Millmow, *The Power of Economic Ideas: The Origins of Macroeconomic Management in Australia* (Canberra: ANU E Press, 2010).
[4] S.J. Butlin, 'The Hundredth Record', *Economic Record*, 42, no. 100 (1966), 509.
[5] D.B. Copland, *Inflation and Expansion* (Melbourne: Cheshire, 1951), 9–10.
[6] M. Corden, *Australian Economic Policy Discussion: A Survey* (Melbourne: Melbourne University Press, 1968), 58–9.

Professor L.F. Giblin, portrait by Sir William Dobell, c1945

Source: University of Melbourne Archives, UMA/I/1026

While the inter-war generation of economists were great practitioners they were not renowned as theoretical innovators. The genius of inter-war Australian economists came in adopting theoretical tools to deal with these problems. Giblin summed up the axioms and values that characterised his contemporaries:

> In Australia economists are a peculiar tribe. Rarely are they nourished by the pure milk of the word. Mostly they have been advisers to governments for many years – permanently or intermittently, publicly or privately. Governments do not love them but are inclined to believe

them honest ... They are frequently more practical and realistic than businessmen ... They are resented, of course, by sectional business interests. The word of complaint or abuse is 'academic'; but, in truth, they are the least academic of God's creatures.[7]

Following the relative success of the Premiers' Plan, Keynes invited Copland to give the 1933 Marshall lectures at Cambridge. As the 'public relations man of Australian economics', Copland reported on the rehabilitation of Australia from near bankruptcy to one of the first economies to recover from the Depression.[8] The process had been helped by having four key economic agencies coming under the influence of independent economic advice. One of those tribunals, the Conciliation and Arbitration Court, ordered the emergency wage cut of 10 per cent in 1931.

Copland was the expert witness appointed by the Court to urge the necessity for wage cuts. This advice confirmed Labor opinion that Copland was in the pay of employers and the banks. And they would never let Copland forget it. In the post-war years Arthur Calwell and Bert Evatt made reference to it, though the former, more kindly, could not believe how much Copland had changed. This was a Copland trademark: to change his position and be open to charges of inconsistency.

By the mid-1930s Australia was regarded by one Indian economist, B.P. Adarkar, as 'the Utopia of practical economists' because problems like wage fixation, tariff setting, monetary management and federal finance were dealt in a scientific way by experts and governments working together.[9] The English economic historian, C.R. Fay, congratulated his Australian counterparts for their 'good fortunes to live in a country where economists are occasionally heeded.'[10]

Australian economists did not commit the same mistake as their American counterparts in 1937 by advising the federal government to cut spending now that recovery was underway. The former prime minister and treasurer,

---

7 T. Hytten, 'Giblin as an Economist', in D.B. Copland, ed., *Giblin; The Scholar and the Man* (Melbourne: Cheshire, 1960), 96.
8 N. Cain, 'Australian Keynesian: The Writings of E.R. Walker', *Working Papers in Economic History*, 13 (Canberra: Australian National University Press, 1983), 2.
9 C. Goodwin, *The Image of Australia* (Durham: Duke University Press, 1974), 236. In a letter to Keynes in November 1941 the English-born and raised economist, Colin Clark, explained how he had fallen in love with Queensland: 'When you leave England for Australia you get a strange feeling you have somehow jumped ten years into the future, and when you come to Queensland you jump ten years further. Queensland is a predominantly rural and small enterprise economy, with a very equalitarian distribution of income and property, very generous social services, compulsory Trade Unionism, and all matters of wages hours and working conditions judicially controlled by the Arbitration court, which now has such prestige that both sides always accept its decision'. C. Clark to J.M. Keynes, 10 November 1941, University of Queensland Library, Colin Clark Papers, UQFL87.
10 Goodwin, *The Image of Australia*, 236.

R.G. Menzies, always wary about economics, dryly observed that '[i]n the economic history of the last fifteen years nothing will be more notable than the rise in influence and authority of the professional economist'.[11]

Giblin encouraged the Commonwealth Public Service to recruit more graduates instead of being a repository for returned servicemen. The growing professionalisation of economics was matched by gradual placement of economists within the CPS. The first two appointees had been outstanding academic economists. Leslie Melville joined the Commonwealth Bank in 1931 and, in the following year, Roland Wilson joined the Treasury. Coombs, a doctoral graduate of the London School of Economics, found employment in the Commonwealth Bank working under the supervision of Melville.

The rising Turks of the Australian economics profession were all more receptive to Keynes' *General Theory* than their older colleagues. Names like Trevor Swan, Heinz Arndt, Peter Karmel, Gerald Firth and Richard Downing come to mind. The most eminent, though, must be Coombs and Wilson. The Keynesian revolution would, in J.E. King's words, 'conquer Australia like the Spanish inquisition'.[12]

Certainly, by 1939, Melville and Downing would independently recall that the small corps of economists in Australia were all Keynesian in policy persuasion, if not analytical framework.[13] It was helped in that process both by Keynes' dealings with Copland and Giblin and also by having two of his associates, Colin Clark and Brian Reddaway, spend time in the Antipodes. Reddaway's thoughtful and incisive précis of what Keynes was saying became the first published academic review of *The General Theory*. Clark had gone to Australia in 1937 on a visiting lectureship but was expected to return to Cambridge to head a department of applied economics. When Keynes asked when Clark would be coming home, he could only sing of the attraction of remaining in Australia: 'People have minds which are not closed to new truths ... and with all the mistakes Australia has made in the past, I still think she may show the world, in economics ... in the next few years.'[14] They were poignant words.

---

11   R.G. Menzies, 'The Australian Economy During War', *Joseph Fisher Lecture in Commerce* (Adelaide: Hassell Press, 1942), 6.
12   J.E. King, 'Notes on the History of Post-Keynesian Economics in Australia', in P. Arestis, G. Palma and M. Sawyer, eds, *Capital Controversy: Post-Keynesian Economics and the History of Economic Thought* (London: Routledge, 1997), 298.
13   S. Cornish, 'The Keynesian Revolution in Australia Fact and Fiction', *Australian Economic History Review*, 33, no. 2 (1993), 19; R.I. Downing, 'Review of M. Keynes (ed.), *Essays on John Maynard Keynes*', *Economic Record*, 52, no. 137 (1972), 11–12.
14   J.M. Keynes, in D. Moggridge, ed., *The Collected Writings of John Maynard Keynes*, Vol. 27, *Employment and Commodities* (London: Macmillan, 1981), 808.

War finance

The last year of peacetime in Australia was marked by difficult economic choices and political turbulence. The necessity to divert resources into defence as the security environment grew darker was jeopardised by the federal structure of government and traditional ideas about public finance. By the end of 1939 there came, however, a moment of economic revelation. As Copland later styled it:

> The lesson of the war is unmistakable in its demonstration that, given a clear and generally accepted objective, we can erect an economic structure far superior to that which we knew during the dark days of the thirties.[15]

In 1939, Australia smoothly switched to a total war economy because economists serving on a key advisory committee known as the Financial and Economic Committee were uncommonly influential. Formed in late 1938, the F and E Committee under Giblin's leadership convinced the then Acting Federal Treasurer, Percy Spender, that, before resorting to taxes and borrowing expedients, the war effort could be met by putting all human and physical resources to work.

Coombs was adamant that the committee gave 'economic planning of the war' a Keynesian pedigree. The idea for the committee came from Wilson. It was the realisation of his 'central thinking agency' that he had spoken of in 1934.[16] Wilson had in mind a 'small thinking committee to which all sorts of problems could be submitted for general advice.'[17]

The committee's primary task would be to advise the treasurer and his department. Eventually this would amount to the committee challenging the Treasury's orthodox canons of war finance. While Giblin is credited with leading the way, some influence should be credited to E.R. Walker who had written a book on war economics. Singing its praises, Copland said the 'great virtue' of Walker's book was that it got 'behind the veil of money' and put the defence problem 'in real terms'.[18]

Copland reckoned that a war effort of 15 per cent of resources was possible before any strain on resources would emerge. Australian economists advised the government therefore to shepherd resources by borrowing until the economy reached full employment. This was around the same time Keynes applied the *General Theory* framework to war economics in *How to Pay for the War* (1940).

---

15 D.B. Copland, *The Road to High Employment* (Melbourne: Angus & Robertson, 1945).
16 W.G.K. Duncan, *National Economic Planning* (Melbourne: Angus & Robertson, 1934).
17 G. Whitwell, *The Treasury Line* (Sydney: Allen & Unwin, 1986), 2.
18 D.B. Copland, 'News and notes', *Economic Record*, 15 (1939), 230–1.

In short, Spender assimilated a physical resources view as distinct from a monetary view. It was Giblin, then, who encouraged Spender to attempt more with fiscal policy. Giblin demonstrated how Australia, with 10 per cent unemployment, could painlessly increase its defence budget without facing resource pressures. Instead of a heavy-handed resort to economic controls that would intimidate business, Giblin felt that expenditure could be raised through credit expansion. Convinced, Spender raised the matter with Menzies, highlighting how the financial costs of the war effort could be lightened by putting the unemployed back into work. While the unemployed had, hitherto, been a state matter, Spender believed the initiative 'would not only be good politics on our part, but sound economics, if we take the lead in this matter'.[19]

Spender took Giblin's proposal to Cabinet and announced, in dramatic words, 'One of the objectives of our present policy is to restore and increase the national income. This will enable us to divert resources to defence without encroaching unnecessarily on existing standards of consumption'.[20] Spender made it clear in a submission to Cabinet how borrowing for defence would be from the central bank thus sparing private enterprise from a greater tax burden. Once capacity and full employment were reached, however, taxation would assume its rightful duty and prevent any inflation. This 'changeover' point was projected to occur by May 1940.

Cornish has identified this as the moment when a Keynesian revolution in economic policy 'arrived' in Australia. An English newspaper hailed Spender's budget as 'the answer to an economist's prayer'.[21] Until then, at the official policy level, there had been little recognition of expanding economic activity by bringing idle resources into circulation. It revolved around the necessity of how quickly, and the means by which, to increase military spending. Raising taxes, issuing public loans or recourse to credit finance, that is, budget deficits, would disrupt economic activity. This spelt sacrifices not only to programs but also political reputations. Indeed, the Commonwealth Bank, then Australia's central bank, recycled a version of the British Treasury's view; namely, that using resources for defence needs, even amidst 10 per cent unemployment, would reduce the amount of consumer goods that could be produced when the economy recovered.

Before the outbreak of the war Copland had wanted the same array of economic controls Nazi Germany had. With the outbreak of war he had his wishes partly granted. Menzies asked him to come to Canberra as Commonwealth Prices Commissioner and also as economic consultant to the prime minister. The need

---

19   Cited in Millmow, *The Power of Economic Ideas*, 263.
20   Ibid., 263.
21   Cited in P. Spender, *Politics and a Man* (Sydney: Collins, 1942), 45.

for price control was immediate, albeit taking place in an environment of suitable macroeconomic policies. The need for price control was urgent if production was to be directed to areas of greatest national need rather than to areas of greatest profit. As Prices Commissioner, Copland recognised that a leading problem of price control was that of limiting increases in the price structure to the unavoidable increases in costs while preventing, as far as possible, a general upward movement in prices brought about by the operation of outside influences. He saw that a general increase in the prices of basic commodities would cause a rise in the cost of living and a consequent rise in the basic wage, which was automatically adjusted to the cost of living.

With the coming to office of the Curtin Labor Government, and the entry of Japan into the conflict, Australia entered a more difficult and demanding stage of the war. The government resorted to planning and regulations, and newly created government departments, headed by the likes of Wilson, superseded the work of the F and E Committee. As the Japanese threat receded, planning for post-war reconstruction received increasing attention.

The post-war challenge

There was a general fear that the end of hostilities would see, after a brief post-war boom, the return of the slump. It gave urgency to the task of preventing a rerun of the 1930s, with governments undertaking to make elimination of unemployment 'a fundamental aim' of economic policy. Australia reached the crowning glory of Keynesianism when the Chifley Government presented the White Paper on Full Employment. As Selwyn Cornish has detailed, the document took an inordinate amount of redrafting with plenty of material from economists, along with Curtin and Chifley. The White Paper was a more circumspect and considered document than its British counterpart, with clauses on fiscal balance, the mobility of resources, productive efficiency, wage stability, stabilisation by government spending and concerns about the external account. The successful management of war finance alleviated concerns about the efficacy of fiscal policy to fulfil the promise placed on it.

Memories of widespread unemployment in the inter-war years cut deeply. Australian economists invested their hopes in the White Paper and the political authorities observed the target. Indeed, the economic history of the post-war era was that the authorities were too zealous in pursuing it. The reluctance to consider checking aggregate demand policies might have had something to do with anxieties about the return of depression. There was an element of a depression mentality in the air. It is astonishing to recall that the Menzies

Government nearly lost office because it let unemployment reach 3.1 per cent by 1961–62. In contrast, the collective consciousness held little fear of severe inflation yet it became the prevailing problem during the Keynesian era.

Inflation had been contained during the war years by a comprehensive prices and rationing system. The Labor Government had allowed excessive liquidity to build up in the economy which was kept in check by controls on prices, wages and capital. This problem carried over into the peacetime economy with economic activity potentially excessive. The post-war economy was marked, therefore, by high levels of economic activity, full employment and inflation. Inflation was suppressed by retaining the wartime administrative controls including price and capital controls.

The Chifley Government was reluctant to engage in containing demand by fiscal and monetary means even though the White Paper had envisaged their use. The 1948–49 budget was stimulatory and involved capital spending on infrastructure to further development. The Menzies Government also embraced developmentalism, a mindset that was promoted by the Treasury. It was only after the inflationary boom of 1951 that both the Treasury and the Commonwealth Bank persuaded the Menzies Government to cut back outlays.

The tendency, though, towards maintaining the economy at a high pitch of activity was the outstanding pattern of macroeconomic policy during the Keynesian era. It was compounded by commitments to a high rate of immigration and development without resorting to credit restrictions and import controls to counteract inflationary pressures and balance of payments problems. Neither the electorate nor politicians found the prospects of budget deficits too galling in the early post-war years. The prevailing political milieu was to oppose raising taxes and to regard budget surpluses as the opportunity to reduce taxation. Perhaps it was reasoned that with rationing still in tow there was enough austerity being administered. The Chifley Government also had ideological concerns about using interest rates to choke off excessive aggregate demand. The Menzies era, too, was also marked by a perceptible reluctance to use market controls to fine-tune aggregate demand.

Overall, the political economy of the first 15 years after the war was one of continuous economic growth coupled with inflation and pressures upon the external account. Coombs identified that there was both political resistance and interest group resistance to undertaking the necessary deflationary measures that the Australian economy needed. The short life of the electoral cycle reinforced the reluctance to act just as officials were hesitant about advice unacceptable to ministers. In the same vein, Gerald Firth spoke in 1951 of an asymmetry problem, in that every interest group backed expansion but there was resistance to confronting inflation.[22] It partly derived from the unwillingness of most Australian economists during the post-war reconstruction era to speak about the dangers of inflation. Only the Menzies Government in 1951 and again in 1960 was prepared to bite the bullet but only after the Treasury and Commonwealth Bank were pulling in concert to curb a boom.

Keynes and the Australian Keynesians

Not all economists in Australia adhered to the early post-war consensus about Keynesianism. The old guard were not totally swept away by *The General Theory* as the young were. There was the added question of interpreting Keynes and, on that note, the difference between Keynes and the Keynesians. There was Keynes' famous jibe that, after attending a dinner party in Washington with American Keynesians, he recollected 'I was the only non-Keynesian there'. Keynes had told Hayek that he would put the young heretics in their place but he did not live long enough to do so. Nor did Keynes get round to writing a sequel to *The General Theory*.

Giblin was worried that full employment would trigger a wages problem and asked Keynes about it. Keynes demurred, saying the control of wages at full employment was ultimately 'a political problem'.[23] Keynes was equally concerned about avoiding inflation at full employment as he was about avoiding another slump. He felt that the workers and trade unionists would show a degree of community-mindedness.

James Brigden's reaction, later encapsulated in a short and querulous article in the *Economic Record*, noted how credit expansion would result in rising wage costs as full employment was approached. The problem was that there was 'no coordination between wages policy and finance policy' to prevent wage inflation from occurring. Consequently, Brigden concluded that if credit expansion and, thus, full employment, were pursued, there would have to be controls upon labour, foreign exchange and investment.[24]

In Brisbane, Colin Clark, director of the Queensland Bureau of Industry, state statistician and economic adviser to the Queensland Treasury, was working on the thesis that too much spending by the federal government ultimately meant inflation. The idea had come from Premier Hanlon, who was concerned that the

---

22 G.G. Firth, 'Disinflation in Australia: A Democratic Dilemma', Paper presented to the ANZAAS Conference 1951, Brisbane, Queensland.
23 Cited in A. Millmow, 'The Evolution of John Maynard Keynes' Wage and Employment Theory, 1920–1946', *History of Economics Review*, 71 (1992).
24 J.B. Brigden, 'The credit theory of full employment', *Economic Record*, 15 (1939).

mooted post-war expenditures on social goods and nationalisation reminded him that it had been excessive taxation that had been the undoing of empires and countries in the past.

Clark investigated and subsequently deduced that the maximum rate of taxation was 25 per cent of net national product and submitted his research to the *Economic Journal*, which Keynes edited. If a nation did engage in over taxing, he predicted that, after some lag, rising inflation would result. In other words, it was high and rising taxation that stimulated rising prices; and rising government expenditure was the main cause for this rising taxation.[25]

Clark was adamant that Keynes agreed with his contention and that he had been working on the matter when he had died in April 1946. Clark never deviated from being 'Mr. 25%'.[26] Whether Keynes would have stayed constant with the principle is debatable given his penchant to change his mind when the circumstances changed. Clark, who had worked with Keynes, would later write that his mentor was a liberal who believed in the free market 'because it provides the maximum possible decentralisation of economic decision'.[27]

The most vocal dissident to the Keynesian crusade, though, was Copland. In his Godkin lectures, given at Harvard in 1945, Copland focused upon the eternal problem of the relation of state control to private enterprise or, more broadly, the relationship between the private and public sectors. Copland contended that the pre-war economy failed to operate in the best interests of the community at large, that it could not avoid depressions, and that it would not employ all available factors in the long run. To stabilise the economy and ensure a certain measure of security for all, he continued, it would be necessary for the nation as a whole to engage in public investment and not be fearful of national debt. While praising the power of entrepreneurial talent, Copland argued that some degree of social control, expressed through a large public sector, would give capitalism a more benign, ordered traverse. Copland, however, was not enamoured of full employment, preferring high employment.

Unlike many others in the profession, Copland quickly realised that it was rapid, almost unnerving, economic progress that would be the normal state of affairs for market economies, not stagnation of the pre-war era. Contrary to fears of a post-war depression, the new era was marked by astonishing rates of technological and economic growth for most countries, none more so than Australia, which would grapple with a bold development and migration program in the post-war

---

25   A. Millmow, 'Colin Clark and Australia', *History of Economics Review*, 56 (2012).
26   A. Millmow, 'Mr. 25%', *Australian Financial Review*, 2 July 2010.
27   C. Clark, 'Keynes and Others: A Personal Memoir' (1982), 18, University of Queensland Library, Colin Clark Papers, UQFL87.

period. Australia, though, found itself in the early post-war period beset by bouts of inflation and external deficits, which led to corrective action followed by another spurt of expansionism.

As the first vice-chancellor of The Australian National University, Copland was not expected to engage in public debate about economic management but no one dared silence him. His views rubbed hard against those of the 'inside' economists. Copland, however, was not the only isolated voice. Heinz Arndt has argued that in the post-war era, until the 1970s, economic policy was conducted by the inside economists with academic voices shut out. He goes on to remark:

> The Commonwealth Government in the 1950s and 1960s had the advice of better economists inside than were to be found outside – seven of the best, as it happened all men of good minds but short stature, were nicknamed 'Mr Menzies's Seven Dwarfs'. They did not feel the need for outside help, so that university economists were more remote from government than in most other western countries.[28]

There was also a chasm in how economists within the Department of Post-War Reconstruction, headed by Coombs, interpreted the 'new economics' of Keynes and how Copland did. Copland was seen as somewhat detached from the great post-war 'crusade' of Keynesian economic thought and practice led and propagated by Coombs.[29] There was undoubtedly some animus between the two that sprang from the bureaucratic power struggle during the war years. While he was economic consultant to the prime minister during the war, Copland had never been part of Chifley's circle of advisers. For his part, Coombs felt Copland was a rather pedestrian economist.

Copland wanted to participate in the 'dynamizing' of Keynes' conceptual revolution. For Australia, this meant channelling resources into investment, rather than consumption; of having capacity-building rather than full employment. Copland lamented that 'Keynes didn't live to castigate his followers who turned his theory of full employment into one of economic stability and security at all costs'.[30] Copland would further maintain that the Chifley and Menzies governments did not address the full criteria and economic challenges set out in the White Paper on Full Employment. He bemoaned that post-war Australia was not meeting the economic objectives contained in Part IV of the White Paper, which covered questions like fiscal balance, the mobility of resources, productive efficiency, wage stability, stabilisation by government spending and concerns about the external account. Coombs and Walker felt a

---

28   'Antipodean Economics' (1987), National Library of Australia, Papers of Heinz Wolfgang Arndt, 1933–2002.
29   H.C. Coombs, *Trial Balance* (Melbourne: Sun Books, 1981).
30   D.B. Copland to Michael Barkway, 15 February 1961, Copland Papers, National Library of Australia (NLA) MS 3800, Box 11, Series 1, Folder 88.

state of full employment was more likely with extensive planning. Copland felt that this was unnecessary and that the maintenance of high employment would not require any extensive state authority over the prerogative of capital, only a degree of regulation.

The ragtime of Australian economic policy, 1948–1952

When Copland became vice-chancellor of The Australian National University in 1948, he told a businessman how he 'was appalled at both the state of the economy and the state of the mind of economists'.[31] He campaigned to get Australian economic policy on a more fundamental footing and waged a critique of 'the younger brethren' of economists in a series of speeches and provocative articles. The earliest of these articles were designed to make 'a splash' in order to further a political ambition as a prospective Senate candidate for the Coalition in the forthcoming election. Apart from this, however, the string of commentaries mirrored his deep concerns about the orientation of the Australian economy and the rubric of economic policy. He informed Menzies there was a 'deplorable state of affairs' in Canberra with the Chifley Government struggling with post-war demands on the economy.[32] Copland later told the English economist, Edith Penrose, that the period from 1948 to 1952 was 'the ragtime of Australian economic policy' – a period of immense policy error.[33] He had a point. Australia would endure aberrations like an attempt at bank nationalisation, coal strikes, raging inflation, a needless devaluation against the American dollar, relaxation of physical controls and then their reimposition, and a boom and bust within the space of five years.

Back to Earth in Economics: Australia 1948 was a critique of the supposed Keynesianism practised by Australian economists. They were to be 'brought back to earth'. In short, Copland felt that the post-war economic forecasts had been much too dire about the Australian economy and that the subsequent 'obsession with security' and pumping up aggregate demand was no basis on which to develop the nation. That is, there should be an equal stress upon raising the rate of economic growth and augmenting the supply side of the economy. There would be difficulties, too, he noted, if the government had to curtail expenditure to contain inflation.

---

31   D.B. Copland to G. Foletta, 10 May 1954, Copland Papers, NLA MS 3800, Box 8.
32   D.B. Copland to R.G. Menzies, 9 January 1949, Copland Papers, NLA MS 3800, Box 8.
33   D.B. Copland to E. Penrose, 28 November 1955, Copland Papers, NLA MS 3800, Box 9.

Copland also set out to dispense with the 'depression psychology' permeating the Australian economic policy establishment, which held back the embrace of growth and development. To develop his case, Copland took the line that the post-war boom was more a case of accident than design, that is, full employment was basically inevitable. It had been achieved by creating a business environment conducive to an increase in private investment above pre-war levels. While there was a post-war investment boom it was not, Copland argued, 'a good ground on which to claim the success of a full employment theory of full employment' when that condition was inevitable. The main reason for the buoyant level of economic activity was due to the legacy of the war economy, demands of reconstruction and expansion of universal welfare.

There was also the ephemeral fortune of high export prices. Copland's argument anticipated that of R.C.O. Matthews' controversial paper in 1968 that the reason why unemployment had been low in the post-war years in Britain and elsewhere was a prolonged investment boom as countries made good on the war damage and that 'the decline of unemployment ... is to a large extent not a Keynesian phenomenon at all'.[34] Copland also wanted to deride the idea that, with simple demand management, Australia was bound for a 'golden age' in economic performance when, in fact, the objectives of post-war reconstruction were 'not being attained'. Copland feared that Australian policy-makers were becoming complacent with the return of good times, which masked underlying weaknesses within the economy. Post-war advantages had been frittered away by labour unrest, the wasting of record high export earnings and lower taxes. Nor was Australia investing sufficiently in key industries to secure vigorous and sustained growth. The culprit was the doctrine of over-full employment — that is, more jobs than people to fill them — which prevented resources flowing to the most productive ends and enticed absenteeism, overmanning and labour indiscipline. There were shortages of coal and steel in 1948, which gave the lie to the government's obsession that maintaining full employment was sufficient to maintain productive well-being. More importantly, the doctrine of full employment lulled policy-makers into a false sense of security that they had the means to handle exogenous economic shocks. Copland was concerned that the veneer of prosperity made policy-makers blind to Australia's low productivity which apparently lagged behind other western economies and that, once the export price boom passed, the nation would find itself in a familiar set of difficulties. So it proved.

Copland was, moreover, apprehensive about the possibilities of implementing a stabilisation package if the economy needed to be wound back because of an external deficit. By the same token, the old 'pioneering spirit' that kindled Australia's economic development in the past had to be revived. Copland

---

34 D.B. Copland, *Back to Earth in Economics: Australia, 1948* (Melbourne: Cheshire, 1948).

identified three matters that needed immediate attention: first, to secure more supplies of coal and other materials; secondly, more housing; and, finally, the need to develop more export potential instead of relying upon the existing staples. This meant ridding the economy of rationing and regulation and setting the sails for growth. Copland's overall recommendation was to develop a general plan to recruit resources that were basic to immediate needs and long-term priorities. It was a classic long-term Keynesian program that shunned short-termism. Copland seemed quite unaware that Coombs also lamented that Australia did not seem to be following the dictates of Keynesian functional finance which underpinned the White Paper. There was too much focus on full employment and too little on inflation. Consequently inflation within the economic system was suppressed by the use of controls.

In 1949, Copland made another telling comment about the fabric of Australia's economic development, drawing attention to the imbalance in production patterns between capital goods and consumption goods, arguing that it was impairing Australia's development. He memorably stigmatised Australia's post-war economy as a 'milk-bar' one, preoccupied with meeting consumption needs rather than overall development. The imbalance could only be rectified by redirecting resources to the basic industries, by allowing more access to foreign borrowing, more immigration, and a longer working week. It remained a perennial issue throughout the 1950s.

Elsewhere Copland adumbrated upon the new social and economic framework for a private enterprise economy and deviated slightly from his long-run bearings. Copland outlined six areas where 'social control' or state activity in various spheres of the economy had been largely beneficial, not only in terms of economic development but also remunerative for the business sector. Those spheres were macroeconomic management and stability; public investment spending; establishment of state-owned utilities; social security and redistribution; arbitration and conciliation; and, lastly, restraints upon the power of monopolies. While he welcomed increasing the degree of social control, Copland believed there was an optimal level of intervention. Copland now felt that Australia, at least, had reached that level and that 'a stay order' on further extensions of state activity was now warranted. More intervention or social justice in the economy, he felt, would enfeeble the entrepreneurial spirit that had made Australia.

There was little support from most of his peers about the need to make fundamental adjustments to the economy to secure long-term growth, productivity and development. The neglect of the younger economists bemused him. Their complaints ignored his heroic efforts to change economic policy in the mid-1930s. Whilst reading Roy Harrod's biography of Keynes, Copland wrote to a friend:

> Still reading Keynes and I remember most of the controversy and the discussion he was involved from the 1920's onwards. A few of us had been working on similar lines and I have somewhere a set of memorandums to the government of NSW from 1932 to 1936 urging with all the persuasion I could muster an expansionist policy, but we could not get past the Commonwealth Treasury. It would be fun to dig them out now and circulate for the younger brethren who still think we are past praying for. I'm sure he [Keynes] would disown Coombs and his school if he was with us now.[35]

Some time later, Copland would suggest that 'the over-enthusiasm for the Keynesian theory and its extravagant expectations in a theory of full employment would have been disowned by the Master'. Copland was unrepentant about his differences with the younger economists even if he was guilty of over-dramatising them.

There was no spring clear-out of the economic mandarins when the Menzies Government came to power in 1949. Coombs remained as governor of the Commonwealth Bank and sought to be within earshot of Menzies. Copland would have some intermittent influence especially with the new Federal Treasurer, Arthur Fadden. Moreover, Copland lobbied to get Roland Wilson into the Treasury as secretary in a bid to counter Coombs' influence over the prime minister.

Copland returned to assailing the economic perfectionists in May 1950 in a speech marking the 25th anniversary of the founding of the Victorian Branch of the Economic Society. He warned how the 'more extreme devotees' of planning were 'much too confident of their ability to control the powerful forces arranged against them'. Apart from an illusion about their omniscience, they had not factored into their analysis the requisite degree of public acceptance needed for the new doctrine, especially from the business sector. Copland feared that the planners would not have the courage to prune expenditure when it was needed most, nor would there be public acceptance for doing so. Maintaining the economy at over-full employment would jeopardise price stability and put pressure on Australia's external account. Finally, acute supply shortages interfered with development while full employment meant that workers had little incentive to raise productivity.

Copland, in addition, sought to redress the social balance within the economy, arguing that the entrepreneurial spirit was still the engine that powered a mixed economy. This signified his embrace of a mild form of corporatism. He reaffirmed his long-held faith in the restorative and civilising powers of public

---

35   D.B. Copland to M. Lundy, 1951, courtesy of Marjorie Harper.

investment for economic development and dismissed notions that the increase in public debt would impoverish future generations. Since the early 1930s, Copland had consistently praised the role of public investment as the means to economic recovery from the slump. Now he saw it spearheading Australia's economic development.

In July 1950, in an address entitled 'Problems of an Expanding Economy', Copland demonstrated how he differed from the policy outlook of his contemporaries. With a large-scale immigration policy in train, Copland felt it imperative that policy-makers not be hidebound by the past. More importantly, Australia had to become a high investment economy instead of a high consumption one. The migration program spelt huge outlays in housing and infrastructure, meaning that consumption had to be cut, if necessary, by taxation. The 'motto of the age', he suggested, might be 'Houses before hotels, tractors before motor cars, electricity before refrigeration'. If not cut voluntarily, consumption could be wound back by taxation and some inflation. Copland felt that the attendant risks of becoming a high investment economy, namely, a lack of final demand, would not eventuate, and that Australia could easily revert to a high consumption economy.

The last requirement needed for a rapidly expanding economy was to draw upon foreign supplies of capital goods and, if need be, to access foreign funds to acquire them. Here Copland contemplated a new financial nexus with the United States. He was particularly damning of the 'anti-borrowing psychology' and, with one eye on the stalled Australian National University construction program, he vented his spleen, asking, 'How can you develop this country with picks, shovels and wheelbarrows?' He closed by stating that Australia had to choose between stability and progress. To his mind, the instability that comes with large-scale development must come first. He never wavered on this. Four years later he maintained that '[w]e are apt to concentrate on the instability and to ignore the development, as though a high rate of development and stability were natural bedfellows'. The debate about the scale of Australian post-war immigration mirrored, therefore, the divide between the meek and mild 'planners' and the 'brave' advocates of development.

One of the slogans on which the Coalition had campaigned in the 1949 election was 'to put value back into the pound'. It would come back to bite them. By mid-1950 the Menzies Government was caught by their own inflationary crisis stemming from the Korean War boom reflected in high wool and metals prices. The Chifley Government had unwisely devalued the currency by 30 per cent to align Australia with the sterling bloc. Besides encouraging exports, it led to a speculative inflow of capital in anticipation of revaluation. With a fixed exchange rate, the terms-of-trade boost meant exporters' foreign exchange receipts flowed directly into the monetary system fuelling consumption.

Apart from poor productivity growth, inflation ensued from the levels of social investment needed to absorb a large immigration intake, along with increased defence spending incurred amidst a full-employment economy.

One solution would have been revaluation, which all Australian economists, bar Copland, recommended. He dismissed the idea, stating that an appreciation would have damaged other exporters and also jeopardised the profitability and development of Australia's manufacturing industries. If Australia really wanted to stifle inflation, it had to resort to more domestic options like monetary tightening. Working through the back channels, Copland's advice might have swayed Wilson and Fadden, though the latter would by definition always uphold rural exporting interests.

The more intelligent expedient to both an appreciation and terms-of-trade boom was to quarantine the wool export bonanza into a price stabilisation fund, which would immobilise spending power and thereby contain its inflationary effect. First outlined in September 1950, some of the fund could also be used for rural betterment. Funds could then be released when the fortunes of wool exporters turned against them. While the Menzies Government adopted a variation of Copland's prescription, implementing a wool stabilisation plan came too late to prevent an inflationary impulse surging through the economy. Ultimately, inflation would be quelled by the collapse of commodity prices, a surge in imports and the so-called 'horror budget' of 1951–52.

In the meantime Copland called for radical measures like Australia leaving the sterling bloc because it aligned Australia's trade with the empire and led to trade discrimination against non-members. He thus called into question the old imperial connection with Britain, believing that Australia should strike out into the Asia-Pacific where its economic destiny lay. Relying upon the British market and the sterling area meant limited export growth and constrained development of the Australian economy. This stand raised eyebrows. When he first raised the idea of an American loan in 1948 to deal with Australia's own dollar shortage, the result of a trade imbalance with the United States, he reported much later that his then critics felt he 'had gone over the edge'.[36] Australia, he motioned, should leave the sterling area, free up the exchange by means of dollar loans and bargain with the United States for further dollars on the basis of the Australian immigration program, which relieved the refugee problem in Europe. He held that 'the one unused resource' of productivity could break the logjam of competing inflationary pressures, which were the product of the boom in export prices, a huge investment program and the very absence of productivity gains.

Copland returned to a variation of the 'milk-bar economy' theme when his book, *Inflation and Expansion* (1951), was published. The overriding theme of the

---

36   D.B. Copland to H. Cox, 15 April 1954, Copland Papers, NLA MS 3800, Box 8.

book of essays was how mixed economies, like Australia, became constrained in meeting their welfare and full employment obligations such that they could not channel enough resources to meet their development aspirations. There was none of the impelling urge there had been in wartime to allocate resources to basic industries. Australia, in particular, faced this imbalance, though it was, Copland stressed, primarily a political problem of collective choice. The logical outcome was inflation, which could only be dealt with by higher productivity.

Given his outspoken views on growth and expansion Copland would have been bemused to find himself singled out by the press and the Australian Labor Party leadership for the Australian economy's maladjustment during 1951–52. In the reaction to Fadden's budget of 1951–52, when a counter-cyclical budget surplus was implemented, the *Sydney Morning Herald* held Copland, along with other academic economists, responsible. It was a strange line of attack when it was really all the Treasury's handiwork. Wilson had told Fadden shortly after he had been appointed secretary that inflation was out of control and endorsed the deflationary measures taken in the 1951–52 federal budget.

Copland must have felt some sense of vindication, however. For some time he had anticipated the likely anger from Australians unaccustomed to cutting expenditure outlays consistent with fiscal restraint. The commitment to full employment meant that exuberance could only be checked 'in the last resort' by the exercise of 'a measure of restraint for which there was no precedent in the history of Australia'. Such was the prospect presented by Fadden's federal budget.

In an ABC radio commentary, Copland praised the budget as 'economically sound', 'courageous', and a 'landmark in Australian finance'. The budget strategy of increasing taxes and deferring public works would allow more resources to be channelled towards development and defence. Moreover, the tax imposts could be easily reversed and had a low disincentive effect.

Copland's praise of the budget was not contrived. He saw the circumstances of over-full employment, coupled with inflation, as posing a distinctly new challenge to economists:

> But on the problem of preventing undue expansion we have yet to learn a good deal more about technique and still more about how to influence government and public opinion to accept restraints ahead of danger. This was the new task confronting the new generation of economists. If they succeed they will achieve even more than their predecessors.[37]

It was a challenge only partly met.

---

37   D.B. Copland, 'Economic Study and Public Opinion in Australia: The Role of the Economist', *Australian Highway*, 34, no. 2 (1952).

By 1952 Australia faced what Copland called 'the old Adam of the Australian economy' – a liquidity crisis brought about by a deteriorating external account. Wool prices had steadily fallen since April 1951 while there had been a flood of imports resulting from buoyant economic activity. The Menzies Government responded to the challenge by resorting to import licensing.

The announcement resulted in a quite extraordinary attack upon Copland by Australia's new business newspaper, the *Australian Financial Review*. The editor, Jack Horsfall, penned a front-page story, entitled 'The Dire Economic Consequences of Sir D. B. Copland'.[38] Horsfall's attack had followed a Copland address, 'The Balance of Payments and Money Incomes in Australia', which had been reproduced in the same paper. Surveying the economic conditions that had led to the government imposing trade controls, Copland concluded that Australia was facing a fundamental disequilibrium which necessitated either devaluation or deflation. Full employment, cheap money, an ambitious development and migration policy and a short-lived export price boom had led Australia to this crisis. The 'grievous expedient' of import controls, Copland argued, did not address the true cause of the malaise. Copland drew vindication from what he had been saying over the past seven years, namely, that economic activity had been run too strongly and that productivity had been falling because of the unbalanced nature of investment and poor work practices. Without sourcing enough foreign capital to keep the expansion going, Copland had already warned that an external deficit was imminent.

In a long public diatribe against Copland's views upon economic expansion, Horsfall pinned the imposition of import controls on Copland's crusade for growth and expansion. Horsfall did not pull his punches:

> No single voice has been more responsible than his for bringing Australia to the point where import restrictions were unavoidable. He has persistently plugged the case for unbridled development and unlimited immigration in face of disastrous inflation and the dissipation of overseas funds.[39]

In accusing Copland of pushing the cause for expansion even when Australia had not secured dollar loans and when he had just supported the Fadden budget, Horsfall questioned Copland's reading of the economy. Copland, Horsfall suggested, might have to give away his policy advocacy skills. Few Australian economists have been subject to such front-page denigration in Australia's national press. Horsfall had been a former student of Copland's at the University of Melbourne and differed strongly on the growth parameters needed for Australia.

---

38   'The Dire Consequences of Sir D.B. Copland', *Australian Financial Review*, 20 March 1952.
39   Ibid.

With a life-long interest in rural exports, Copland had long anticipated the problem of the external deficit and bemoaned how Australia's trade pattern was hamstrung by imperial preferences when its development aspirations far exceeded the scale of the 1920s. Australia, for instance, received fixed prices for her wheat, butter and meat in the British market while the bulk of her imports came from there. Copland felt that expedients like credit restriction, import restrictions and special trade arrangements to deal with the yawning trade deficit were only 'playing with the problem' and their ultimate effect would be to dampen the pace of economic development.[40]

With the bursting of the wool export boom Copland sensed a new reality in Australian economic management. Australia was returning to 'traditional policy' of coping with 'the vigorous forces of the outside world' away from a 'naïve' Keynesianism of instruments and controls.[41] Apart from pursuing full employment, other distortions like the sheltered markets of the sterling bloc, the lack of sectoral balance within the economy, and cheap money were being discarded. All this reminded Australian economic planners that, apart from being compatible with the social milieu, economic policies had to be tailored to fit the fact that Australia was still a small, open, vulnerable economy. With a fixed exchange rate, Australia had to ensure it did not get its price and cost structure out of alignment with the rest of the world. Expanding global trade meant that, for commodity exporting countries like Australia, the long-term prognosis was mostly good. Moreover, with better macroeconomic control over expenditure and the establishment of a viable manufacturing sector, the Australian economy would be more stable than in the past.

The golden age

The age of the mandarins was the age of Keynes. Two of the mandarins, Coombs and Wilson, had different visions of economic management. Wilson, however, seemed more a big picture man like Copland than Coombs, who focused on short-term macroeconomic management. Both agreed, however, that, with continuous economic growth, it was inflation rather than unemployment that had to be monitored. Academic economists reinforced this view and occasionally sought to impress a point. In a manifesto issued in February 1956, 'The outlook for the Australian economy', eight leading professors of economics recommended an increase in taxation and interest rates in a bid to dampen 'spendthrift prosperity' and generate more savings. As government investment spending had not been rising rapidly, and because there was a desperate need

---

40 'Copland Urges a Grand Course', *Australian Financial Review*, 12 December 1951, 12.
41 D.B. Copland, 'The Australian Post-war Economy: A Study in Economic Administration', *Canadian Journal of Economic and Political Science*, 20, no. 4 (1954), 436–7.

to implement various infrastructure projects, the manifesto opposed cuts in government expenditure. It also dismissed direct controls as a solution for excess demand. Not long afterwards, the government brought down a mini-budget of deflationary measures to strike at the 'root cause' of Australia's current account deficit problem.

Upon returning home from a diplomatic posting in 1956, Copland was amazed to find that the main policy debate among academic economists was still whether Australia was growing too fast. Not for the first time, he preached adventure and expansion. He was convinced that economic progress since 1953 had been 'relatively sound and vigorous' and in no need of restraint.[42]

Neither the Treasury nor his academic colleagues shared his optimism. The new generation of economists, he continued, worshipped 'the false god of stability' when 'there was no future in stability'.[43] It was much better, Copland reasoned, to be discussing growth and expansion 'than to be worrying about the problems of devastating depression' of 25 years ago. Copland was concerned that the authorities were going to suppress expansion because of worries about inflation. Heinz Arndt represented academics expressing concern that Australia's creeping inflation rate, if left unchecked, would compound economic difficulties, particularly with the external account, in the near future. Copland was not just on the outer but fast losing his credibility. Coombs warned that community passivity about tolerating 'creeping inflation' would build into something monstrous.

Copland remained unrepentant and urged policy-makers to push on with 'the adventure of economic expansion on the grand scale whilst enduring the restraints that are necessary for its success'. This meant that consumption and the obsession with security and employment took a lower priority. Ideally, the title of his co-edited anthology, *The Conflict between Stability and Expansion* (1957), encapsulated the dilemma facing Australian economic policy-makers.

He repeated his prescription of expansion before stability in one of his last scholarly contributions. After discussing the conflict between growth and stability Copland listed the policy settings needed for Australia to focus upon the former. Fiscal policy, perhaps in the form of higher personal income tax, would channel a higher level of savings into capital formation, which, in turn, would realign the balance between consumption and investment. This policy, if successfully implemented, would make it unnecessary to resort to a credit squeeze to ensure proper distribution of resources between consumption and investment.

---

42   D.B. Copland, 'The Australian Economy: A New Look', *Economic Record*, 33, no. 65 (1957), 141–52.
43   D.B. Copland to W.S. Robinson, 23 January 1961, Copland Papers, NLA MS 3800, Box 11, file 85.

Despite the warning about the build up of excessive demand there was to be another stop-go episode that was almost comical. In a bid to free up supplies Roland Wilson urged the new treasurer, Harold Holt, to abandon import controls in February 1960. There was an immediate surge in imports, which led to a deficit on the trade account. In November 1960, Holt had to announce a mini-budget, which amounted to Australia's first post-war credit squeeze. 'Holt's Jolt' quickly turned into recession. Copland told Fadden, who had only just retired as treasurer, that the current policy pronouncements seemed to him one of 'the most confused' he had ever witnessed.[44] He argued that import controls should not have been relaxed when Australia's export prices had fallen 25 per cent since 1952. Now Copland queried how a credit squeeze could ever promote growth and development.[45] He felt that the Commonwealth Government had become easily intimidated by a slight increase in inflation and a balance of payments deficit problem. With his friend and mentor, W.S. Robinson, Copland dismissed the threat of inflation, vouching that he would rather have a slight lift in prices than dampen economic growth.[46] Menzies was unrepentant about the credit squeeze:

> Nobody can get rid of inflationary booms without treading on someone's corns. It is the duty of the practical statesman to select the corns and not be afraid of treading on them. To achieve this I must be content to annoy thousands.[47]

In 1963, Copland turned his mind towards economic planning and growth targets but no one in the bureaucracy (except perhaps Crawford) was much interested. He rather crudely lamented to Robinson:

> It is very funny that nobody in Australia is seriously interested in growth: but then we must remember that we have among the economists the Seven Dwarfs, who naturally would hardly be interested in growth.[48]

Some of the 1960s imbroglio was repeated the next decade with the Whitlam Government but this time it spelt the end of the Keynesian era. It was elected against a backdrop of a fully employed economy and a balance of payments in surplus. The economic bounty suggested that it would be practical to implement Whitlam's election promises. The only apparent bugbear was that their predecessors had allowed an inflationary problem to linger. Annual inflation rates of 7.3 per cent were significant for the time, coming from both domestic

---

44   D.B. Copland to Sir A. Fadden, 15 December 1960, Copland Papers, NLA MS 3800, Box 11, Series 1, Folder 88.
45   'The Credit Squeeze and the Balance of Payments: A Key Problem in Economic Statesmanship', *Sydney Mirror*, 15 February 1961.
46   'Import Controls Best', *Age* (Melbourne), 11 May 1961.
47   Cited in A. Millmow, 'Eye on the Money', in A. Cornell, ed., *The Best Australian Business Writing 2012* (Sydney: New South Publishing, 2012), 222.
48   D.B. Copland to W.S. Robinson, 21 March 1963, Copland Papers, NLA MS 3800, Box 12.

cost pressures and rising import prices. By refusing to deal with average wage increases of over 10 per cent for 1972 and then by not revaluing, the McMahon Government exposed the economy to underlying tensions. Whitlam was committed to significant social reform through government spending despite these economic clouds on the horizon. Gerald Firth had identified the incipient problem of stagflation in May 1972. He recommended greater wage discipline to disarm it.[49]

With the economy in boom through 1973, the Federal Treasury, aghast at the growth in outlays, advised caution. In his first budget as treasurer, Frank Crean allowed the inflationary problem to loom larger by allowing a significant growth in federal outlays financed by Treasury notes and cash balances with the central bank. Fred Gruen, Whitlam's economic adviser, later recalled that the demand pressures building in 1973–74 were of 'a greater intensity' than anything since the end of the Second World War. A 25 per cent tariff cut and a further revaluation helped alleviate matters by diverting demand pressures to imports. There was also price control aimed at big business in the form of the Prices Justification Tribunal, which might have reduced the inflation rate from what it otherwise would have been. However, on the fiscal policy front, Crean was not sufficiently tough enough to exercise restraint of the growth on outlays which the Treasury felt advisable.

With fiscal policy already prescribed, the Labor Government endeavoured to contain the inflation problem by sharply increasing interest rates. The subsequent credit squeeze went on for far too long and thus led to the subsequent recession. Firms and businesses were caught short, having built up their stocks and over-ordered to catch up with a booming domestic demand. Given the sudden weakening of markets, Australian firms could not easily pass on wage and other cost increases.

The quadrupling of oil prices by the Organisation of Petroleum Exporting Countries (OPEC) cartel in the year from December 1973 exacerbated Australia's domestically generated inflation and unemployment problems. Continuing strong wages expansion in the first two years of the Labor Government further facilitated a booming economy. As a result, the wages' share of national income rose at the expense of profits.

The 1974–75 budget, described by Crean as 'a budget of many hands', was an inappropriate response to the situation. By this time the Treasury had been marginalised because the government had lost faith in its approach. Cairns replaced Crean at the end of 1974 largely because the latter was perceived as dominated by the Treasury. The Labor Party caucus did not feel that containing

---

49   'The Problem of Stagflation: Unemployment with Rising Prices', May 1972 Public lecture at University of Tasmania, Firth Papers, NLA.

inflation should be the priority when unemployment was rising. This budget was therefore unorthodox in a period of very high inflation, providing urban renewal to deprived areas, some income tax relief and a 33 per cent increase in government outlays, together with increased taxes for the business sector. The idea was to encourage union agreement for wage restraint, thus limiting the pass-on of international inflation through cost pressures in Australia.

Cairns received a missive from the governor of the Reserve Bank of Australia, Sir John Phillips, with his 'solution' to stagflation. Phillips was an early convert to monetarism and had been tracking money supply growth. The malaise in the business sector, Phillips felt, was deep-seated in character and could not be resolved by a boom in spending led by government expenditure. Phillips felt it advisable that government expenditures and the rate of monetary expansion be reined back as inflation was badly disrupting business planning. Apart from keeping wage pressures under check, reducing the rate of government spending would restore confidence to the private sector.[50]

Phillips' advice stemmed from the Reserve Bank of Australia's 1973 *Annual Report* that was noticeable for joining with the Treasury in arguing that inflation mattered more than unemployment. The dominant culture amongst the RBA's economists had recently become monetarist. It was symbolised the year before (1973) by the presence of a leading English monetarist, Michael Parkin, within the Bank's Research Department.[51]

Economists and senior officials within the RBA were the first to accept 'inflationary expectations' as a significant factor within the policy domain. Treasury economists, too, accepted the importance of inflationary expectations before comparable acknowledgement by their academic brethren. Despite its misgivings about some of Milton Friedman's work, the Treasury became more monetarist in outlook following the experience of the late 1973 credit squeeze.

In April 1975, a small-statured man who was neither a dwarf nor a mandarin arrived in Canberra. It was the father of monetarism, Milton Friedman. He had come to administer the last rites of Australian Keynesianism. The message he hammered home was that the choice between inflation and unemployment disappears when inflation is out of control; any action to create more jobs merely adds to inflationary expectations and, in turn, a further rise in unemployment. It was a new wisdom for a new age – full employment was replaced by a concept called NAIRU (the non-accelerating inflation rate of unemployment).

---

50   Sir J. Phillips to J.F. Cairns, 18 December 1974, National Archives of Australia (NAA) A5931 CL 155.
51   'Reserve Bank Backs the Treasury Line', *Australian Financial Review*, 28 August 1974.

Retrospect

Despite two recessions, stop and starts, trade deficits and policy errors, the age of Keynes was, to quote the economic historian Angus Maddison, 'a golden age'. It was thus for Australia as it was for other western countries. Despite Copland's protestations about not growing fast enough, Australia still registered an average growth rate of 4.7 per cent during the period 1945–73, higher than most comparable industrialised countries. During the post-war era Australia's population grew on average at 2.5 per cent, one of the highest growth rates in the world. Inflation averaged 4.6 per cent over the same period. In the 1970s, macroeconomic performance deteriorated markedly as growth fell to 3.1 per cent while inflation soared to an average of 9.7 per cent.[52]

While the post-war period enjoyed propitious factors like reconstruction, pent-up demand and the liberalisation of international trade, Ian MacFarlane also notes that there was widespread restraint in economic behaviour along with governments committing themselves to full employment and robust economic growth. There was a high savings rate and little reliance upon foreign savings. MacFarlane says fiscal and monetary policies were adjusted to smooth the business cycle but this did not mean that fiscal policy was too expansionary. If anything, demand management was restrained. In the 12 years between 1961 and 1973, the budget was, on balance, in surplus. In the earlier period, 1950 until the 1970s monetary and fiscal policy could not be too expansionary without threatening inflation, the balance of payments or the exchange rate. When, moreover, there was a recession, there was also a quick recovery. While in recent times there has been talk of 'The Great Moderation' in macroeconomic performance from the mid-1990s onward without any explicit Keynesian economic management, one should point out that it only lasted for less than half the period known as the Keynesian golden age.

---

52   I. Macfarlane, 'The Economics of Nostalgia', *Reserve Bank of Australia Bulletin*, 2 (1997).

4

An Age of the Mandarins? Government in New Zealand, 1940–51[1]

John R. Martin

The passage of more than half a century allows us to view the period following the end of the Second World War until the 1950s genuinely as history. Research materials, principally in archives, are supplemented by official histories, and biographies, with a few interviews enriching the story. I have been struck by the number of leading public servants of the period who were still in office during the 1950s and 1960s and who influenced the public service in which I spent 35 years. I was privileged to have known a number of them.

In this chapter, after sketching the political and economic situation in New Zealand in 1945, I identify two principal challenges – managing the economy and national development – facing the Labour Government led by Peter Fraser. I also examine changes in organising government business made after the National Government came to office late in 1949. I then describe briefly the state of the public service as New Zealand emerged from the war. I consider the role played by several prominent public servants – a team to set against the Seven Dwarfs – and reflect on what we know about their working relationships with ministers.

In essence, the picture is, first, of a group of outstanding and long-serving public servants who worked very closely with Prime Minister Fraser and his deputy, Walter Nash, the minister of finance, through the war and afterwards. With the change of government in 1949, the close, personal and somewhat haphazard methods of working under Labour were succeeded by a more conventional (in the Westminster model) relationship between ministers and officials, conducted within a more formal machinery for the handling of Cabinet business – a change sought unsuccessfully by officials when the Labour Government was in office.[2]

---

1   In writing this chapter I have benefited greatly from discussions with Dr Brian Easton, Professor Gary Hawke, Sir Frank Holmes and Mr Noel Lough. Needless to say the responsibility for what is said rests entirely with me. I have also gained much from two books by a Canadian scholar, J.L. Granatstein, *The Ottawa Men: The Civil Service Mandarins* (Toronto: Oxford University Press, 1984); *A Man of Influence: Norman A. Robertson and Canadian Statecraft 1929-68* (Deneau Publishers, 1981).

2   A recent discussion of New Zealand's constitutional arrangements in the immediate post-war period is H. Kumarasingham, *Onward with Executive Power: Lessons From New Zealand 1947–57* (Wellington: Institute

Peter Fraser, c1940

Source: S.P. Andrew Collection, Alexander Turnbull Library

of Policy Studies, 2010).

I conclude with reflections about the influence that the immediate post-war period had on New Zealand public administration at least until the 'revolution' of the mid-1980s. This was, in part, a matter of personalities: the heads of departments in the 1960s and 1970s were the 'bright young men' of such agencies as the Economic Stabilisation Commission of the 1940s; they were shaped by the mandarins of that period and, in turn, guided key public servants of the 1970s and 1980s. Beyond personalities, the 'mildly corporate' style of government — some would say, in Keith Middlemas' phrase, 'corporatist bias'[3] — that persisted for nearly half a century owed a great deal to the conventions and arrangements that emerged during the war and in the transition to peace.

Setting the scene

New Zealand entered the Second World War in a state of 'economic emergency'.[4] Although commodity prices had improved since the mid-1930s, increased imports (flowing from expanded government activity and guaranteed dairy prices) and an upturn in capital withdrawal during 1938 led to an exchange crisis. In December 1938 import and exchange controls were imposed; they remained in place with variations for five decades. After long and humiliating discussions in the City of London seeking to roll over maturing loans, the minister of finance, Walter Nash, returned to New Zealand the day after war was declared.

New Zealand was radically different at the end of the war. Exchange reserves were in a healthy state and loans had been repaid. In 1947, the 'Government and people of New Zealand' were in a position to make a 'gift'[5] of £10 million sterling to the United Kingdom. Export income had been enhanced through bulk purchase agreements under which the United Kingdom purchased exports of meat, dairy products and wool at guaranteed prices. These arrangements remained in place until the 1950s. Imports had been restrained. Fiscal and monetary policies were deflationary[6] and based on 'sound finance'. Crucially they were complemented by stabilisation measures — income and price controls

---

3   In the British context, 'the tendency of industrial, trade union and financial institutions to make reciprocal arrangements with each other and with government while avoiding overt conflict'. Keith Middlemas, *Power Competition and the State*, Vol. 1 (London: Macmillan, 1986), 1.
4   J.V.T. Baker, *The New Zealand People at War: War Economy* (Wellington: Historical Publications Branch, Department of Internal Affairs, 1965), 2. I am indebted to Baker, and also to G.R. Hawke, *The Making of New Zealand: An Economic History* (Cambridge: Cambridge University Press, 1985); and B. Easton, *In Stormy Seas: The Post-War New Zealand Economy* (Dunedin: University of Otago Press, 1997) for their discussions of the New Zealand economy before, during and after the war.
5   The 'gift' was not only an act of generosity; it was linked with negotiations on sterling and bulk purchase.
6   Hawke, *The Making of New Zealand*, 172. Price rises in New Zealand between 1939 and 1945 at 18 per cent (and 5 per cent during the stabilisation period from 1942 to 1945) were significantly below the United Kingdom and United States, and Australia (23 per cent).

– that were supported by a 'willingness of groups within the community to subordinate their interests to the perceived need for resources to be mobilised towards the war'.[7] The machinery of stabilisation and the thinking behind it influenced both economic management and the style of government for many years to come.

New Zealand's first Labour Government held office throughout the war and for four years afterwards – a total of four parliamentary terms. It had won in a landslide at the general election at the end of 1935 and remained in office until 1949. It was led, first, by Australian-born Michael Joseph Savage. He died in 1940 and was succeeded by Peter Fraser, who headed the government for nine years until the National Party led by Sydney Holland defeated it. Fraser, as prime minister and minister of external affairs, and Walter Nash, as deputy prime minister and minister of finance, dominated the Cabinet throughout the war and in the immediate post-war years. Their distinctive styles of leadership and their relations with the public service are considered below.

When Labour came to office, New Zealand was emerging from the Depression. Ministers had no hesitation in using the state as the engine of development. Extensive public works programs (notably roads, housing and hydro-electric power development) got under way. Benefits were increased. Industrial relations legislation was amended to improve the position of workers and unions. Guaranteed prices for dairy products were introduced. The *Industrial Efficiency Act* 1936 signalled the government's commitment to 'the promotion of new industries in the most economic form'. And, in 1938, passage of the *Social Security Act* 'restored New Zealand's status as a social laboratory'[8] and laid the foundations of the modern welfare state.

Mobilisation of the country for war of necessity further extended the role of the state, facilitated by the existence of widespread controls already in place. The wartime framework of public agencies and regulatory instruments was available to the Labour Government to pursue national development in the post-war period.

The post-war challenges

Like all other countries that had been engaged for five years in total war, New Zealand had immediate issues with which to deal in making the transition to peacetime. Employment was at the forefront. Returning servicemen needed to find jobs; the place in the workforce of women (who had filled the gap left by

---

7   Ibid.
8   P.M. Smith, *A Concise History of New Zealand* (Melbourne: Cambridge University Press, 2005), 157.

men called into the forces) required attention – a particular issue for the state services; and 'manpower' controls had to be unwound. Unlike the situation after the Great War, the shortage of labour after the Second World War was 'to make the problem of rehabilitation comparatively simple'.[9] Indeed, the persistence of 'full employment'[10] – most economists at the time and later would say '*over*-full employment' – and the consequential threat of inflation preoccupied policy-makers in the post-war period.

To illustrate the nature and style of governance in New Zealand in the post-war years I have focused on economic management (the short term) and national development (the long term). But there were also activities of interest in other fields of public policy – and the public service – to which I will allude below.

Economic management

At what point was the influence of Keynes on New Zealand economic management felt? We know that when the minister of finance, W. Downie Stewart, and the secretary to the Treasury, A.D. Park, were in London in 1932, they met Keynes who offered views on New Zealand's exchange problem (including 'to approximate the Australian rate of exchange').[11] We know, too, that Keynes' ideas (*The Means to Prosperity*)[12] – to stimulate growth through increased government spending – influenced representations to the minister of finance, Gordon Coates,[13] early in the 1930s, but were dismissed as irrelevant. Keynesian views on the place of 'cheap money' (low interest rates) were understood by officials such as Ashwin (see below) and shared by the apostles of Douglas Credit.[14] But the influence of economists on the New Zealand governments of the 1930s was largely confined to recommendations to devalue the New Zealand pound against sterling that came from a government-appointed committee in 1932. The New Zealand Treasury was more inclined to deal with bankers and businessmen than economists.

---

9   Baker, *The New Zealand People at War*, 504.
10 Hawke, *The Making of New Zealand*, 190. After the Second World War and until 1967 not more than 0.2 per cent of the labour force was registered as unemployed.
11 M. McKinnon, *Treasury: The New Zealand Treasury 1840–2000* (Auckland: Auckland University Press in Association with the Ministry of Culture and Heritage, 2003), 137. Downie Stewart, who resigned his ministerial post when the Cabinet decided to devalue, described Keynes in his diary as 'a peculiar looking man, very tall, with dark hair and black moustache'.
12 J.M. Keynes, *The Means to Prosperity* (London: Macmillan, 1933).
13 J.G. (Gordon) Coates (1878–1943), Reform Party prime minister between 1925 and 1928, was minister of finance in the Coalition Government between 1933 and 1935. He served in the war cabinet from 1940 until his death in 1943.
14 Hawke, *The Making of New Zealand*, 154.

B.C. (Sir Bernard) Ashwin, c1955

Source: New Zealand Treasury

There is no evidence that the influence on economic policy of economists, Keynesian or otherwise, increased after Labour assumed office in 1935. Indeed, McKinnon, in his history of the New Zealand Treasury, contrasts the 'movement of young Keynesians into other British Commonwealth Treasuries' with their absence from the New Zealand Treasury. In particular, the 'exciting' experience of H.C. Coombs in Australia in the mid-1930s is recalled.[15]

At this point the first of the 'mandarins' around which this chapter is constructed enters the narrative. B.C. (later Sir Bernard) Ashwin had been an influential adviser to the United/Reform Coalition Government, which held office from 1931 to 1935, a period which included negotiations over establishment of the Reserve Bank. Although Ashwin did not become secretary until 1939 – at the age of 42 – there is no disagreement with the proposition that he was the principal official advising New Zealand governments on economic management from the early 1930s until his retirement in 1955.

Brian Easton, writing about Ashwin as one of New Zealand's nation-builders, states that he was the Treasury's only economist in the 1930s.[16] Ashwin had graduated as a Master of Commerce in economics in 1925 from Victoria University (part-time study). He was a member of the Economic Society of Australia and New Zealand from the 1920s and a contributor to the *Economic Record*.

Ashwin worked in close association with the Labour Government throughout its long period of office. Walter Nash was the minister of finance for the entire 14 years. Ashwin was deeply involved in the *Social Security Act* 1938 (seeking to moderate the claims on the public purse); in buying out the private shareholders in the Reserve Bank and increasing the Bank's powers over the trading banks; in the exchange crisis of 1938–39, meeting ministers daily while negotiations proceeded in London; and in the various aspects of what is generally accepted to be a 'symbolic' new direction of economic management that can be dated from the decisions in December 1938 to impose import and exchange controls that continued long after the initial crisis.[17]

'Insulationism' (or 'planned insulation')[18] was the term in use from the late 1930s through to the post-war period to represent 'a broad decision that the course of the New Zealand economy should be determined less by events overseas and more by the choice of local people, especially those holding official positions'.[19] By contrast, with the onset of the Depression in 1930, the government at the end of the war in 1945 had at its command not only the levers of fiscal policy, but

---

15 McKinnon, *Treasury*, 159, citing G. Whitwell, *The Treasury Line* (Sydney: Allen & Unwin, 1986), 10, 11, 61–5.
16 B. Easton, *The Nationbuilders* (Auckland: Auckland University Press, 2001), 47.
17 Hawke, *The Making of New Zealand*, 163.
18 J.B. Condliffe, *The Welfare State in New Zealand* (London: Geo. Allen & Unwin, 1959), 58.
19 Hawke, *The Making of New Zealand*, 163.

also control of monetary policy (through the Reserve Bank and, in theory, the ownership of the Bank of New Zealand – nationalised in 1945 and responsible for 40 per cent of banking business), import, exchange and price controls, and, in effect, an incomes policy through the instrument of the Arbitration Court.

The Reserve Bank, established in 1934, perhaps surprisingly, does not feature prominently in this story. In matters of general monetary policy, Ashwin was undeniably the principal adviser:

> He had been prominent in the foundation of the bank, and he looked on it as to some extent his child. But he considered that it had had an unfortunate beginning and he did not regard it as playing a major role in economic policy in the 1940s. By the late 1940s and the early 1950s … Ashwin was too well established as the senior financial adviser to Government to regard the bank as a rival …[20]

The role of the Arbitration Court warrants recognition here. The Court (a judge flanked by nominees of the social partners, the employers and unions), with its power to issue general wage orders, played a significant role in the economy. Judge Arthur Tyndall shared a number of characteristics with other 'mandarins' who feature in this chapter. He was a long-time public servant (an engineer, lawyer and accountant). After some years in road construction, he was successively secretary of Mines (1934–36), and director of Housing (1936–40) – heading a flagship program of the Labour Government – becoming judge of the Arbitration Court in 1940 and remaining in that position until 1965.

In the words of J.B. Condliffe, one of New Zealand's most eminent economists, writing in 1959, '[t]he New Zealand economy emerged from the war taut with suppressed inflation'.[21] With international reserves at very comfortable levels, a balanced budget, and the continuation of an assured market for primary products in the United Kingdom, there were pressures on the government to ease wartime restraints. But, by comparison with the situation when Labour assumed office a decade earlier, notable for under-employment, resources, including the workforce, were now fully employed. There was also an appreciation among the policy-makers of the

> lesson of Keynesian economics that fiscal policy could be used to balance aggregate demand and supply in the economy as a whole, and that the

---

20   G.R. Hawke, *Between Governments and Banks: A History of the Reserve Bank of New Zealand* (Wellington: Government Printer, 1973), 223. Particularly after Ashwin's retirement in 1955 and on the technical aspects of monetary policy E.C. Fussell (deputy governor, 1941–48 and governor, 1948–62) was a respected adviser.
21   Condliffe, *The Welfare State in New Zealand*, 99.

budget was not merely a matter of government housekeeping. But this was grafted on to an economy where official controls were widespread and not regarded as a transitory phenomenon.[22]

At the centre of the government machinery that administered this web of controls was the Economic Stabilisation Commission (ESC) – 'that very remarkable institution'.[23] In December 1942, a comprehensive economic stabilisation scheme was announced and a six-person commission established with Ashwin as director of Stabilisation. Ashwin took over as chair of a three-person commission in July 1943.[24]

The ESC had what may now seem to be a disproportionately large influence on economic policy making and public administration during the next 30 years. First, as an 'independent semi-representative body'[25] it demonstrated the 'mildly corporate'[26] nature of New Zealand politics that persisted until the Rogernomics revolution in the 1980s. One interpretation is that 'the government was engaged in an elaborate piece of social engineering. Ministers were attempting to construct a wartime economy that would treat all sections as fairly as possible'.[27] The government – represented by Ashwin – was in the chair flanked by F.P. Walsh[28] representing the Federation of Labour and a representative of the farming industries. This was an expression of the agreement between the trade union movement and the farmers underpinning the stabilisation policy of the government. The unions, notably the Federation of Labour, and farming, through the producer boards and Federated Farmers, carried a great weight in determining economic policy through the next four decades.[29]

---

22   Hawke, *The Making of New Zealand*, 173.
23   L.C. Webb, 'The Making of Economic Policy', in R.S. Parker, ed., *Economic Stability in New Zealand* (Wellington: NZIPA, 1953), 24.
24   In some respects there is an affinity between the ESC and the Australian 'F and E' (the Financial and Economic Advisory Committee) – see Whitwell, *The Treasury Line*, 65–79.
25   M.J. Moriarty, 'Administering the Policy of Economic Stabilization', *New Zealand Journal of Public Administration*, 7, no. 2 (March 1953), 30.
26   A term attributed to John Roberts, Professor of Public Administration at Victoria University of Wellington (1966–88). Roberts also wrote about 'the stabilization game' – 'a symbolic construction of policy consensus among a broadly dispersed political elite' – a consensus of 'fair shares'. See John Roberts, 'Society and its Politics', in *Thirteen Facets: Essays to Celebrate the Silver Jubilee of Queen Elizabeth the Second 1952–77* (Wellington: Historical Publications Branch, DIA, 1978).
27   M. Bassett and M. King, *Tomorrow Comes the Song: A Life of Peter Fraser* (Auckland: Penguin, 2000), 202.
28   G. Hunt, *Black Prince: The Biography of Fintan Patrick Walsh* (Auckland: Penguin Books, 2004), 133. Fintan Patrick Walsh (1896–1963), a founding member of the Federation of Labour and president from 1953, and member of the ESC (1942–50). His key role in economic policy making in the immediate post-war period is exemplified by the publication of *Economic Stabilization in the Post-War Period* in early 1946. Soon known as 'The Walsh Report' but written by ESC officials, Lloyd White and Alan Low, the report warned of the dangers of inflation. Walsh, with Fraser's endorsement, 'sold' the report to reluctant trade unions.
29   This proposition as it applies to the union movement may be challenged by citing the conflict with the National Government that reached its peak in the waterfront strike of 1951 followed by a 'snap' general election. The industrial relations system based on the Arbitration Court remained, however, and the Federation of Labour without doubt had a very large influence on the administration of the 1960s, 1970s and early 1980s.

Secondly, the commission played an important role 'in easing the pressure on the political executive: it carries out negotiations on prices and payouts with representatives of the farming industries, the manufacturing industries, and other economic interests'.[30] McKinnon suggests that negotiations at the level undertaken by the ESC in New Zealand were carried out by ministers in the United Kingdom, Canada and Australia (cf. the role of the Australian price stabilisation committee).[31]

Thirdly, the ESC reached across the whole range of government agencies. While other tribunals and departments administered the regulations on prices, wages, goods and services – there were 18 controllers in the Ministry of Supply and Munitions – the commission called the shots. As Moriarty wrote at the time:

> Economic Stabilization covers prices, wages, rents, transport – in fact every economic activity of the individual. The Departments dealing with these activities all have problems which are also the concern of the Commission. The Commission is the central intelligence and 'economic general staff' service for the Government. It must maintain contact, through its officers, with the various departments dealing with economic affairs, recommend particular courses of action which it believes to be in harmony with the general policy, and withal keep the Government continually informed of the economic state of the country.[32]

The ESC in this respect clearly foreshadows the coordinating role of the Treasury in future, both as the 'principal economic and financial adviser' and as chair and secretariat of the Officials Economic Committee structure that developed in the 1940s and took a central place in economic decision-making (see below).

Fourthly, the ESC was a fruitful training ground for a remarkable number of public servants[33] who would lead the public service in the 1960s and 1970s (as well as Robert Parker[34] and Leicester Webb,[35] who had distinguished academic careers

---

30   L.C. Webb, 'Politics and Administration', in Horace Belshaw, ed., *New Zealand* (Berkeley: University of California Press, 1947), 288.
31   McKinnon, *Treasury*, 173.
32   Moriarty, 'Administering the Policy of Economic Stabilization', 30.
33   Among the names are: M.J. Moriarty (secretary of Industries and Commerce, 1965–72), H.G. Lang (secretary to the Treasury, 1968–76), N.V. Lough (secretary to the Treasury, 1976–80), Sir Alan Low (governor, Reserve Bank, 1967–77), G.D.L. White (deputy secretary, Foreign Affairs, 1964–72, Ambassador, Washington, 1972–78), A.C. Shailes (controller and auditor-general, 1975–83), K.C. Durrant (deputy director-general, Ministry of Agriculture and Fisheries, 1969–82).
34   R.S. (Robert) Parker was lecturer in public administration at Victoria University College, Wellington from 1939 to 1945, with some years in war service (including time at the Economic Stabilisation Commission), and returned as professor of political science from 1949 to 1954 when he took up the position of reader (later professor) in political science at The Australian National University.
35   Leicester Webb (1905–1962), after a career in journalism and study in Europe, became director of stabilisation from 1945 to 1948 and later professor of political science at The Australian National University. See J. Warhurst, 'Leicester Webb and the Foundation Years of Australian Political Science', *Australian Journal of Political Science*, 37, no. 3 (November 2002).

in Australia). The staff of the ESC featured a number qualified in economics – the Treasury was then, and for a decade into the future, predominantly a department of accountants. But this was a generation of public servants whose formative years were spent in an environment of regulation born not of ideology but of a pragmatic resort to the apparatus of the state to deal with the problems of the day. Such an approach was not incompatible with an underlying belief in the virtues of markets. This eclectic approach characterised the policy stance of people like Moriarty and Lang throughout their influential careers. The commission itself became an advisory committee to the minister of industries and commerce in 1948. It was abolished in 1950 and a number of the staff (including Moriarty, Lang and Lough) transferred to the Treasury.

The heyday of the ESC also marked the dominance of Ashwin within the Wellington governance system.[36] This dominance was starkly emphasised between 1942 and 1944 when Walter Nash, although remaining minister of finance, was also resident minister in Washington DC. While his central role in the business of government remained, in the last years of the Labour Government Ashwin was not always successful in persuading ministers to avoid inflationary spending. Although the head of the Prime Minister's Department, Alister McIntosh, told Sir Norman Brook, secretary to the Cabinet in the United Kingdom, in February 1950, that the 'Treasury have succeeded all too well in scaring the new Government stiff', Ashwin apparently fell out with Holland in his final years.[37]

Among the major economic events that stand out in the five years following the war are the decision in 1948 to revalue the New Zealand pound to parity with sterling, and the Korean War commodity boom in 1950–51 – after Labour had been defeated at the polls and the National Party had begun its uninterrupted period of eight years in office. Many wartime controls were relaxed in Labour's last years. In the early 1950s, the National Government, consistent with rhetoric about 'freedom', reduced price controls and limits on exchange payments and imports. Balance of payments pressures soon led to their tightening. Coupled with monetary controls, constraints at the frontier and regulation of prices and wages continued to mark economic management in New Zealand for the first four decades after the war.

Symbolising the readiness of successive governments to resort to regulatory powers when confronted by problems of economic management was retention until 1987 of the *Economic Stabilisation Act* 1948. This statute retained the wartime emergency powers of the Executive to 'control prices, wages, and take almost

---

36   While Ashwin was secretary to the Treasury he also served as director of the Reserve Bank; director of the State Advances Corporation; chairman of the Local Authorities Loans Board; member of the Dairy Products Marketing Board; and, during the war, paymaster-general of the armed forces.
37   McKinnon, *Treasury*, 216.

every economic measure conceivable (short of raising taxes) by regulation'.[38] Around 200 regulations were made under the authority of this Act. As Sir Robert Muldoon said in 1976, 'you can do anything provided you can hang your hat on economic stabilisation'.[39]

Associated with such controls were policies of industrialisation[40] — behind the mechanisms of 'import selection' or 'import substitution' — central to the broader objective of national development. In this respect, Hawke's observation is apposite. He notes that the best reason for import licensing 'was probably that it was desirable to have a variety of industries so as to provide opportunities for New Zealanders to develop a range of skills and aptitudes' and that the alternative, quoting Drummond[41] on industrialisation programs in general, was:

> A small scattered population of farmers, shepherds and miners, a few market towns, a scanty clutch of civil servants, lawyers, doctors and clerics. New Zealand in 1900 in fact. Or Gold Coast in 1950.[42]

National development

Above all, New Zealand was a 'dependent economy'.[43] After the war a 'programme of planned development behind the insulation of exchange control'[44] could be built on the foundations put in place in 1938 and later extended. New Zealand's national development in the 1940s and 1950s had three principal components. First, increased productivity in the farming industries (these were the years of aerial topdressing, irrigation, and application of state-funded scientific innovation to the grasslands); second, enhanced infrastructure; and, thirdly, industrialisation.

Expanded public works activity was a key element in Labour's pre-war program: roading, hydro-electric power generation, airport development, irrigation schemes and housing projects. All resumed after the cutbacks of the Depression. But the outbreak of war diverted resources to military requirements. The Public Works Department became increasingly 'the constructional agency of the armed

---

38 G. Palmer and M. Palmer, *Bridled Power* (3rd edn Auckland: Oxford University Press, 1997), 171.
39 Ibid., 172.
40 See S. Leathem, 'Industry and Industrial Policy', in H. Belshaw, ed., *New Zealand* (Berkeley: University of California Press, 1947) and Michael Bassett, *The State in New Zealand 1840–1984: Socialism without Doctrines?* (Auckland: Auckland University Press, 1998), 208–10.
41 I.R. Drummond, 'The British Empire Economies in the "Great Depression"', in H. van der Wee, ed., *The Great Depression Revisited: Essays in the Economics of the Thirties* (The Hague: Martinus Nijhoff, 1972), 233.
42 G.R. Hawke, *Government in the New Zealand Economy*, Planning Paper No. 13 (Wellington: New Zealand Planning Council, 1982), 44.
43 H. Belshaw, 'Stabilisation in a Dependent Economy', *Economic Record Supplement*, April 1939; C.G.F. Simpkin, *The Instability of a Dependent Economy: Economic Fluctuations in New Zealand, 1840-1914* (London: Oxford University Press, 1951).
44 Condliffe, *The Welfare State in New Zealand*, 63.

4. An Age of the Mandarins? Government in New Zealand, 1940–51

services'.[45] The extent of military requirements and the claims from overseas theatres on manpower and equipment were an unparalleled challenge. The departmental structure was demonstrably inadequate and, from March 1942, wartime arrangements were put in place.

A Defence Construction Council was established with the prime minister as chairman and with the newly appointed commissioner of defence construction as vice-chairman. This latter appointment, with sweeping powers, had a significant influence on post-war organisation of public works. James (later Sir James) Fletcher, the founder of what is still a major construction company, had been a dominant figure in the government's state housing schemes. He was instrumental in creation of a new statutory agency – the Ministry of Works[46] – to 'establish more appropriate control over the execution of all construction works, including housing construction', and became the first commissioner of works. The Ministry, separate from the Public Works Department (PWD), worked with the Treasury in examining the economic and technical aspects of all projects from central government agencies, local government or subsidised from the public purse. Responsibility for carrying out public works remained with the PWD.

It was envisaged from the outset that the ministry would continue after the war and, from 1946, the commissioner of works took over the responsibilities of the permanent head of the PWD. Thus was born the Ministry of Works, the powerful department that played such a major part in New Zealand's development until its demise during the 1980s 'Revolution'.

From its inception the ministry – and its minister, the redoubtable Robert Semple – aspired to a 'planning' role. Semple, indeed, referred to it as the Ministry of Works and Planning.[47] He spoke of the haphazard way in which public works had proceeded and of 'political roads and bridges'. Initially, it was envisaged that Fletcher as commissioner would supervise the execution of a plan for post-war recovery approved by Cabinet. Some credence was given to the 'planning' function of the ministry when administration of the *Town Planning Act* 1926 was transferred from the Department of Internal Affairs to the Ministry of Works in 1946 (the Act was not amended until 1948). The Town and Country Planning Branch was an integral part of the ministry until the 1980s.

Despite Semple's claims, there was some uncertainty about where 'planning' should be located in the governance structure of the post-war period. Early in 1944 Cabinet established the Organisation for National Development

---

45 R. Noonan, *By Design: A Brief History of the Public Works Department, Ministry of Works 1870–1970* (Wellington: Government Printer, 1975).
46 *Ministry of Works Act* 1943.
47 Noonan, *By Design*, 188.

(OND) as a branch of the Prime Minister's Department — the counterpart to Australia's Department of Post-War Reconstruction. The initiative seems to have come from the Department of Industries and Commerce (and Ministry of Supply) that carried the major burden of administering wartime controls. The mandate was 'not only to study and plan for long-range development of the Dominion but also to make special preparation for practical measures to meet the period of transition which will occur on the cessation of hostilities.'[48] The Organisation itself, working within policy set by a Cabinet sub-committee of the prime minister, and the ministers of Finance, Industries and Commerce, Works, Agriculture, and Rehabilitation, consisted of a chief executive officer, a coordinating committee of five permanent heads (chaired by Ashwin), and a small research staff. Planning was to be undertaken by a series of committees chaired by ministers: construction, power development, rehabilitation and personnel, transport, tourism and publicity, immigration and labour, imports and shipping.

On 19 November 1945, Cabinet disbanded the OND. Cabinet committees already established would deal with any 'major problems involving rehabilitation and post-war reconstruction'. The executive committee was replaced by a special departmental committee chaired by the secretary to the Treasury 'and making recommendations to Cabinet whenever necessary'. Various planning committees continued at the discretion of the appropriate responsible minister. The Ministry of Works would assume all 'physical planning functions'. Regional councils set up under the auspices of the OND were 'to take full responsibility for managing their own affairs'.[49]

Polaschek, writing in 1958, assessed the OND as having 'accomplished a good deal' despite its short life, specifically important surveys of coal mining and forestry, population estimates and demobilisation plans.

> Nevertheless, New Zealand governments must face an election every three years. This coupled with their typical pragmatic approach to problems gives them a preference for action rather than plans. So the existence of a purely planning body divorced from the carrying out of policy is always likely to be precarious. Particularly is this so if its functions cut across those of old established departments, like Treasury and Works, which are concerned both with forming policy and applying it.[50]

---

48 Hon. D.G. Sullivan (Minister of Industries and Commerce and acting Prime Minister) announcing the establishment of the Organisation for National Development in 1944 (quoted by Leathem, 'Industry and Industrial Policy', 174).
49 Archives New Zealand, AAFD 816/1, Shanahan's personal file on Cabinet organisation.
50 R.J. Polaschek, *Government Administration in New Zealand* (Wellington: New Zealand Institute of Public Administration, 1958), 49.

The OND failed, in Polaschek's view, 'primarily because too much was expected from it too soon' – in announcing its demise to the House of Representatives, Fraser spoke of impracticability; he wanted quick results – but also 'because it cut across the lines of departmental authority and responsibility'.[51] Permanent heads were already overburdened. This is consistent with Sutch's comments that underline the location of power in Wellington:

> Sullivan [Minister of Industries and Commerce] as Acting Prime Minister, established the OND early in 1944, when Nash was busy as New Zealand Minister in Washington and Fraser was at a war conference. When Fraser returned to find an economic planning group in his own department he was more than displeased and by 1946 he had disbanded it. He was supported in his action by the older and stronger government departments, for example, Treasury and Works, but had he wanted to, Fraser could easily have made an economic unit the most important part of the machinery of state.[52]

Similar impressions were recorded in a discussion in 1964 of a paper by Foss Shanahan (see below).[53] There was a feeling that the OND had been 'suffocated' by senior officials in the Ministry of Works and the Treasury, 'partly because it sought to interpose itself between major Departments and their Ministers, partly because it seemed to usurp departmental responsibility for implementing plans, partly because its plans (which were not always discussed with departments responsible) were too ambitious and unreal, and partly because the youth and experience of some of its officers caused jealousies'.[54]

As 'indicative planning' came into vogue in the 1950s and 1960s – the New Zealand manifestations are found in sectoral planning conferences, the National Development Conference (1968–72) and the New Zealand Planning Council (1977–91) – there were echoes of the issues that surrounded the OND.

Cabinet and coordination

Leicester Webb, writing in 1940, observed that:

> It might be expected that, notwithstanding the variety of a cabinet minister's work, it would be possible for a dozen men to govern New

---

51   Ibid., 270.
52   W.B. Sutch, *The Quest for Security in New Zealand 1840–1966* (Wellington: Oxford University Press, 1966), 345, 346.
53   F. Shanahan, 'Planning in War and Peace', in J.P.M. Cornwall, ed., *Planning and Forecasting in New Zealand* (Wellington/London: NZIPA/Oxford University Press, 1965), 19–32.
54   Cornwall, *Planning and Forecasting*, 10.

> Zealand, which has fewer inhabitants than Liverpool, is not troubled by racial minorities, and has no pressing problems of foreign policy, without shortening their lives by overwork and lack of sleep and without creating around themselves an atmosphere of flurry and crisis. But it is not so. The machinery of government in New Zealand works with as much jamming and overheating as the machinery of government in a great empire.[55]

Five years of war were years of achievement but, if anything, they highlighted the problems of the machinery of government suggested by Webb. At the ministerial level, the credit for achievement can largely be attributed to two people: Peter Fraser[56] and, to a lesser degree, Walter Nash.[57] 'In effect, throughout the war, the key political decisions were made most of the time by two men. The pressure flicked from one to the other according to whichever was in New Zealand at the time.'[58] The situation did not change significantly in the aftermath of the war.

Fraser's health declined and both men conducted their business with a degree of idiosyncrasy that was the bane of officials. Fraser's sight was not good and officials, notably A.D. (later Sir Alister) McIntosh, head of the Prime Minister's Department and secretary of External Affairs, were on call late into the evening to read telegrams to him. Nash was a hoarder of files, a habit that continued in his one-term prime ministership between 1957 and 1960. These characteristics simply underlined the need, obvious to officials, for a more systematic conduct of government business.[59]

> What detracted from an atmosphere of dignity in conducting cabinet meetings was [Fraser's] lamentable disregard for method and order. This led to endless rambling discussion and excessive waste of time with himself as the most notable offender leading the pack in the pursuit of many a hare. He just would not be organized. An agenda was an affront, and any attempt by an official or a colleague to introduce order would only make him mulish and antagonistic ...[60]

---

55 L. Webb, *Government in New Zealand* (Wellington: Department of Internal Affairs, 1940), 67–8.
56 For an account of Fraser in New Zealand politics see Bassett and King, *Tomorrow Comes the Song*.
57 For a similar account of the life of Nash see Keith Sinclair, *Walter Nash* (Auckland: Oxford University Press, 1976).
58 Bassett and King, *Tomorrow Comes the Song*, 223.
59 'For my part I wished that [Nash's] good intentions had not rested on his egregious inability to organise his work. As with Fraser, time meant nothing to Nash. As a Minister he boasted that he never went home on the day he left it ... Papers piled up in his office. They stayed there for days and weeks, or months or years, and sometimes forever ... This habit of holding papers caused serious dislocation of public business.' Sir Carl Berendsen in Hugh Templeton, ed., *Mr Ambassador: Memoirs of Sir Carl Berendsen* (Wellington: Victoria University Press, 2009), 7.
60 A.D. McIntosh, 'Working with Peter Fraser in Wartime', in M. Clark, ed., *Peter Fraser: Master Politician* (Wellington: Dunmore Press, 1998), 163 (reprinting a 1973 address by McIntosh). There is a resemblance to the practice of Mackenzie King in Canada: 'King's lack of, and aversion to, system.' Granatstein, *The Ottawa Men*, 203.

But in the domestic Cabinet for which there was no secretariat, until after the end of the war, chaos often prevailed.

This provides an opportunity for introduction of three mandarins who made an indelible mark on the New Zealand public service. C.A. (later Sir Carl) Berendsen, 'an Australian New Zealander', departed from New Zealand as the first high commissioner in Canberra early in 1943 and retired as ambassador to the United States in 1952. But through the 1930s and until he left Wellington, he was the government's adviser on external affairs. From 1935, Berendsen was also permanent head of the Prime Minister's Department and, from June 1940, secretary of the War Cabinet. Berendsen was something of a one-man band. As his successor (McIntosh) commented, 'Berendsen had always been reluctant to take on staff not only because he was more competent than anyone else to handle the drafting and the decision-making involved but there was, in fact, no room physically within the Prime Minister's Department in Parliament Buildings in which to put staff'.[61]

McIntosh, a librarian and historian, was effectively Berendsen's deputy in all roles. In 1943, at the age of 37, he became secretary of the War Cabinet and permanent head of the newly created Department of External Affairs. In 1945 he also became head of the Prime Minister's Department. He remained in the dual roles, heading the two departments, until 1966. McIntosh laid the foundations and built the department now known as the Ministry of Foreign Affairs and Trade, and guided New Zealand foreign policy for more than 20 years.[62] He was at the right hand of four prime ministers – Fraser (for six years), Holland (for eight), Nash (for three) and Holyoake (for seven). It is his part in establishing the machinery that institutionalised the way in which New Zealand cabinets and officials have, in fundamental respects, functioned to the present day that is of interest.

Even more directly concerned with the organisation of Cabinet than McIntosh was the third of the trio of diplomat-cum-prime ministerial advisers, Foss Shanahan. A lawyer, Shanahan transferred from the Customs Department to the Prime Minister's Department in 1938 as assistant secretary to the Organisation for National Security (ONS), established within the Prime Minister's Department in 1937 to prepare the 'War Book'. In 1940, at the age of 30, Shanahan became

---

61   A.D. McIntosh, 'Origins of the Department of External Affairs and the Formulation of an Independent Foreign Policy', in *New Zealand in World Affairs*, Vol. I (Wellington: Price Milburn/NZIIA, 1977), 17.

62   McIntosh's place in New Zealand's administrative history is well covered in his published correspondence: *Undiplomatic Dialogue: Letters Between Carl Berendsen and Alister McIntosh 1943–1952* (1993) and *Unofficial Channels: Letters Between Alister McIntosh and Foss Shanahan, George Laking and Frank Corner* (1999) both volumes edited by Ian McGibbon; McIntosh's own story of the early years in 'Origins of the Department'; McIntosh's speech accepting an honorary degree from Canterbury University in 1965, reprinted in M. Templeton, ed., *An Eye, an Ear and a Voice: 50 Years in New Zealand's External Relations 1943–93* (Wellington: MFAT, 1993).

secretary of the ONS. He then became assistant secretary to the War Cabinet and secretary of the Chiefs of Staff Committee and, in 1945, secretary to Cabinet and assistant (later deputy) secretary of External Affairs. In the 1950s Shanahan served abroad but tragically died at the age of 54 in 1964 (still deputy secretary of External Affairs, with McIntosh's retirement from the New Zealand public service only a couple of years away).

The archives tell a story of persistence by McIntosh and Shanahan in their efforts to persuade the government 'to establish a Cabinet Secretariat with a view to placing Cabinet business on an orderly basis, in contrast to the notoriously haphazard procedures which had characterised the War Cabinet'[63] – and the peacetime Cabinet.

In a file note of 30 September 1946,[64] Shanahan observed that the British Cabinet Secretariat 'had now, with experience in the Second World War, reached a very high stage of perfection' and that the Whitehall model was paralleled in Canada and Australia, particularly the former. Wartime experience, Shanahan argued, had emphasised the need for coordination among departments and the formal machinery in place on defence questions had proved its worth. But the work was more than one person could handle. The range of Cabinet standing committees recently established was serviced through arrangements organised by the minister in the chair. The 'weakness' of these committees was that 'they may trend [sic] in their discussions to proceed without the Ministers concerned always being informed of developments in sufficient time … there is scope for a Cabinet Secretariat in New Zealand'.

A further paper of 5 June 1947 pointed to 'the number of important policy matters with which Cabinet must deal, some reorganization of the business could be effected so as to reduce the amount of time spent by Cabinet on matters not of the same relative importance' and again commended the British system and developments in Australia.[65] Specific proposals were made for the approval of expenditure with delegation to individual ministers. A formal agenda should be circulated in advance. Ministers should be required to 'formulate precisely' recommendations and circulate papers five days in advance. Minutes on the British model should be prepared. The secretariat should check that effect had been given to decisions made by Cabinet.

---

63   McGibbon, *Unofficial Channels*, 28. A War Cabinet had been formed in July 1940 with three Labour members and two from the National Party. It was to deal not only with service matters but also production for war purposes, financing the war and generally to implement the policy of parliament in relation to New Zealand's participation in the war. This was not a 'national government' as the National Party Opposition was seeking: the Labour Cabinet continued as 'the government'. The War Cabinet held its last meeting on 9 August 1945 and, despite Holland's unwillingness to participate a degree of bipartisanship was achieved.
64   Archives New Zealand, AAFD 816/1, Shanahan's personal file on Cabinet organisation.
65   Ibid.

McIntosh and Shanahan made little progress in the remaining days of the Labour Government in setting up a secretariat on the Whitehall model although Shanahan was present at Cabinet meetings from January 1948. The results of the 1949 general election presented the opportunity for officials to take the initiative.

In a memorandum of 2 December 1949 – between election day and the swearing in of the new government – McIntosh, acknowledging that this was 'substantially Mr Shanahan's draft', put before the prime minister-elect, Sydney Holland, a number of proposals 'to assist in the conduct of Cabinet business'. The memorandum:

> presupposes that the concern of Cabinet with routine details would be reduced and the attention of Cabinet would be concentrated mainly on policy questions ... Ministers would be informed of problems before they were discussed and thus be in a better position to discuss them when they were being considered in Cabinet. Under a system where minutes were made and circulated the Ministers would be better informed and could better instruct Permanent Heads.[66]

McIntosh associated Ashwin and R.M. Campbell, chairman of the Public Service Commission, with his urgings

> that some such procedure should be instituted, with a view not only to increasing the efficiency of the Cabinet itself but, more especially, to enabling the Public Service to carry out the policy decisions Cabinet wishes Government Departments to implement.

Shortly afterwards, Shanahan (who had been abroad and had spent time with Norman Robertson, secretary to Cabinet in Ottawa) made specific proposals to the prime minister relating to procedures for the agenda, minutes, expenditure control (on which Ashwin was reporting separately) and servicing Cabinet committees. Shanahan was not lacking in ambition for the Cabinet Secretariat. But the trouble-shooting role to which he aspired as Cabinet secretary – perhaps emulating the dominance in Whitehall of Norman Brook (on whom he had called) – was not something that commended itself to such 'mandarins' as Ashwin in the Treasury or, it can be supposed, E.R. McKillop, the commissioner of works (1945–55). Although Shanahan, as deputy to McIntosh in the Prime Minister's Department and External Affairs, remained a powerful figure within the Wellington bureaucracy until his death, the Cabinet secretary and the secretariat were essentially there to service the Cabinet and its committees, a role executed efficiently and effectively, but not to set the directions for the path of government.

---

66 Ibid.

A further definition – and restriction – of the role of the Cabinet Secretariat was associated with another important and long-enduring institutional innovation from the early post-war years. This was the Officials Economic Committee that became a central feature of the policy making machinery in Wellington for 30 years. The origins of this committee can be traced to a Balance of Payments Working Party formed in 1947 to forecast overseas exchange transactions (OET) in the context of the Sterling Area difficulties in the aftermath of the Second World War.[67] Members represented the Treasury, the Reserve Bank, Industries and Commerce, Customs and Agriculture.[68] It continued into 1949, focusing on OET forecasting and the import licensing schedule. After the change of government various arrangements were made to advise the Holland Government on economic matters including an Import Advisory Committee, and the Board of Trade. From 1952, the Cabinet Economic Committee, initially the Cabinet Committee on Economic Policy, usually chaired by the deputy prime minister, was supported by a standing Officials Economic Committee, itself served by a standing working party. Officials participated in discussion in the Cabinet Economic Committee, which met monthly.[69]

When Shanahan, in his capacity as secretary to Cabinet, called on the secretary to the Treasury in 1952 to discuss the arrangements for servicing the Cabinet Economic Committee, Ashwin agreed to Shanahan's proposals with one exception – he was insistent that the secretariat for the Officials Committee and the Working Party should be in the Treasury, not the Cabinet Secretariat.[70] From the outset, the Treasury chaired and provided the secretarial services for the committee and the working party (and signed all submissions to the Cabinet Committee).[71]

On some issues from the 1940s to the 1980s there was a long-standing divergence between departmental 'lines' – notably on industrial policy and border protection between the Treasury and Industries and Commerce – and some 'patch protection' between Industries and Commerce and Foreign Affairs on

---

67   B. Galvin, *Policy Co-ordination, Public Sector and Government* (Wellington: Institute of Policy Studies, 1991), 12; Baker, *The New Zealand People at War*, 569.
68   McKinnon, *Treasury*, 187.
69   For a contemporary discussion of the official economic policy making arrangements in the early 1950s see G.J. Schmidt, 'Some Administrative Problems Associated with a Vulnerable Balance of Payments', Paper presented for Diploma of Public Administration, Victoria University of Wellington (1952).
70   Personal information: H.G. Lang ONZ, Secretary to the Treasury (1967–76).
71   Other departments represented on the Officials Economic Committee (OEC) were Industries and Commerce (from 1972 Trade and Industry), Agriculture, External Affairs (from 1972 Ministry of Foreign Affairs), Customs and Statistics. The Reserve Bank attended when internal economic policy was under discussion. Permanent heads or their deputies usually attended meetings of the OEC; the working party was chaired by a divisional director in the Treasury. The range of topics was very wide with a heavy emphasis on overseas trade policy as well as the more obvious matters such as regular reporting on the economic situation and the overseas exchange forecasts. Significantly, the budget and taxation fell outside the scope of the committee – these were matters for the Minister of Finance and the Treasury.

trade policy.[72] Nonetheless, the machinery of coordination among departments, especially on economic matters, through the post-war period until the fourth Labour (Lange) Government's 'Revolution' in the 1980s can be given a strong pass assessment.

The post-war public service

On the cessation of hostilities an immediate problem facing the government and the controlling authority, the Public Service Commission, was absorption into the permanent staff of 'the huge temporary army of public servants' that had entered the public service during the war.[73] This was not an easy task. The Public Service Commission had to balance the claims of the temporaries – often not meeting the criteria for permanent employment – with the equity promised to those returning from military service. After intense negotiations with the public service trade union, the Public Service Association (PSA) – whose significance in this period cannot be overstated – the necessary statutory amendments were enacted in the *Public Service Amendment Act* (1946).

The principal change[74] ushered in by the 1946 amendment – the first major change to the governing statute since 1912 – was replacement of the sole Public Service commissioner by a three-man commission, one of whom was to be a representative of the PSA (following a precedent set in some Australian states).[75] Appointed as chairman for a seven-year term was the last of the 'mandarins' in this particular narrative, Dr R.M. (Dick) Campbell – 'an unusual choice', in the words of the State Service Commission's historian.[76] Campbell, at the time, as he had been for some 10 years, official secretary (effectively deputy high commissioner) in London, had worked with Reform Party minister Coates during the 1920s and 1930s (latterly as one of the 'brains trust').[77] An economist

---

72 T. Woodfield, *Against the Odds: Negotiating for New Zealand's Future* (Palmerston North: Dunmore Press, 2008).
73 J.H. Boyes, Public Service Commissioner, quoted by Alan Henderson, *The Quest for Efficiency: The Origins of the State Service Commission* (Wellington: Historical Branch, Department of Internal Affairs, 1990), 173.
74 Other changes were the opening up in a limited way of the appointment of people from outside the service who were shown to be 'in great degree' more suitable than applicants from within, and the exemption of a number of Permanent Head positions from the *Public Service Act* – thus leaving the way open for political appointments. (Those excluded were the Secretary to the Treasury, the Solicitor-General, the Secretary of External Affairs, the head of the Prime Minister's Department, the Commissioner of Works, the Director of Broadcasting and the Commissioner of Supply.)
75 Webb, 'Politics and Administration', 282.
76 Henderson, *The Quest for Efficiency*, 189.
77 In 1934–35 Gordon Coates, as minister of finance, employed in his private office advisers who collectively became known as the 'Brains Trust'. They were Campbell, Professor Horace Belshaw from Auckland University (with a Cambridge doctorate and an association with Keynes), and Dr W.B. Sutch, a 27-year-old graduate of Columbia University and later secretary of Industries and Commerce (1958–65).

(with a doctorate from the London School of Economics), he had no experience of administration on the scale of the public service. Fortunately, another commissioner was very experienced; George Bolt had been with the commission since 1916.

There was no doubting Campbell's sharpness of mind (and of pen). '[H]e was consistently innovative, if unpredictable and unorthodox in his methods. In matters of efficiency and economy, he was a breath of fresh air, with his enthusiasm to promote change tempered constructively by Bolt's experience.'[78] J.K. (later Sir Jack) Hunn, then on the staff of the commission and later a commissioner, observed that 'Dick Campbell was an inspirational force in either trying out ideas of his own or invigorating others. He was the soul of unorthodoxy … Dick Campbell tried hard to humanize the Public Service but it was a Sisyphean uphill struggle.'[79]

What was the direction of change in which Campbell sought to take the service? Campbell placed considerable emphasis on improving departmental efficiency and introduced the O&M ('Organisation and Methods') approach thus emulating innovations of the British Treasury. Long overdue, the commission also embarked down the devolution route, delegating personnel authority to departments and establishing the commission's presence in offices in Auckland and Christchurch. More controversially, Campbell sought to open up the service with proposals to remove provisions that were solidly embedded in the regime. Among these were abolition of appeal rights above a certain salary ceiling and reduction of the statutory protection against competition from outside applicants; opposed by the assertive PSA, neither proceeded into legislation.

In the longer view, the most interesting questions that might be asked about the New Zealand Public Service of the immediate post-war period concern its quality. Leicester Webb, though not unkind, had been a consistent critic through the 1940s:

> The genius of the New Zealanders expresses itself in the sphere of government, not in a capacity for solving difficult problems of sociology or economics, but in a capacity for carrying through successfully projects requiring organising ability and technical skill and resource … since the nature of the problem is clearly defined and the type of ability needed for its solution easily measurable. But when the task involves excursions into abstract thought and calls for ability of the type which is difficult either to define or measure, government in New Zealand is

---

78   Henderson, *The Quest for Efficiency*, 191.
79   J.K. Hunn, *Not Only Affairs of State; An Autobiography* (Palmerston North: Dunmore Press, 1982), 55, 62–3.

frequently at a loss and tends either to fall back on shallow definitions of common sense or to become dominated by ideas which are ingenious and misleading simplifications.[80]

In 1944, Webb defined 'two public services in New Zealand today': one, the new agencies set up to deal with the issues of wartime 'staffed in a large measure by men and women without public service training'; and the 'old-fashioned departments', a public service that had been

> markedly reluctant to prepare itself for the work of regulating or actively directing economic enterprises; in these respects it is still very much the product of the reforms of 1912 – reforms conceived by men whose instinct was to set the narrowest possible limits to State activity.[81]

While Webb was focusing particularly on economic policy making, Lipson[82] in 1948 raised a general concern about the impact of an undue preoccupation with a 'perverted equalitarianism'.[83]

> New Zealand is notoriously ungenerous to talent. In its anxiety to raise minima, the country has deemed it necessary to lower maxima ... There is not enough encouragement for each to do his best and for the ablest to display their full capacity. Everything tends toward a norm, and deviation from the average becomes a cardinal sin.[84]

This was to return to an issue that was high in the agenda in the years immediately before the Second World War, namely the perceived disadvantages faced by graduates who, after full-time study, sought to join the state services; they could be appointed only if there were no suitable internal candidate. While there was a place for science and professional graduates, this was not the case for those who were majoring in arts or 'cultural'[85] disciplines. Discussion between the university and the Public Service Commission continued until the war. The minister of education (Fraser) set up a representative committee, chaired by the vice-chancellor of the University of New Zealand, Professor T.A. (later Sir Thomas) Hunter, and including the ubiquitous Bernard Ashwin. It did not report and was overtaken by the outbreak of war. The commission had continued to emphasise the value of work experience – from cadet to permanent head.

---

80   L.C. Webb, *Government in New Zealand* (Wellington: Department of Internal Affairs, 1940), 158–9.
81   L.C. Webb, 'The Future of Wartime Control', *NZJPA*, 7, no. 1 (September 1944), 17.
82   Leslie Lipson, an Oxford graduate teaching at the University of Chicago, was appointed in 1938, at the age of 26, as the first Professor of Political Science at Victoria University College, Wellington.
83   L. Lipson, *The Politics of Equality: New Zealand's Adventures in Democracy* (Chicago: Chicago University Press, 1948), 456.
84   Ibid.
85   Ibid., 491.

The recently formed Institute of Public Administration submitted that 'preferential treatment for the university graduate, such as is given in the administrative grade in England is not suitable to New Zealand conditions'.[86]

> Any suggestion that New Zealand initiate some aspect of the administrative class at once runs afoul of strong antipathy to the British method of recruitment ... the Public Service Association will assail this insidious advocacy of a privileged class ... In general, those who have joined the service at the age of eighteen or under have felt that they had a prior claim on opportunities for promotion and have sought to exclude the holders of nonprofessional degrees.[87]

The view of the Public Service Commission (PSC), the Institute of Public Administration and, no doubt, the generality of public servants appeared to have been shared by Labour ministers. McIntosh's efforts after 1943 to establish a distinctly New Zealand diplomatic service received no encouragement from Peter Fraser who decided that no permanent appointments should be made to External Affairs until the returned servicemen became available.[88] (From 1946 External Affairs, almost alone among departments, recruited a very high quality of graduates as well as some outstanding officers discharged from the military.)

While arts graduates were not welcomed into the New Zealand Public Service until the 1950s, accountants were ranked highly. Before the war the professional accountant's qualification (Accts. Prof) was earned by part-time study at private colleges rather than the university (which took over accountancy education in 1946). By the end of the 1930s about 65 public servants acquired accountancy diplomas annually while something like 40 gained qualifications in other fields. 'Usually the expert was employed on expert work but accountancy training became a recognised qualification for advancement on administrative duties.'[89]

After the war the reliance on accountancy began to be questioned. As Sam Barnett, then superintendent of Staff Training in the PSC and later secretary of Justice, wrote in the Institute of Public Administration's journal in 1946, 'the education of the Public Service in New Zealand has for the past 30 years been conducted under the auspices of the N.Z. Society of Accountants, if it can be said that that professional body educates anyone'.[90] Nonetheless, Acct. Prof. remained a common hallmark of a very high proportion of senior management in the New Zealand Public Service into the 1960s at least.

---

86   J.R. Martin, *Spirit of Service: A History of the Institute of Public Administration New Zealand* (Wellington: IPANZ, 2006), 23.
87   Lipson, *The Politics of Equality*, 457–8.
88   McIntosh, 'Origins of the Department of External Affairs', 19.
89   Polaschek, *Government Administration in New Zealand*, 112.
90   S.T. Barnett, 'Education for the Public Service', NZJPA, 9, no. 1 (1946), 6; quoted by Polaschek, *Government Administration in New Zealand*, 122.

An important development in the preparation of officials for leadership came with the establishment of the Department of Political Science and School of Public Administration at Victoria University, Wellington, in 1939. Strongly urged by the Institute of Public Administration and supported by the PSC, the School inaugurated the Diploma of Public Administration (DPA) that continued until the 1970s when the Master of Public Policy (MPP) replaced it. One course ran in 1940–41. After wartime suspension, the DPA resumed in 1947. The initial staff was Leslie Lipson and R.S. Parker from the University of Sydney (later to succeed Lipson as professor). Of the eight students on the first course, two became chairmen of the State Services Commission, one headed the Post Office, one became the secretary of Industries and Commerce, one headed the South Pacific Commission, and one became Professor of Political Science at Victoria. Later courses, if not quite matching this record, provided a number of permanent heads and their deputies.

Conclusion

From the distance of more than 60 years, revisiting the aftermath of the Second World War provides some insights into the development of the governance of New Zealand – particularly the public service – in the succeeding decades. An obvious, but often forgotten, proposition is that history is continuous. In this case, we cannot ignore the experience of the war or the long-term impact of the 1930s. First, the damage to New Zealand society caused by the Depression and prolonged and widespread unemployment. Second, the first Labour Government's willing resort to instruments of the state – willing but driven by the issues rather than doctrinaire socialist ideology. And, third, the exchange crisis of 1938 and the imposition of controls at the frontier.

Writing in 1953, Leicester Webb correctly observed that 'the content of political action in our time is almost wholly economic'.[91] This chapter has, therefore, concentrated on the post-war challenges to the system of governance posed by, first, economic management in the short term ('insulationism' and 'stabilisation') and, secondly, the issues of development for the longer term ('planning'). There are, however, other issues that could have repaid more detailed examination: the issues raised by the urbanisation of Maori, for instance; the expansion of the welfare state; or the 'formulation of an independent foreign policy'.[92] But the focus of this chapter has been on the way in which policy was made and executed rather than on its substance – on the machinery, mechanics and style of government rather than the outcomes.

---

91 Webb, 'The Making of Economic Policy', 12.
92 McIntosh, 'Origins of the Department of External Affairs'.

In political terms exploration of these matters has been almost exclusively with the latter period in office of the first Labour Government (1935–49). The general election of late 1949 brought the National Government to power. National occupied the Treasury benches for 27 of the next 34 years and this study identifies the central core of continuity in style and approach of Labour and National governments. This is thrown into relief by the contrast with the 'revolutionary' years between 1984 and 1990 when the fourth Labour Government (Lange, Palmer, Moore) was in office.

As Simkin observed, 'New Zealand is a singularly pure example of a dependent economy'.[93] From the 1930s on, New Zealand governments sought to 'insulate' the country from the effects of the instability that went with dependence. Creation of the Reserve Bank in 1934; the advent of exchange and import controls to deal with the 1938 run on the currency; the action taken by Labour to centralise commodity marketing and introduce guaranteed dairy prices; and the *Social Security Act* 1938 all symbolise acceptance of the role of the state in mitigating external influences on New Zealand's welfare. Thus, when the resources of the country were mobilised to meet New Zealand's wartime obligations, the basic elements of the machinery of 'insulation' were already in place.

Central to economic management from 1942 through the 1940s was the Economic Stabilisation Commission (ESC). Its all-embracing range over the activities of producers and consumers was, during the war, effectively under the control of a triumvirate of appointed office-holders: Ashwin together with representatives of the labour movement (F.P. Walsh) and the farming industries. Ashwin and Walsh during 1945 worked on a post-war stabilisation regime, retaining most controls, which Walsh, with difficulty, sold to the union movement – which was, however, to chafe at the restraint applied to wages that led to the confrontation between the watersiders and the National Government in 1951.[94]

Ashwin and Walsh were both close to the prime minister, Peter Fraser; Ashwin saw him almost every day during the war.[95] '[Fraser] established a working relationship with the able if unlovable F.P. Walsh of the Seamen's Union at an early stage in the life of the government.'[96] Ashwin was directly responsible to the minister of finance but Nash was in Washington DC between 1942 and 1944.

The tripartite nature of the ESC signals the crucial role played in New Zealand public policy and politics in the post-war period by 'the three great economic

---

93 C.G. Simkin, *The Instability of a Dependent Economy: Economic Fluctuations in New Zealand 1840–1914* (London: Oxford University Press, 1951), v.
94 Bassett and King, *Tomorrow Comes the Song*, 298.
95 B. Easton, 'Fraser and the Development of the Nation-Building State', 125; quoting from a 1970 interview of Ashwin by John Henderson.
96 M. Bassett, 'The Political Context of the Prime-Ministerial Years', in M. Clark, ed., *Peter Fraser, Master Politician* (Wellington: Dunmore Press, 1998), 47.

pressure groups, the Federation of Labour, Federated Farmers, and the Employers' Federation'[97] – with the government holding the ring. Parallel with the ESC, and central in industrial relations until the 1980s, was the Arbitration Court. Providing an essential background was, as John Roberts argued persuasively, 'a society of fair shares' that endured until the 1980s upheaval.[98]

The Economic Stabilisation Commission did not survive the arrival of the National Government. But the significant array of controls that remained and the influence of the officials who had served their formative years in the ESC ensured that its influence continued to be felt. The policy of insulationism in the cause of stability also persisted. Balance of payments crises in 1957–58 and at intervals through the 1960s and 1970s meant that import and exchange controls, administered with varying degrees of severity, remained in place. Similarly, persistent bouts of inflation saw governments of different persuasions intensify price and incomes controls. Pragmatic recourse to the instruments of the stabilisation policies of the 1940s was the hallmark of economic policy until the 1980s. At the same time, what can be identified broadly as Keynesian fiscal and monetary policies were subscribed to.

Taking the longer view, at one level, wartime initiatives resulted in a 'permanent'[99] addition to the machinery of government – the role of the Ministry of Works as a planning influence on physical investment.[100]

At a broader level of national planning of the economy, to which some at least believed the short-lived Organisation for National Development (OND) should aspire, the record is patchy at best. In bureaucratic terms, the demise of the OND can be attributed to the ability of Ashwin (and the Treasury) in particular to influence government thinking. They probably shared Leicester Webb's judgment expressed in 1947 that 'perhaps because the scope of its activities was both too wide and too nebulous, it did not have much effect on administration and was finally allowed to lapse.'[101] The output of the OND was likely to have been contrasted with the very practical responsibilities being assumed by the Ministry of Works.

At the political level, the Fraser Government was well aware that once the war had ended, there would be strong pressures from the business community in

---

97 J. Roberts, 'Society and its Politics', in I. Wards, ed., *Thirteen Facets: The Silver Jubilee Essays Surveying the New Elizabethan Age; A Period of Unprecedented Change* (Wellington: Government Printer, 1978), 71.
98 Ibid., 73.
99 The Ministry of Works was privatised in 1988.
100 For a discussion of the Ministry's role see R. Noonan, *By Design* and Polaschek, *Government Administration*, 260–70.
101 Webb, 'Politics and Administration', 288.

particular, in concert with the National Party, to reduce the extent of controls.[102] The narrow majority achieved at the 1946 general election underlined the first Labour Government's declining hold on office.[103] But the OND would have converted New Zealand's economic policy into a centrally coordinated detailed plan. Commenting on a 1944 document, *Interim Report on Post-War Reconstruction and National Development*, J.V.T. Baker, historian of the war economy (and later government statistician), observed 'though the Labour party has often been accused of being socialistic, it was not ready for this.'[104]

A striking feature through this period is the continuity of public service leadership. Ashwin in the Treasury was a towering figure for three decades. McIntosh and Shanahan were at the centre of New Zealand governance from the outbreak of war to the 1960s. Others such as Moriarty, Lang and Lough were central figures in economic policy making into the 1970s. The same continuity features in other areas of public policy. Dr C.E. Beeby, director of Education, 1940–60, was synonymous with education in New Zealand for more than 20 years. Sir Joseph Heenan, secretary of Internal Affairs (1935–49), was the Labour Government's 'go to' person in many matters. In the labour and employment field, James Hunter, then Herbert Bockett, played leading roles from the 1930s to the mid-1960s.[105] A.R. (Pat) Entrican[106] was director of Forests from 1939 to 1961 and E.J. Fawcett, director-general of Agriculture from 1943 to 1957.[107] All made major contributions and were individuals with personalities that could not be ignored.[108]

Others have identified the contribution of this group of key public servants to governance in the 1940s and 1950s. John Roberts, for example, writing in 1978 in the aftermath of the first oil crisis, was pessimistic about the prospects for reform in economic management in New Zealand 'in the face of the inert administrative system'.

> New Zealand has an honest, intelligent and public bureaucracy which is incapable of major reform. This is largely due to the insulation of the service from politics instituted in 1912 and confirmed in 1962. The effects were masked in the crisis of the depression and war, *partly*

---

[102] The public too was restless. As early as 1944, Webb noted that '[t]here are signs that the public generally, irrespective of their economic interests or political opinions, have grown very weary of coupons, forms and regulations'. Webb, 'The Future of Wartime Control', 10.

[103] Labour had a majority of four – the four Maori seats. Bassett and King, *Tomorrow Comes the Song*, 312.

[104] Baker, *The New Zealand People at War*, 531.

[105] J.E. Martin, *Holding the Balance: A History of New Zealand's Department of Labour 1891–1995* (Canterbury: Canterbury University Press, 1996), 235.

[106] J.R. Martin, 'Entrican, Alexander Robert', in *The Dictionary of New Zealand Biography, Vol. 5*, (2000), 164–5.

[107] Tony Nightingale, *White Collars and Gumboots: A History of the Ministry of Agriculture and Fisheries 1892–1992* (Wellington: Dunmore Press, 1992), 237–8.

[108] Entrican, for example, wore bow ties and a broad-brimmed cowboy-style hat.

because the Labour Party simply circumvented the rules and brought their men into administrative power, and partly because obsessive institutional separatism had to be abandoned in the face of wartime exigencies.[109]

Certainly, these outstanding public servants give the lie to the generally held belief that appointments in the 'old' public service were made in accordance with 'Buggins' turn in the five years or so before superannuation became available. Ashwin was appointed as secretary to the Treasury at the age of 42; Berendsen, secretary of External Affairs and head of the Prime Minister's Department at 38 and 42 respectively; McIntosh, to these positions at 37 and 39 respectively; Beeby, director of Education at 37; Heenan, secretary of Internal Affairs at 47, and Entrican director of Forests at 41.

It is beyond dispute that these public service leaders of the 1940s and 1950s all enjoyed a close relationship with Peter Fraser. Equally, there are indications that the same permanent heads may not have had a comparably easy relationship with the Holland-led National Government after 1949. One overseas commentator, after spending some time in New Zealand, noted that 'like the Republicans in 1953 [in the United States], the Nationalists in 1950 were imbued with a suspicion of, almost a hostility towards, the administrators'.[110] But this can be attributed, on the experience of other changes of government after a long period, to quite understandable doubts about the enthusiasm for new masters that would be shown by those so close to the previous administration. Perhaps not surprisingly, by 1949 only one permanent head had been in office before Labour had come to power in 1935.

Nevertheless, all the permanent heads mentioned above except Beeby (who had been director of the Council of Educational Research until invited by Fraser to apply for the position of assistant director of Education with the expectation of ascending to director)[111] were career public servants. All except Campbell (appointed as chairman of the Public Service Commission by the governor-general on the advice of ministers in accord with statute) were appointed by the Commission.

Since the 1980s the bureaucratic memory in New Zealand has become focused on the present and what came immediately before. The people who form the subject of this essay, and the context in which they carried out their important

---

109 Roberts, 'Society and its Politics', 96 (emphasis added).
110 Political scientist, P. Campbell, 'Politicians, Public Servants and the People in New Zealand: II', *Political Studies*, 4, no. 1 (February, 1956), 21, quoted by McKinnon, *Treasury*, 206. Also conversation with Dr Beeby.
111 Beeby was appointed under the usual public service procedures, a point he emphasised later in his life. See Noeline Alcorn, *To the Fullest Extent of his Powers: C.E. Beeby's Life in Education* (Wellington: Victoria University of Wellington, 1999), 90–2. The influence of the prime minister, is, however, suggested by a reference to 'Peter Fraser's stacking the interview panel to ensure that C.E. Beeby became Director of Education'. I. Carter, *Gadfly: The Life and Times of James Shelley* (Auckland: Auckland University Press, 1991), 224.

public responsibilities, are virtually forgotten. Nonetheless, an exploration of governance in the immediate post-war period has served to emphasise the continuity in public service as well as acknowledging the contribution to New Zealand society of those who have gone before.

Part II

5

Sir Frederick Shedden: The Forerunner

David Horner

Sir Frederick Shedden occupies an interesting and perhaps unique place in any consideration of the great mandarins of the Commonwealth Public Service who flourished, exercised their power, and helped to build modern Australia in the quarter of a century after the end of the Second World War.[1] In many respects he fitted neatly into this characterisation – he was the secretary of the Department of Defence from 1937 until 1956; he wielded great power in the Defence group of departments; he was a key adviser to the prime minister; and he helped shape many of the instruments of government. But in other respects he was different. Unlike his contemporaries from this period, he had been secretary of his department since 1937, that is from before the Second World War. Although he had almost completed a university degree in commerce, he was not especially concerned with economic issues. By the mid-1950s, his power and influence were waning, and he stepped down as departmental secretary almost two years before he formally retired. Further, unlike other mandarins, he refused to move permanently to Canberra, and worked in Melbourne for his entire career.

While it might be debated as to whether Shedden was actually one of the legendary seven dwarfs he was, arguably, the greatest public servant of his time. Whether he was the greatest ever, is another matter. Some would give that accolade to Sir Robert Garran, the joint author of the classic treatise on the new Commonwealth Constitution (1901). Garran was a close adviser to the prime minister, W.M. Hughes, during the First World War and was secretary of the Attorney-General's Department for an unrivalled period of 31 years – from 1901 to 1932.[2] Shedden's eminence relates only partly to his long 19 years as secretary. It is true that Garran, Sir Roland Wilson and Sir Arthur Tange – each of whom was a permanent head for some 20 years – served for a longer period, and many others served well beyond 10 years: Sir Kenneth Bailey, Sir

---

1   This paper is based on D. Horner, *Defence Supremo: Sir Frederick Shedden and the Making of Australian Defence Policy* (Sydney: Allen & Unwin, 2000).
2   Sir Kenneth Bailey, a later secretary of the Attorney-General's Department, wrote that Garran was 'revered in his lifetime as one ... of the Fathers of Federation. His repute as the wise and trusted legal counsellor of successive Federal Governments, moreover, became almost a legend'. K.H. Bailey, 'Sir Robert Garran', *The Australian Quarterly*, xxix, no. 1 (March 1957): 11.

Henry Bland and Sir Richard Kingsland each served for 18 years, although, except for Bailey, they all served in more than one department. To put their achievements in perspective, Professor R.N. Spann, an expert on Australian public administration, writing in 1979, noted that even 'in 1965, at a time of great government stability, Commonwealth permanent heads had only occupied that position in their existing department for an average of 5.5 years; in mid-1975 it was only 2.7 years'.[3]

Shedden's importance relates primarily to the fact that he was defence secretary during all of the Second World War, the onset of the Cold War, the Korean War and the early part of the Malayan Emergency, rather than to the longevity of his tenure. During the Second World War, prime ministers Robert Menzies and John Curtin also held the Defence portfolios and Shedden was their key adviser. As well as heading his department, Shedden became secretary of the War Cabinet and the Advisory War Council and was thus the principal coordinator of the war effort. He probably had more influence over the running of the government's main business for a longer period of time than any other public servant; and the government's main business – the conduct of the Second World War – was the biggest enterprise in Australian history. The fact that Shedden's influence had declined by the mid-1950s should not detract from his wartime achievements.

Education of a public servant

Shedden was a public servant from the old pre-war school. Educated at Kyneton State School and Kyneton Grammar School, in Victoria, he was placed fourth out of 300 candidates in the Commonwealth Public Service examination, and began work in the Department of Defence, Victoria Barracks, Melbourne, in March 1910. He was aged 16. Apart from service abroad he worked at the barracks in the same government department until 1971, that is, for 61 years. It is a record unlikely ever to be matched.

In his own time he gained accountancy qualifications and also learned shorthand, but the heavy workload caused by the outbreak of the First World War forced him to terminate studies for a law degree at the University of Melbourne. Promoted in the finance section, he arranged a temporary exchange with a member of the pay staff of the Australian Imperial Force (AIF) headquarters in London, and he served briefly in France. By December 1917 he was back in Australia and was discharged from the AIF. In later years he was proud of this very limited military experience.

---

3   R.N. Spann, *Government Administration in Australia* (Sydney: George Allen & Unwin, 1979), 331.

Sir Frederick Shedden (centre) with Prime Minister John Curtin and Mrs Curtin, 1944

Source: National Archives of Australia, A5954, 661/12

Shedden was promoted further within the Defence finance section, while he almost completed, part-time, a commerce degree at the University of Melbourne. The Professor of Economics, Douglas Copland, was so impressed that he offered Shedden a scholarship to undertake postgraduate studies, but a major change in Shedden's career prevented him taking up this opportunity. In December 1927 he sailed to Britain to attend the Imperial Defence College. Shedden was the first Australian civilian to attend the Imperial Defence College, which had opened in 1927 and took senior military and civilian officers from across the Empire for its year-long course. He established a friendship with the college's commandant, Vice-Admiral Sir Herbert Richmond, who reported that Shedden had worked 'indefatigably' and had entered into all studies with 'acuteness and zeal'.[4] Shedden was one of the few public servants of his era who received formal training to prepare him to take on leadership of his department. Indeed, this was probably only possible in the Defence Department but, even then, few public servants received this opportunity.

---

4   Imperial Defence College, Confidential Report on Mr F.G. Shedden, 19 December 1928, National Archives of Australia (NAA) A5954, 46/21.

After the course, Shedden spent nine months in London preparing a paper on the principles of imperial defence with special reference to Australia, and studying British public expenditure, under the tutorship of Dr Hugh Dalton, later British minister for economic warfare during the Second World War. Returning to Melbourne in October 1929, he became secretary of the Defence Committee, which included the Chiefs of Staff of the three services. He witnessed the efforts of the new Labor Government led by James Scullin to cut costs during the Depression and took part in the debates between senior Naval and Army officers over the most appropriate strategy for the defence of Australia. Shedden was an advocate of imperial defence, which relied on building up the Navy so that it could cooperate with the Royal Navy in time of threat.

In 1932, following the defeat of the Labor Government, the new external affairs minister, John Latham, was nominated to attend the League of Nations Disarmament Conference in Geneva. Shedden accompanied him as his assistant, but Latham was absent for much of the meeting and Shedden acted in his stead. Shedden was also secretary to the Australian delegation at the World Monetary and Economic Conference in London. In addition, he was appointed the Australian representative in the British Cabinet Office and Committee of Imperial Defence, where he established a friendship with the legendary Sir Maurice Hankey, who showed him how power could be wielded behind the scenes and taught him which sort of organisations needed to be developed to manage a nation's security policies.

Back in Australia in September 1933, Shedden resumed work with the Defence Committee and accompanied Hankey during the British official's visit to Australia in 1934. Shedden tried to model himself on Hankey and was later nicknamed 'the pocket hanky'. In November 1936 Shedden became first assistant secretary and prepared the Defence Department's briefing papers for the 1937 Imperial Conference in London. The Australian delegation included the prime minister, Joseph Lyons, the defence minister, Sir Archdale Parkhill, and the treasurer, Richard Casey. Shedden was the delegation's defence adviser and had discussions with Hankey about preparing Australia for war.

Secretary to the Department of Defence

In November 1937, aged 43, Shedden succeeded Malcolm Shepherd as the Defence department's fifth secretary. Since 1929 he had worked to expand the secretary's influence and authority. He had proven to be a skilful bureaucrat, not afraid to challenge the military chiefs, but usually working behind the scenes. Preparation for war dominated his first 20 months as secretary. He accelerated work on the War Book that set out procedures to be followed on the outbreak of war. He was instrumental in the appointment of inspectors general for the Army and for defence works and supplies, and helped to arrange the visit of a senior British air force officer to inspect the Royal Australian Air Force. He encouraged more frequent meetings of the Defence Council, which included senior ministers, military chiefs, defence officials and industry representatives. Shedden was its secretary.

As Defence secretary, Shedden was an aloof and distant figure who 'eschewed publicity'. His whole life revolved around his work and he spent most of his time at the office. The Sheddens had no children and lived modestly. He was short (170 cm), always well dressed in suit and tie, and conscious of his status. Some military chiefs such as Major-General John Lavarack and Air Vice-Marshal Richard Williams resented his power. In 1936, Lavarack had clashed with the government over how to handle Colonel Henry Wynter, who had criticised the government's reliance on the Singapore strategy. The defence minister, Parkhill, had recommended that Lavarack be created a Companion of the Bath. Shedden, who had not yet been appointed secretary, was instrumental in having the recommendation withdrawn. The Navy chief, Admiral Sir Ragnar Colvin, noted that Shedden 'always had the ear of the Prime Minister and could generally get the Chiefs of Staffs view and wishes overridden. Still … he was an able and knowledgeable man and though one couldn't trust him personally his views were generally sound.'[5] Of course, as Shedden supported the 'blue water' strategy, he was sympathetic to the Navy's views.

War Cabinet secretary

The outbreak of the Second World War in September 1939 brought Shedden to the position of Australia's most important and influential public servant. As Defence secretary his role in bringing Australia to a war footing during the following months was crucial, but the prime source of his power and influence was his role as secretary of the War Cabinet – a post he held throughout the war. The prime minister, Robert Menzies, took over the Defence portfolio, now called Defence Coordination, and additional ministries were formed to administer the three services. Shedden became Menzies' principal adviser, while as War Cabinet secretary he ensured that War Cabinet decisions were promulgated and executed by the various government departments. In that sense, he was the key coordinator for the war effort. As secretary to the Defence Coordination Department he exercised a measure of control over other Defence-related departments. Indeed, he was at the heart of the strategic decision-making process, coordinating advice from the Service chiefs.

---

5   R. Colvin, *Memoirs* (Durley, Hampshire: Wintershill Publications, 1992), 119–20.

In many ways, Shedden invented the method of conducting Cabinet business. Before each meeting he prepared detailed cabinet agendum papers. He attended almost all the meetings of the War Cabinet, took notes of proceedings, prepared the minutes confirming the outcome of the discussions and then, as mentioned, from his position as secretary of the Department of Defence, set about ensuring that the decisions were implemented.

Shedden's orderly mind, unrivalled understanding of bureaucratic processes and knowledge of Defence administration resulted in a highly efficient secretariat, which gave increased authority to the work of the War Cabinet. Reflecting Shedden's insistence on accurate agenda and minutes of Cabinet submissions and decisions, and his highly efficient filing system, Menzies was once quoted as saying 'Documentation, thy name is Shedden'.[6] During the war the need to house the extensive War Cabinet minutes resulted in establishment of the War Archives Committee. This led to appointment of an archives officer in the Commonwealth Library, and eventually to the Commonwealth Archives Office, now known as the National Archives of Australia.

While not always agreeing with Shedden's approach as secretary of his department, other senior defence public servants have praised him highly. Sir Frederick Chilton, who worked under Shedden for more than a decade and was later head of the Department of Repatriation, wrote that Shedden:

> had a real presence and powerful personality. He was ruthless with those who crossed him, and devastating with those in his Department who could not rise to his exceptional standards of performance ... Shedden's 'forte' was top level policy and its broad application. He was not a good administrator in the sense of leadership of a team ... He ruled by fear – and this stultified initiative. But as a head of a small policy Dept of Defence, he was superb.[7]

Another senior defence public servant wrote: 'Shedden's brilliance as a Secretariat Co-ordinator and his tremendous capacity to maintain order in all work with which he was associated, more particularly in the chaos of war, was a very significant factor.'[8]

After the September 1940 federal election, in which Menzies retained office but was head of a minority government, he and the leader of the Opposition, John Curtin, agreed to establish the Advisory War Council in order to involve the Opposition in the crucial decisions affecting the nation's security. Shedden

---

6 J.P. Buckley, 'Sir Frederick Shedden, KCMG, OBE: Defence Strategist, Administrator and Public Servant', *Defence Force Journal*, 50 (January/February 1985), 27.
7 Letter, Sir Fredrick Chilton to author, 28 July 1979.
8 Transcript of lecture by Garry Armstrong, Australian Staff College, 8 May 1978.

became secretary of the Advisory War Council. Later, after the outbreak of war with Japan, by which time Curtin was prime minister, the Advisory War Council took on many of the functions of a War Cabinet.

In January 1941, Menzies departed for a visit to the Middle East and Britain in which he hoped to persuade the British Government to reinforce Malaya and Singapore. Shedden was his principal adviser throughout this journey. In the Middle East they visited Australian troops and discussed war developments with Lieutenant-General Sir Thomas Blamey (GOC AIF) and senior British officers. In London, Menzies approved the decision to send forces to Greece. Shedden gained first-hand experience of how the British Government was conducting the war and was critical of British generalship in the Middle East.

After they returned to Australia, Menzies created five new ministries, and Shedden became secretary of the new Department of Home Security, while retaining his previous responsibilities. Also, Menzies agreed to allow a minute secretary to attend the War Cabinet meetings, thus relieving Shedden of this burden. The hand-written notes of the minute secretaries reveal that during the next four years Shedden played a significant role in War Cabinet discussions – he was not just a silent secretary.

Advising the Curtin Government

Conservative by nature, Shedden had been a long-time supporter of imperial defence, but when the Labor Government came to power in October 1941 he soon established himself as the prime adviser to John Curtin, prime minister and minister for defence. Shedden helped the new government in its transition to power and his influence was demonstrated after the outbreak of war with Japan. Following a War Cabinet meeting on 8 December 1941 he advised Curtin that the information presented by the Chiefs of Staff was 'scrappy and meagre … the Government must press it right home that this is a new war'.[9]

When the American general, Douglas MacArthur, became Commander-in-Chief of the Southwest Pacific Area in April 1942, Shedden assumed an even more important role. Curtin established the Prime Minister's War Conference, which consisted of himself, MacArthur and any other minister he thought should be invited. The Prime Minister's War Conference became the key decision-making body with regard to war strategy, exceeding even the War Cabinet. In practice, Shedden attended all meetings of the conference. As Curtin advised MacArthur, 'if I should not be readily available, Mr Shedden has my full confidence in regard to all questions of War Policy'.[10]

---

9   Memo, Shedden to Curtin, 8 December 1941, NAA A5954, 555/10.
10 Letter, Curtin to MacArthur, 10 April 1942, NAA A5954, 1598/2.

In July 1942, MacArthur moved his headquarters to Brisbane and the Prime Minister's War Conference met less frequently. Instead, Shedden travelled to Brisbane on several occasions for discussions with MacArthur. In December Curtin told Shedden that, but for his assistance, 'he could not have carried on', and later said 'that he was his right hand and left hand and head too'.[11]

In June 1943, Shedden was made a Knight Commander of the Order of St Michael and St George – the only civilian to be knighted by the Labor Government. He received a flood of congratulatory letters from politicians, military leaders, other government officials, academics and businessmen.[12] General Blamey, for example, wrote that the knighthood was 'fitting recognition of the grand services you have rendered during the last few years. All of us who know the background of Australia's effort utter a prayer of thanks for your guiding presence there'. Typically, Shedden assembled extracts of these letters and distributed them to various people such as S.M. Bruce and Vice-Admiral Richmond, and then sent copies of Richmond's laudatory reply to MacArthur. Professor Kenneth Bailey, Dean of Law at the University of Melbourne, might have admired Shedden for working 'anonymously and in silence, without publicity or boosting', but Shedden was making sure that those in influence knew what others thought.

In the second half of 1943 Shedden played an influential role in encouraging the War Cabinet to establish principles for reshaping the war effort. In fact, when the relevant departments failed to agree, Shedden and his staff drafted the paper that was approved by the War Cabinet. He then accompanied Curtin to Washington and London in April–May 1944 to seek Allied approval for these measures. On return he tried to ensure that manpower was redeployed from the Services to essential industries, but his attempts were hindered by Curtin's illness. Shedden provided valuable assistance to the acting prime minister, Ben Chifley, and continued this function when, following Curtin's death, Chifley became prime minister.

Post-war defence policy

During the war Shedden had argued that Australia's future defence policy should be based on three pillars: collective security through the United Nations; British Commonwealth cooperation; and local defence. The government approved these principles and, after the war, Shedden restructured the Defence Department in order to improve cooperation with Britain. Chifley and the defence minister, John Dedman, largely gave him a free hand. He accompanied Chifley to a Commonwealth Prime Ministers' Conference in London in April–May 1946.

---

11 Shedden's Diary, 25 February 1943, NAA A5954, 16/1.
12 Extracts from the letters are in NAA A5954 654/7.

Shedden continued to gather more power and authority. Early in 1948 he was appointed chairman of the Defence Committee – the first non-serviceman to hold the position. The Navy chief, Admiral Sir Louis Hamilton, claimed that he engineered the appointment so that 'that little bastard Shedden' would be locked into the Committee's decisions and would not undermine them.[13] In fact, Shedden had already arranged his appointment long before Hamilton proposed it.

Lieutenant General Sydney Rowell, who succeeded Vernon Sturdee as Chief of the General Staff (CGS) in 1950, but had already been identified by Shedden as the next chief, was unwilling to criticise Shedden's chairmanship too strongly. He recalled that Shedden was 'a great Australian public servant' with whom he had enjoyed the 'happiest personal relationship'. Shedden:

> had an unrivalled knowledge of matters associated with Commonwealth defence and he was a tireless and meticulous worker. If it could be said that he had a fault it was in his complete absorption in the work he was doing, leaving little time for outside activities. He had critics at home and abroad; in the main these were service people who could not match his intellect or who were jealous of his power and influence.

Rowell thought strategy was best left to those 'who are trained in it, namely the Chiefs of Staff', but saw Shedden as a special case; Australia was 'not likely again to have someone of the calibre and background of Shedden to fill the post'.[14] It has to be remembered that Shedden had saved Rowell's career after the 1942 Kokoda campaign when Blamey had wanted to reduce him to the rank of colonel. Shedden played a role in having Rowell appointed Vice-CGS in January 1946 and recommended him as CGS in 1950. Rowell had good cause to remember Shedden favourably.

During 1948 and 1949, Shedden spent much time dealing with a leakage of information to the Soviet Union and the consequent reduction in the flow of classified information from the United States. He was instrumental in the formation of the Australian Security Intelligence Organisation (ASIO) in March 1949, and later that year travelled to the United States and Britain in an effort to restore the flow of information. Initially he was unsuccessful and access to American information only began to be restored after the election of the Menzies Government in December 1949.

---

13   Letters, Hamilton to Foley, 16 August 1947, and Hamilton to First Sea Lord, 27 November 1947, Foley Papers (held by Rear Admiral James Goldrick).
14   S.F. Rowell, *Full Circle* (Melbourne: Melbourne University Press, 1974), 194–5.

The Menzies Government and the Cold War

Frustrated by the Chifley Government's reluctance to enter into full-scale defence planning with Britain, particularly concerning committing forces to the Middle East, Shedden welcomed the election of the Menzies Government. For several years he was in his element. Following the outbreak of the Korean War in June 1950, the government stepped up defence preparations and Shedden accompanied Menzies to a Prime Ministers' Conference in London in January 1951. On return Menzies claimed that the nation had only three years to prepare for war. Eventually, in December 1951, the Cabinet agreed to commit forces to the Middle East in time of war. During this period Shedden was closely involved in setting up the Australian Secret Intelligence Service (ASIS), ensuring that it remained part of the Defence Department.

The strategic situation was changing. The threat of a world war declined and the government began to focus more on strategic planning in South East Asia. Also, the signing of the ANZUS Pact with the United States and New Zealand offered the prospect of increased cooperation with the United States. Shedden was closely involved in these aspects of defence planning, but his personal influence was waning. He and his department remained in Melbourne, while Menzies in Canberra sought advice from the senior ministers and the secretaries of his own department and External Affairs located there.

The decline of a mandarin

By 1954 Shedden had lost much of his previous influence and, during a visit abroad with Menzies in January and February 1955, was disappointed to find that he was upstaged by the External Affairs secretary, Arthur Tange. He had to fight off several attempts to remove him from his position as chairman of the Defence Committee. Menzies thought that the problem with Defence was 'the dead hand of Fred Shedden',[15] and tried unsuccessfully to persuade Shedden to become ambassador to Japan or high commissioner to Canada. Tange later wrote disparagingly about Shedden:

> Shedden was committed by past decisions and by his war-time experience with the War Cabinet, to Australia's engagement to Imperial (later Commonwealth) Defence. Led by Britain, this called for priority after the war to blocking Soviet expansion. Within these parameters Shedden was vigilant in protecting Australia's interests, such as control of Australian forces, from being submerged by British strategic priorities.

---

15   Vice Admiral Sir John Collins, interview with author, 9 October 1978.

> When I came to deal with him I noted how much Shedden cultivated his personal access to figures prominent in the wartime Anglo-American alliance. I perceived no intellectual questioning by him – an industrious administrator, rigid in this, and defender of turf …
>
> During the years in which I had discussions with Shedden I did not hear any opinion on Australia's strategic outlook or priorities. In the Defence Committee he expected opinion to come up from subordinate committees comprised of uniformed officers. Shedden saw his role as chairman being to obtain a decision, giving either approval or disapproval without encouraging discussion of the substance – an attitude which I could do little to resist, as he had the support of the Chiefs.

Tange also criticised the Defence organisation and, by implication, Shedden's role in moulding it:

> Defence seemed to value procedure and precedent over analysis and rethinking about a vastly changing world.
>
> Defence personnel were a mixture (so it seemed to us in Canberra) of a handful of perceptive and questioning officers accompanying a larger number exercising the modest role of guiding Service officers in the unfamiliar terrain of public administration and accountability.
>
> Shedden's system laid down the discipline that past opinion should be piled one upon the other before reaching a conclusion … There was much turgid prose.[16]

Having read many of the Defence papers from this period I can confirm that the usual process was for the documents to work their way though all the previous decisions before arriving at their conclusion. While a struggle with the young, ambitious, capable and acerbic Tange was probably inevitable, Shedden's old friend, Richard Casey, who was once again a Cabinet minister, was also losing patience in him. In February 1953, Casey noted in his diary that he had discussed with Shedden 'the question of speed of decision on strategic questions in the Defence Department'.[17] On 30 July 1954, after trying for some days to secure additional funds for defence, Casey wrote in his diary: 'The Chiefs of Staff have no opportunity to give their undiluted non-political professional advice as to what money is necessary for defence. All they have to say is filtered through Fred Shedden.'[18]

---

16   Sir Arthur Tange, 'Defence Memoir', draft manuscript.
17   Diary entry, 13 February 1953, p. 27, Casey Papers, NAA (Melb) M1153/0, 33.
18   T.B. Millar, ed., *Australian Foreign Minister: The Diaries of R. G. Casey, 1951–1960* (London: Collins, 1972), 173.

In July 1956 the government announced that Shedden would be stepping down as secretary in order to write a history of the development of Australian defence policy. He would continue on full pay until he reached retirement age in August 1958. He handed over to Edwin Hicks in October 1956, after serving 20 days less than 19 years as Defence secretary. But his retirement made little practical difference, as he continued his work for the next decade without obvious change in his routine. Each year he continued to advise Hicks when he was going on 'annual leave'.[19] While researching my biography I had another insight into Shedden's mindset. In the University of Melbourne Archives I found several boxes of his papers that had not been included in the much greater number that were lodged in the Defence Department. In one of the boxes, which included the contents of Shedden's desk drawer, I found some small cardboard boxes, each with its own label – rubber bands, paper clips, pins, etc.

Shedden failed in the task of writing his history but not through lack of effort. He carried out research in the United States and Britain in 1958 and continued collecting documents, researching and writing. When he submitted the first volume (covering the period to 1939) to the publisher in October 1967 and running to a grand total of 426,431 words, he was advised that it was unpublishable; it was more a linking together of documents than a piece of historical writing. He kept working until May 1971 – two months before his death, by which time he had brought the story (over 2,400 typed pages) up to the end of the Second World War. It is preserved in the National Archives of Australia along with his official papers, which consist of over 2,400 boxes and are the most important documentary source on Australian defence policy from the mid-1930s to the mid-1950s.

Shedden's failure to complete his book should not overshadow his outstanding achievements over a long working life. For 20 years he had dominated defence decision-making, giving it purpose and consistency. He had shaped a Defence organisation that persisted largely unaltered until the 1970s. He had played a principal part in the defence of Australia during the war. In the opinion of Sir Paul Hasluck, Shedden was 'one of the few outstanding men in the civil side of the Australian war effort. Discretion, orderly arrangement and careful groundwork were so large a part of his training and his method that his achievement was often hidden.'[20] Shedden devoted his life to the defence of Australia, and no other person has played, or is likely again to play, such an important part in the making of Australian defence policy for so a long period.

---

19 For example, memos Shedden to Hicks, NAA A5954, 63/4.
20 P. Hasluck, *The Government and the People, 1939–1941* (Canberra: Australian War Memorial, 1952), 444.

6

Sir Roland Wilson – *Primus Inter Pares*

Selwyn Cornish[1]

When Roland Wilson was inducted into the military cadets at age 14 he weighed scarcely 25 kg; at full height he was only 158 cm.[2] He was clearly a person of slight build and short stature. But he frequently reminded those who drew attention to these facts that his endowment of brainpower was more than adequate compensation. He could run intellectual rings around ministers, business leaders, academics, public servants and journalists. Yet he was not only highly intelligent; he also possessed moral courage and had a biting wit. According to Douglas Copland, Wilson at an early age exhibited 'force of character and capacity for leadership'.[3] As to wit, a colleague remarked that Wilson used it 'for many a devastating one liner', adding that the 'one-liner could be humorous, or it could be like a whiplash'.[4]

Wilson stood up to some of the most powerful men in this country and abroad, including Eddie Ward and John Foster Dulles. Tom Fitzgerald, the finance editor of the *Sydney Morning Herald,* accurately summed up Wilson when he said that '[b]y his intelligence and force of character, Sir Roland Wilson has been the outstanding public servant of his generation'.[5] John Maynard Keynes, who observed Wilson in action at a conference in London during the war, reported that he and other Whitehall officials had 'the greatest respect for his wisdom and for his pertinacity'.[6]

---

1 This paper draws heavily on the following three publications: S. Cornish, *Sir Roland Wilson: A Biographical Essay* (Canberra: The Sir Roland Wilson Foundation, 2002); W. Coleman, S. Cornish and A. Hagger, *Giblin's Platoon: The Trials and Triumphs of the Economist in Australian Public Life* (Canberra: ANU E Press, 2006); and S. Cornish, 'Roland Wilson', in J.E. King, *Biographical Dictionary of Australian and New Zealand Economists* (Cheltenham: Edward Elgar, 2007). These publications relied strongly on Roland Wilson's personal papers, which at the time were privately held and not catalogued. The National Library of Australia (MS 1155) now holds the papers, and a descriptive list is available. Unless otherwise indicated, quotes are drawn from these papers.
2 A. Reid, 'The Czar of the Treasury', *Bulletin* (Sydney), 21 December 1960, 10. See also J. Hetherington, 'Roland Wilson: A Matter of Money', in Hetherington, *Uncommon Men* (Melbourne: F.W. Cheshire, 1965), 187.
3 D. Copland, 'Confidential Statement' to Rhodes Scholarship Selection Committee, 28 October 1924, University of Tasmania archives, Tasmanian Archive and Heritage Office, file 34/5/50.
4 R.J. Whitelaw, Farewell Address to his Treasury Colleagues, 7 November 1986, held by author.
5 T. Fitzgerald, quoted in John Farquharson, 'Outstanding Public Servant of his Generation', *Canberra Times*, 27 October 1996.
6 J.M. Keynes to L.F. Giblin, 13 November 1942, Reserve Bank of Australia Archives, RBAA C. 3.7.6.33.

Sir Paul Hasluck, a minister throughout the entire period of Wilson's tenure as secretary to the Treasury, wrote that Wilson

> gained in authority among inexpert ministers firstly because he gave an impression of having no political motive of his own but a scientific detachment when describing the economic outlook and the problems to be faced and secondly because he never "squared off" to ministers, or flattered, or cajoled them, or tried to ingratiate himself with them. He was polite but uncompromising and ... left the feeling that he was treating them as though they could understand the ... issues, even when he was exposing the flaws in some remark a minister had made.[7]

For John Stone, a later Treasury secretary, the predominant reason for the Treasury's power and prestige during the 1950s and 1960s was the fact that, with Wilson at its head, it 'had a brilliant economist and outstanding public servant'; 'one felt that as the head of one's department, one was extraordinarily fortunate to have a highly distinguished man', for he was

> seen and regarded in and around Canberra, as being not merely ... an intellectual giant to some degree, but also in the Public Service, a bureaucratic giant ... That simply derived from his personality and his force of mind and indeed, his force of expression also. He was an extraordinary lucid thinker and writer, and on occasion, speaker.[8]

According to Stone, 'Wilson's contribution to the Treasury ... was that he gave it a sense of being led by an outstanding figure – someone, so to speak, that the department could look up to. He gave it intellectual quality.'[9]

Education

Wilson was born at Ulverstone, Tasmania, on 7 April 1904 and died in Canberra on 25 October 1996, aged 92. He was the first of his immediate family to complete secondary school and attend university. His formal education began at the convent school in Ulverstone, the same school that the state premier and later prime minister Joseph Lyons had attended many years before.[10] Upon completion of primary school he won a junior bursary, which allowed him to proceed to the public high school in Devonport. There he topped the state junior examination

---

7   P. Hasluck, *The Chance of Politics* (Melbourne: Text Publishing, 1997), 55.
8   J. Stone, interviewed by B. Schedvin, 17 May 1991, National Library of Australia (NLA).
9   J. Stone, Eulogy: Sir Roland Wilson, St John the Baptist Anglican Church, Reid, ACT, 1 November 1996, Papers of Sir Roland Wilson, NLA MS 1155.
10 The Wilsons were Protestants. Wilson's mother thought that by attending the convent school her son would associate with a rather more refined group of fellow pupils than he would were he to attend the local state primary school.

and was placed second in the senior (matriculation) examination. Again, he secured a state scholarship, which enabled him to enrol for the commerce degree at the University of Tasmania. He studied economics under two of Australia's leading economists, D.B. Copland and J.B. Brigden. He had not planned to go to university, and his father was reluctant to allow him to do so. It was only after Copland came to Ulverstone to meet his father that he was allowed provisionally to attend the university for one year, which was extended for a second and then a third and fourth year when success followed success.[11]

Wilson was awarded the 1925 Rhodes Scholarship for Tasmania, the first Tasmanian Rhodes scholar to come from a state school, and the first to be selected from the Faculty of Commerce. He possessed neither Greek nor Latin. For these reasons his selection was attacked in an unsigned letter to the *Mercury*, Tasmania's leading newspaper. He was so badly stung by the criticism that he considered rejecting the scholarship. But he changed his mind after receiving a stern lecture on the meaning of moral courage by a member of the Rhodes selection committee, the substance of which he was never to forget.

In his referee's report to the Rhodes committee, Copland wrote that Wilson

> is certainly the most brilliant student that has passed through my hands since I came to Tasmania. His record of High Distinctions is evidence of this, but it does not convey at all an adequate impression of his remarkable mental powers.
>
> … His analytical powers are marked, and will eventually give him a high place among economists if he continues with the subject. He has shown balanced judgements and some degree of original thought which will doubtless become more evident as his studies progress. I am convinced that he will possess to quite an unusual degree the ability to do higher work in economics and that his election to a Rhodes Scholarship will ultimately bring distinction to the country.[12]

When Wilson reached Oxford he discovered that the university did not recognise the commerce degree from the University of Tasmania and he was compelled to take the Diploma in Economics and Political Science (which he completed with distinction) before being permitted to enrol for postgraduate studies. In his first year at Oxford he wrote an essay on the subject of 'Social and Economic Experiments in Queensland from 1860' for the Beit Prize in Colonial History, one of the university's most prestigious prizes. The essay was successful; one of the judges considered it to be 'the best Beit Essay that has been submitted for some years'. Having won the Beit Prize, Wilson was then permitted to enrol for the

---

11 University of Tasmania archives, Tasmanian Archive and Heritage Office, file 34/5/50.
12 University of Tasmania archives, Tasmanian Archive and Heritage Office, file 34/5/50.

degree of Doctor of Philosophy (D.Phil). He undertook research on the subject of 'The Import of Capital' and devoted a considerable amount of time to collecting statistical data for his thesis. His examiners agreed that he had 'handled an intricate subject with great ability', and that his work was 'worthy of publication'.[13]

Before finishing his degree at Oxford, Wilson was elected to a Commonwealth Field Scholarship (later known as the Harkness Scholarship) to undertake postgraduate studies at the University of Chicago. There he decided to enrol for another doctorate. He chose the topic of 'Capital Movements and their Economic Consequences', which allowed him to pursue some of the themes that he had foreshadowed in his work at Oxford. His supervisor was the redoubtable Jacob Viner, who held Wilson to be 'one of the two or three best students I have ever encountered'. He predicted that Wilson would 'have a highly successful career as a teacher and scholar'. According to Viner, Wilson was 'an exceptionally able student and researcher, quick, original, industrious and systematic. He writes freely and well, and expresses himself easily and effectively. He has an unusual degree of intellectual maturity for a person of his age.'[14]

Contributions to economic research

After completing his degree at Chicago, Wilson was offered a lectureship at the University of Tasmania and returned to Hobart. He commenced publishing articles based on the research he had conducted for his doctorates. In 1931, Melbourne University Press published a book based on his Oxford and Chicago work entitled *Capital Imports and the Terms of Trade*. Sir Roy Harrod, the eminent Oxford economist, reviewed the book in the *Economic Journal*. He wrote that it was 'a notable contribution to the statistical study of international payments', and 'a valuable addition to the literature of international trade'.[15]

Of Wilson's contributions to economics, perhaps the most arresting was his examination in *Capital Imports* of the effect of capital inflows on the terms of trade of the borrowing country. Received accounts asserted that the terms of trade – that is, the ratio of export prices to import prices – of the borrowing country would improve. In contrast, Wilson found for Australia that the terms of trade tended to be correlated inversely with inflows of capital. His main interest, however, was not with the external terms of trade, but rather with the internal terms of trade: what would happen to the price ratio of 'domestic' (or non-tradeable goods) to tradeable goods (exports and import-replacement goods)

---

13 D.H. Macgregor, Reference for Roland Wilson, 3 December 1931, NAA 1606, AJ25/1.
14 J. Viner, Reference for Roland Wilson, 5 January 1932, Wilson Papers, NLA MS1155.
15 R.F. Harrod, Review of *Capital Imports and the Terms of Trade*, by R. Wilson, *Economic Journal*, 42, no. 167 (1932).

in the case of a capital importing country? On the basis of hypothetical models, supported by empirical data, he concluded that, in Australia's case, 'domestic' (or non-tradeable) prices tended to rise relatively to prices for tradeable goods. Whereas movements in the prices of internationally traded goods tend to be constrained by international competition, there were usually no such constraints on the costs and prices for many 'domestic' goods and services.[16]

Professor Trevor Swan argued in his review in 1972 of Treasury Paper No. 1, entitled *Overseas Investment in Australia*, that it should have been called Treasury Paper No. 2, since the Treasury's explanation of the adjustment process, by which the balance of payments accommodated overseas borrowing, was the same as the one that had been elucidated by Wilson in his book published in 1931.[17] Swan himself had drawn on Wilson's explanation in his own work on internal-external balance. Indeed, H.W. Arndt referred 'to the quite significant Australian contributions — by Roland Wilson and Trevor Swan — to the development of the "small country case" in the theory of balance of payments adjustment'.[18] It has also been claimed that Wilson's work was the precursor of what has since been termed the 'Dutch disease' or 'the Gregory effect'.

Public servant

Wilson was not entirely comfortable working as an academic economist. He later admitted that he 'never felt deeply attracted to scholarship for its own sake'.[19] Instead of an academic career, Wilson thought he might prefer to work as a policy adviser to governments. An opportunity arose in 1932 when L.F. Giblin, the acting Commonwealth statistician, invited him to take the position of economist in the Statistician's Branch of the Commonwealth Treasury in Canberra. The offer was accepted and he was quickly promoted to assistant Commonwealth statistician. He was the first economist to be employed at a senior level in the Commonwealth Public Service. His appointment — which was to be for six months — was not accepted with equanimity. Several members of the Public Service Union who worked in the Statistician's Branch called a strike, and Eddie Ward criticised the appointment in the parliament. Later, however, when Ward was minister for Labour and National Service, and Wilson was the head of his department, Ward declared that Wilson was 'the most able man I have met'.[20]

---

16 R. Wilson, *Capital Imports and the Terms of Trade* (Melbourne: Melbourne University Press, 1931).
17 T.W. Swan, 'Overseas Investment in Australia', Treasury Economic Paper No. 1, *Economic Record*, March 1976, 7.
18 H.W. Arndt, 'Non-Traded Goods and the Balance of Payments', *Economic Record,* March 1976, 89.
19 Address at the Commemoration Ceremony, University of Tasmania, Hobart, April 1969.
20 I. Castles, 'Menzies' Economic Commander', *Australian*, 30 October 1996, 14; Elwyn Spratt, *Eddie Ward: Firebrand of East Sydney* (Adelaide: Rigby, 1965; reprinted by Seal Books, Adelaide, 1978), 70.

In 1935, after declining the chair of economics at Tasmania and the associated post of financial adviser to the Tasmanian Government, Wilson was appointed economic adviser to the Commonwealth Treasury. Giblin had urged him to stay in Canberra rather than moving back to Hobart, informing Wilson that his work for the Commonwealth was 'the bigger job'. Then, in 1936, at the age of 32, Wilson succeeded E.T. McPhee as Commonwealth statistician, a post he was to hold until he was appointed secretary to the Commonwealth Treasury in 1951.

When he was Commonwealth statistician in the 1930s, Wilson created the position of 'Research Officer', which allowed graduates to enter the Commonwealth Public Service on the basis of their university qualifications. Until then, graduates could only enter the service as base grade clerks, unless they held professional qualifications, such as medical doctors or engineers; Wilson himself had been an exception. Among the distinguished graduates he recruited to the Bureau were Arthur Smithies, John Burton, Jim Nimmo, Dick Heywood, Mick Shann and Lindsay Brand. On a number of occasions he tried to attract J.G. Crawford, but without success.

Shortly before the outbreak of war, Wilson was appointed, together with Giblin and L.G. Melville of the Commonwealth Bank, to the Advisory Committee on Financial and Economic Policy (the F and E Committee). Wilson had himself proposed the establishment of this committee and had nominated Giblin to chair it. It was to be responsible for planning and coordinating much of the financial direction of the war in its early stages, and for investigating possible approaches to post-war reconstruction. In addition, as part of Australia's defence planning, Wilson was placed in charge of the National Register of the male population. This work included a census of wealth for which Wilson was responsible.

In 1940, Wilson was asked by the government to establish the Department of Labour and National Service and to become its inaugural head. He quickly created a division of post-war reconstruction in the department. It was here that the early planning of Australia's post-war reconstruction was undertaken, and to which Wilson recruited an impressive group of economists and other university graduates, including Arthur Tange, Allen Brown, Gerald Firth, Fin Crisp and John Burton. Earlier, Wilson had been responsible for bringing H.C. Coombs into the Treasury from the Commonwealth Bank in Sydney. It was this group, including Coombs, that was to form the nucleus of the Ministry of Post-War Reconstruction when it was formed at the end of 1942.

Because Wilson had initiated work on post-war reconstruction in the Department of Labour and National Service, he was invited to represent Australia at the first British Commonwealth conference on the international economy in the post-war era held in London in October 1942. It was at this conference that Keynes outlined his proposal for an international monetary institution aimed at securing international financial stability; the idea was to evolve into the International Monetary Fund established at Bretton Woods in 1944. Keynes informed Giblin that, at the London conference, Wilson had taken a 'prominent, indeed a leading part through all the discussions and played a major role in them with the greatest success'.[21]

Wilson did not attend the Bretton Woods conference, but he was at the conference in San Francisco in 1945 that established the United Nations Organization. Here again he distinguished himself. It was largely because of Wilson's skill and tenacity that the Australian Government's objective of full employment was successfully incorporated into the Charter of the United Nations (clauses 55 and 56), the outcome of a battle that Wilson won against powerful American opposition led by John Foster Dulles. Paul Hasluck, who also attended the San Francisco conference, wrote that, of the large Australian delegation led by ministers Forde and Evatt, 'Wilson was quietly the master'.[22]

Secretary to the Treasury

Late in 1948 a selection committee for the inaugural chair of economics at the newly established Australian National University (ANU), comprising the vice-chancellor (Douglas Copland), W.K. Hancock (professor of economic history at Oxford and one of the four advisers to the Interim Council of ANU), J.R. Hicks (professor of economics at Oxford and a later Nobel Laureate) and Sir Henry Clay (warden of Nuffield College, Oxford), decided to offer the chair to Wilson. But he declined the offer, explaining to Copland that, although he had made some contributions to economic knowledge, he doubted that he had the capacity for sustained research in economics of the kind that would be expected of a professor in a research school. 'I do not believe', he wrote to Hancock, 'that I possess in sufficient measure the scholarly instincts and attributes without which one could neither tolerate nor be tolerated in a research school in the social sciences.' Copland, however, tried to reassure Wilson that 'it should be quite possible for you to take charge of a research department in economics even though you have, as you say, been immersed in policy administration for so many years'. But Wilson was adamant, informing Copland that he had 'reluctantly but firmly declined the invitation'. In addition to having 'a sense of inadequacy on the academic side', Wilson confessed to Copland that he

> was also to some extent influenced by my disinclination to break the long association I had with the Commonwealth Service. I feel strongly

---

21   J.M. Keynes to L.F. Giblin, 13 November 1942, Reserve Bank of Australia Archives, RBAA C. 3.7.6.33.
22   P. Hasluck, *Diplomatic Witness: Australian Foreign Affairs, 1941–1947* (Carlton, VIC: Melbourne University Press, 1980), 193.

that I have been too long out of the academic world to make a satisfactory research Professor of Economics, and if I accepted such a position I should always feel that I was holding it under false pretensions. You will have seen enough of Government service yourself to know that one is forced to become rather specialized in certain requirements, and that this specialization does not contribute much to the breadth and profundity of knowledge required in one who is to fill an important academic post. You must not conclude that I am suffering from an inferiority complex, which is far from true. I am merely trying to be honest about my present situation, and to suggest that the National University would be wise to seek someone of less questionable suitability for the position which has so many potentialities for the future of economics in Australia.[23]

Following his rejection of The Australian National University's offer of the chair in economics, Wilson was appointed secretary to the Treasury on 1 April 1951. At 47 years of age, he was the youngest person to hold the position until Bernie Fraser's appointment in 1984. The duration of Wilson's tenure as Treasury secretary – some 15 years – has not been surpassed. Nor have others exceeded his reputation. As secretary he was the nation's senior economic policy adviser; indeed, he was the nation's most senior public servant. These were extraordinary years, marked by full employment, relative price stability and sustained economic growth. It is sometimes suggested that Wilson's reputation is overestimated because of the favourable circumstances that existed during these halcyon days. It is true that Wilson was not confronted with the problems that beset his predecessors during the depression of the 1930s or the two world wars. Nor did he have to confront the upsurge of inflation that began shortly after he left the Treasury. Nevertheless, in an era when public expectations of a benign economy were widely prevalent, the impact of each cyclical fluctuation tended to be magnified in the minds of many Australians. And since the downturns were often policy-induced, as part of the management of aggregate demand aimed at dampening inflationary forces and preserving balance of payments stability, the Treasury, as the responsible department, was frequently the target of public disquiet, and its head was often the subject of personal criticism.

The 'credit squeeze' of 1960–61 was arguably the most difficult event that Wilson had to contend with during his time as Treasury secretary. The recession of the early 1960s was the steepest in 30 years, until it was exceeded by the recession of the early 1980s. Both Wilson and the Treasury came in for heavy criticism. He never denied his responsibilities as secretary to the Treasury. Nor did he panic. Cool as always under pressure, he set about to restore economic stability and the Treasury's reputation. Both objectives were quickly achieved. His close colleagues

---

23   S. Cornish, 'The Appointment of the ANU's First Professor of Economics', *History of Economics Review*, no. 46 (2007). See also Australian National University Archives, ANUA 104/1/8 Pt 3.

wrote to him after the economy began to rebound from the immediate effects of the recession to congratulate him on his judgement and courage. Stanley Carver, the Commonwealth statistician, wrote to him at the end of 1962, saying that the

> outcome has vindicated your clear vision. I truly believe that you averted a boom-collapse of a kind that could have made the burst bubbles of Sydney Guarantee, Hooker and Reid Murray [companies that had recently collapsed] look like incidents … It is a perilous and painful thing to destroy false doctrine – and even harder to revive an economy rotten with little South Sea Bubbles. Yet I think you have succeeded – and prevented collapse.[24]

Similarly, his Treasury colleague, Lenox Hewitt, wrote to him in January 1963 asking

> whether you've now looked back, in leisure, over your achievements in 1962? They should give you great satisfaction … You've built a fine organization in a year of quite extraordinary achievement. How extraordinary, I feel I am one of those able to judge.[25]

Wilson chose to leave the Treasury three years ahead of the compulsory retiring age of 65. The decision reflected in part his wish to allow his deputy, Sir Richard Randall – another of the seven dwarfs – the opportunity to head the Treasury.[26] But there were also other reasons. Menzies had just retired and was succeeded as prime minister by Harold Holt who, in turn, was replaced as treasurer by William McMahon. With these ministerial changes, Wilson thought it was time for a change at the top of the Treasury. Moreover, the chairmanship of the boards of Qantas Airways and the Commonwealth Banking Corporation were about to fall due and Wilson was ready to take on new challenges.

When he retired from the Treasury in 1966 he had already spent many years on the boards of the Commonwealth Bank and Qantas as secretary to the Treasury. Upon retirement he was appointed chairman of both these enterprises. In due course he was appointed to the chairmanship of the Wentworth Hotel, a fully owned subsidiary of Qantas, and to the boards of the insurance company Mutual Life & Citizens (MLC), Imperial Chemical Industries (Australia), and the Australian-European Finance Corporation. As with everything else he did, Wilson took his work as a company director seriously and his contributions to strategic thinking were highly praised both by his fellow directors and by managers in the companies with which he was associated.

---

24 S. Carver to R. Wilson, 21 December 1962, Wilson Papers, NLA MS 1155.
25 L. Hewitt to R. Wilson, 14 January 1963, Wilson Papers, NLA MS 1155.
26 S. Cornish, 'Sir Richard John Randall (1906–1982)', *Australian Dictionary of Biography*, 18 (Carlton, VIC: Melbourne University Press, 2012), 324–5.

Sir Roland Wilson, 1965

Source: National Archives of Australia, A1200, L51130

Wilson's legacy

What is the significance of Wilson's life and work? An obvious one is that high intellectual ability and steadfast determination can transcend limited family circumstances and the obscurity of the place of one's birth. Born the son of a builder and cabinet maker, in an isolated country town in the smallest and least economically equipped of the Australian states, a young man with limited physical presence but with considerable academic ability and a courageous disposition was able to aspire, and later to be offered and attain, positions at the apex of his nation's academic, bureaucratic and corporate worlds. He was fortunate, to be sure, in having as mentors some of the leading names in Australian economics and politics, among them Giblin, Copland and Brigden, Lyons, Casey, Menzies, Spender, Holt, Fadden, Curtin and Chifley. But he had to win their support, which he did as a result of his powerful intellect and strength of character.

Of his principal achievements, the most significant was surely the part he played in the transformation of the Treasury from its traditional accounting and budgetary function to an institution whose chief responsibility was the provision of economic advice to government. Wilson did not initiate this transformation. Nor was the transformation complete by the time he left the Treasury. But as economic adviser to the Treasury in the 1930s and 1940s, and as secretary to the Treasury in the 1950s and 1960s, there can be no doubt that he, more than any other individual, played the dominant role in the evolution of the Treasury from a department of finance and supply to a department of economic policy advice. When he was appointed Treasury secretary, the *Launceston Examiner* – the leading newspaper in the region of his birth – drew attention to the fact that an economist had succeeded an accountant as head of the department. It pointed out that '[f]or fifty years Treasury administration has been in the hands of persons who were predominantly accountants and graduates from the Treasury's accounting departments'. But Wilson's appointment was altogether different, for it 'marks the first Australian experiment of this kind, and it is a good bet as far ahead as one can see all his successors will be economists, too'.[27]

Wilson's direction of the Treasury was heavily influenced by ideas that he had developed in the 1930s. It was then that he had taken an interest in aspects of policy coordination and planning. He wrote two important papers on the subject, one on 'The Economic Implications of Planning', for the Australian Institute of Political Science in 1934, and the other on 'Economic Co-ordination', the Joseph Fisher Lecture, which he presented at the University of Adelaide in 1940.[28]

---
27 *Launceston Examiner*, 2 February 1952, 2.
28 R. Wilson, 'The Economic Implications of Planning', in W.G.K. Duncan, ed., *National Economic Planning* (Sydney: Angus and Robertson, 1934); R. Wilson, 'Economic Co-ordination', Joseph Fisher Lecture in Commerce (Adelaide: The Hassell Press, 1940).

Given the need and inclination of modern governments to intervene in the economy, Wilson was concerned about the scope for policy conflict and the inconsistencies of objectives and decisions that were likely to occur in these circumstances. It was clear to him that planning was required to coordinate the various interventions, and to bring about a greater measure of coherence in economic policy. Planning, he argued,

> may be regarded as the elaboration of methods for securing wise control. Practically, it involves the establishment of some form of central 'thinking agency', which will be better equipped than the existing political organization, to direct where direction is necessary, and to withhold where intrusion would be harmful.

By planning he did not mean the type of planning that had materialised in the Soviet Union. What he had in mind, though of course he could not spell it out, was something like the Treasury of the 1950s and 1960s when Wilson himself was the secretary – a 'thinking agency' that would operate in a market economy and would aim to achieve greater consistency between competing policy objectives. As he put it,

> the new planning demands a reversal of short-sighted economic policies, the abolition of arbitrary and ill-conceived restraints and interferences with the free workings of the automatic adjustments, and, above all, a more vigorous and rational control of the machinery for creating and distributing purchasing power.

The years of Wilson's headship of the Treasury are often regarded as the high watermark of the Keynesian revolution in Australia, and it is sometimes contended that Keynesianism was the guiding principle of the department's approach to economic policy. While it might be argued that Wilson was never a committed adherent to Keynesianism, he was in some ways a purer adherent to the economics of Keynes than many of those who claimed to be dedicated Keynesians. Neither Wilson nor Keynes were supporters of direct controls. Keynes often referred to them as 'Bolshevism', or 'totalitarian' devices, and Wilson no doubt would have agreed. Like Keynes, he was not attracted to the idea of constantly fine-tuning the economy, particularly by manipulating interest rates, doubting as he did the potency of monetary policy. Both men preferred instead to influence activity by fiscal policy. While agreeing that monetary policy had a role to play, where they differed was in their time horizons – Wilson backed the Menzies Government's strong commitment to economic expansion, whereas Keynes was more concerned with achieving short-term stability.

Accordingly, some of Wilson's greatest work was directed at fostering a more efficient and dynamic economy. He was opposed to Australia's high rate of protection, often clashing with the Department of Trade under its minister, John McEwen, and secretary, J.G. Crawford. While endorsing the reimposition of import controls in the emergency circumstances that prevailed in 1952, when a flood of imports inundated Australia following the bursting of the Korean War boom, Wilson opposed quantitative import controls in principle as a permanent feature of the Australian economy, preferring instead a more adjustable exchange rate regime. He was a powerful advocate of the return to convertibility of sterling area currencies, arguing that Australia's adherence to sterling area controls was imposing a straitjacket on the nation's efforts to force the pace of economic growth and development. As well as his support for convertibility, Wilson was an architect of policy aimed at overcoming the dollar shortage of the 1950s by borrowing in the United States, policy advice that the Menzies Government received favourably but which had been anathema to the previous Chifley administration. On wages policy, Wilson believed that the system of arbitration and conciliation, with its support for quarterly adjustments to the basic wage according to movements in retail prices, was contributing both to inflation and to inefficiencies in the allocation of resources.

There continued to be major differences over policy between the Treasury and the Commonwealth Bank/Reserve Bank during Wilson's time as Treasury secretary, particularly between Wilson and Coombs, the heads of the two agencies. These difficulties might have had their origins during the war and over aspects of post-war reconstruction. They were probably heightened when Coombs, shortly after his appointment to the governorship of the Commonwealth Bank at the end of 1948, wrote to Wilson saying:

> I have always felt it essential that there should be another source of economic advice and some authority concerned with the coordination of inter-departmental work other than the Treasury. It seems to me inevitable that the Treasury, however good its intentions and however able its staff, gradually comes to take the traditional 'financial' point of view and there are many times when this point of view is not the most relevant.[29]

As an alternative source of policy advice, Coombs proposed that the prime minister should have attached to him an economic staff. Wilson was to retain a copy of this letter with his personal papers for the rest of his life.

Similarly, Coombs' decision to invite the nation's top academic economists to the Commonwealth Bank/Reserve Bank twice a year for consultations on the state of the Australian economy was regarded with deep suspicion by Wilson, especially when an invitation to participate was extended to Crawford and other officials of

---

29   H.C. Coombs to R. Wilson, 11 January 1949, in Wilson Papers, NLA MS 1155.

the Department of Trade. Alarm bells rang even louder when Wilson discovered attempts in the early 1950s by Coombs to fund from the Commonwealth Bank work at The Australian National University on contemporary economic trends and issues, the results of which were to be published on a regular basis. Such an exercise, Wilson thought, might cause the government acute embarrassment and inevitably weaken the Treasury's authority as the principal economic adviser to the federal government.[30]

The problem of an alternative source of economic advice to government reached its apogee in 1965 when the Committee of Economic Enquiry (the Vernon Committee) recommended that an Advisory Council on Economic Growth should be established to advise the government on economic matters. The Vernon Committee had been established in 1962 in the wake of the credit squeeze of 1960–61. Crawford had been designated by the prime minister to chair the enquiry; when Wilson heard about it he persuaded Menzies to replace Crawford with a businessman, Dr James Vernon, much to Crawford's chagrin.[31] By the time its report was completed the economy had recovered and the econometric forecasts that had underpinned the committee's analysis of the future seemed incongruent with the new economic dispensation. Wilson and his Treasury colleagues exploited the factual deficiencies and logical inconsistencies of the Vernon Report to impugn its major recommendations, including, above all, the arguments supporting the creation of an Advisory Council on Economic Growth. In this endeavour, Wilson was highly successful. For when he tabled the Vernon Committee's report in the parliament, Prime Minister Menzies, drawing upon a Treasury brief, announced that the government did not accept the need for an alternative source of economic advice. For Wilson, there were no grounds for creating new sources of policy advice, since the Treasury itself evaluated different possibilities. Furthermore, the Treasury was not the only public agency advising the government: 'The problem', he argued, was 'not how to get advice but how to evaluate it. To set up competitive evaluations still leaves the task of evaluating the evaluators.'[32] That, Wilson thought, was clearly the role of the Treasury.

Wilson's – and the Treasury's – difficulties with Coombs, and with Crawford, have sometimes been explained simply in terms of powerful egos refusing to yield

---

30 Wilson's contempt for the Bank had already formed before Coombs became governor. In January 1949 he wrote to Coombs about his return to Australia from the United States and the resumption of his seat on the Bank's Advisory Council. Wilson told Coombs that '[t]hese [duties], of course, include at least one lunch per meeting, sherry twice a day, afternoon tea once a day, and the frequent use of the Governor's plane for the transport of myself, my Treasury colleagues and my secretary between Canberra and Sydney. In between other activities no doubt we will find time at the Council to consider some items of business, if there are any on which you have not made up your mind before the Council meets.'
31 Crawford was subsequently appointed vice-chairman, becoming in effect the principal author of the Enquiry's report.
32 Wilson Papers, NLA MS 1155.

to different points of view. There is something to be said for this explanation. After all, Wilson, Coombs and Crawford were the most senior of the seven dwarfs. But there was more to it than that, for there were significant differences in their approaches to economic policy. The Treasury's priority under Wilson and Randall was to facilitate and enhance economic growth and development. Policies that might inhibit this objective were clearly unacceptable to the Treasury. The central bank, when Coombs was governor, was more concerned with short-term stability, being always ahead of the Treasury in wanting to tighten policy for the purpose of reducing inflation. Coombs was generally eager to use monetary instruments for this purpose, but Wilson was concerned that higher interest rates would increase the cost of servicing government debt, much of the debt having accumulated as a result of funding infrastructure projects. Moreover, fine-tuning aggregate demand tended to induce stop-go cycles in activity, which adversely affected decision-making in the private sector of the economy. The Department of Trade, for its part, wanted to provide tariff and other protection – and subsidies – to local industries, both export and import-replacing industries. For Wilson, however, this meant the diversion of resources into less efficient sectors of the economy, a process that would impede Australia's growth and development.

The Treasury's *Economic Survey*, which was published annually from 1956 to 1973, reveals the department's overriding commitment to economic growth and development. In his Foreword to the first *Economic Survey* in 1956, the prime minister (Menzies) put the Treasury's view precisely:

> By reducing the pressure of home demand the Government has sought to reduce the demand for imports, to reduce the external deficit, and at the same time to assist in stabilizing domestic costs and prices. Initially, the only measures which could be used forthwith to safeguard international solvency were negative rather than positive. They included import restrictions, and restraint of domestic expenditures through higher taxes and ceilings on public works. The Government, however, has always been fully alive to the need for a positive strengthening of the bases of our domestic economy to provide for continued economic growth. This calls for greater productivity and output, especially in those lines of activity where our competitive position is strong and through which we can hope to improve our balance of payments position; it calls likewise for selective basic investment which will contribute to this, and for the domestic saving and overseas borrowing necessary to support it.[33]

---

33 Commonwealth of Australia, *Australia 1956: An Economic Survey* (Canberra: Commonwealth Government Printer, 1956), 5.

In the same *Economic Survey*, the Treasury itself argued that, rather than the achievement of full employment, the 'outstanding feature of the post-war Australian economy has been its many-sided and remarkable continuous growth … It has had force enough to thrust aside obstacles and keep going in face of events which, in other times, would have staggered the economy.' While some aspects of this expansion were due to government policy – such as immigration and basic infrastructure – the Treasury asserted that economic expansion

> has been a spontaneous movement, drawing its impetus from many sources within the economy … there has been nothing in the nature of a general plan, drawn up and imposed by the authority of government. Throughout the community there has no doubt been something of a general conviction that the economy ought to grow, had to grow, and should not be hindered from growing and various elements in the economy, including governments, have acted in accordance with that conviction. But apart from that kind of general belief, it would be difficult to say that the movement has had any single source of inspiration, energy or sponsorship. It has nevertheless operated most powerfully to shape the course of events.[34]

The Treasury's enthusiasm for economic growth was expressed dramatically in its 1963 *Economic Survey*: 'Over the past ten years', the Treasury wrote,

> and especially over the past three years, Australia has achieved its greatest break-through in point of resources since the crossing of the Blue Mountains a hundred years ago. That earlier event opened the first doorway to the pastoral and agricultural wealth of the continent and the growth since built upon it. But until not very long ago it was commonly held that Australia could not be a great industrial nation and therefore could not support any greater number of people at Western standards because it lacked industrial resources. The quick succession of rich mineral discoveries – bauxite, copper, iron ore and now oil – go far to dispel that view – these new riches do, beyond doubt, lift the horizons of Australian growth quite incalculably.[35]

In its next *Survey*, the one for 1964, the Treasury identified a problem that was to beset the Australian economy in the years to come. There were 'two divergent possibilities', it said. 'One is that growth will continue … The other possibility is a renewal of inflation and the beginning of a phase of unstable

---

34 Ibid., 13–14.
35 Commonwealth of Australia, *The Australian Economy* (Canberra: Commonwealth Government Printer, 1963), 24–5.

conditions extending far into later years. Clearly there is in this a challenge both to government and to the whole community.'[36] No one could say that Wilson and Randall did not warn Australia of the possible dangers ahead.

Conclusion

In his Giblin Memorial Lecture to the 47th ANZAAS Conference held in Hobart in 1976, Wilson chose to reflect upon the qualities and outlook required of successful economic policy advisers. Though he was speaking of Giblin, his thoughts applied equally to himself:

> [H]e [Giblin] would have felt that, in the application of economic theory to public policy, the need was greater rather than less for the cultivation of people who could combine a basic mastery of theory with knowledge of the mysteries of a constantly changing society, with intimate experience of business and political realities, with intuitive understanding of the behaviour of individuals, and groups within society — and above all with humanity.
>
> … He made a unique mark in government, in economics, in central banking, in statistics and in war … from his vast knowledge and experience was distilled a wisdom which was put without stint at the disposal of those who knew and loved him.[37]

---

36 Commonwealth of Australia, *The Australian Economy* (Canberra: Commonwealth Government Printer, 1964), 3.
37 R. Wilson, 'L F Giblin: A Man for All Seasons', address to the 47th Congress of the Australian and New Zealand Association for the Advancement of Science, Hobart, 12 May 1976; published in *Search* (Sydney, NSW), 7, no. 7 (July 1976), 314.

7

Coombs the Keynesian

Tim Rowse[1]

It is a commonplace fact that H.C. 'Nugget' Coombs was among the first enthusiastic Australian Keynesians. Groenewegen and McFarlane, in their biographical sketch, call Coombs 'a leading figure in the implementation of the "Keynesian Revolution" in economic policy'.[2] I would not dispute this, but I do not find it very helpful either, partly because in none of the 13 references that Groenewegen and McFarlane make to the 'Keynesian revolution' do they tell you what that 'revolution' consisted of. To label Coombs a 'Keynesian' is only the beginning of an effort to understand him as an intellectual.

A golden moment

The transformative impact of *The General Theory* on intellectuals such as Coombs has been much mythologised. By 'mythologised' I do not mean falsely rendered. Rather, the phrase 'Keynesian revolution' works as a conventional narrative device, a shorthand that effectively distances the historian from the people and events of the late 1930s and early 1940s, rather than bringing them into sharper focus. Furthermore, in the uses to which the name 'Keynes' and the soft focus phrase 'Keynesian revolution' are put I detect a yearning for simplicity, for a clear and unproblematic alignment of economic and political reason. The name 'Keynes' and the phrase 'Keynesian revolution' evoke a moment in the twentieth century that was in two ways a golden moment: first, liberalism seemed to have produced a practically workable model of society; and second, economists owned that model and were being invited by governments to apply it. The yearning for that golden moment is at the heart of the mythologising phrase 'Keynesian revolution'.

---

1 This essay was first published in *History of Economics Review*, 30 (1999), 108–25. It is reproduced with the permission of the History of Economic Thought Society of Australia. Tim Rowse has made minor revisions.
2 P. Groenewegen and B. McFarlane, *A History of Australian Economic Thought* (London and New York: Routledge, 1990), 214.

One of the most florid recollections of that blessed conjuncture of reason and politics – the late 1930s, early 1940s – came from *The General Theory*'s indexer, David Bensusan-Butt. In 1967, he wistfully recalled that he had found in *The General Theory*:

> joyful revelation in dark times. We thought that Keynes had, to put it shortly, found the 'flaw in the capitalist system', and had proclaimed its remedy ... The mystery of contemporary iniquity had been unveiled by a masterpiece of sustained intellectual effort. All the other tangled turgid stuff which lesser men were producing to rationalise the mess around us simply faded away.[3]

Butt had found in Keynes' vision of a reformed capitalism

> everything and more the Fabian generation had looked for in socialism: it was morally speaking egalitarian, it was fully employed, it was generous and gay; it was a very new sort of capitalism controlled not by the greedy votaries of Mammon but by the intellect and *joie de vivre* of an intelligent and robust democracy.[4]

The sovereignty of a cheerful reason is Bensusan-Butt's theme.

> [*The General Theory*] was to us less a work of economic theory than a Manifesto for Reason and Cheerfulness, the literary embodiment of a man who, to those who ever saw him, remains the very genius of intellect and enjoyment. It gave a rational basis and a moral appeal for a faith in the possible health and sanity of contemporary mankind such as the youth of my generation found nowhere else.[5]

In 1967, Bensusan-Butt could distance himself from these youthful faiths and yet still find Keynes' book a wonder. 'From the grey depths of my cynical middle age', he wrote, 'I will not let great men account for much in the determinate sweep of history, but I keep a soft spot for *The General Theory*.'[6]

Three years after Bensusan-Butt's recollections, Coombs offered listeners of the ABC Boyer Lectures similar memories. For many of his generation, it had been hard to see 'in Stalin's Russia the model of a Utopia of which the young could dream and, as for revolution, its techniques had been taken over by the irrational right':

> It was at this stage that the star of Keynes emerged as a focus for youthful enthusiasm and sense of revolt. Looking back, what he offered (or at first

---

3   D. Bensusan-Butt, *On Economic Knowledge: A Sceptical Miscellany* (Canberra: Research School of Pacific Studies, Department of Economics, ANU, 1980), 35.
4   Ibid.
5   Ibid.
6   Ibid., 34–6.

merely promised in due course to find) was unexciting enough – only a new understanding of the workings of the economic system. But it gave us justification for and words to express our scorn for the stupidity and ineptitude of our elders and the grounds to believe that we who shared this new enlightenment could end this miserable mean-spirited chaos of the great depression for ever. It made it possible for us to face the war without despair, believing that if we survived we could set mankind fair with following wind on the way to a new society. It seems to me now that the Keynesian reform program was the last hopefully inspired youthful revolt.[7]

Ten years later, Coombs recalled the publication of *The General Theory* as 'for me and many of my generation the most seminal intellectual event of our time'.[8] Though he recalled at first finding the book difficult and deceptive in its structure, it 'did not fail to generate excitement from first contact, and soon I had become convinced that in the Keynesian analysis lay the key to comprehension of the economic system'. In this conviction he was strengthened by a technical breakthrough – the 'almost simultaneous development of the National Income Estimates'.[9] Coombs went on to tell the story of the Financial and Economic (F and E) Committee, which 'progressively gave the economic planning of the war an *essentially Keynesian character*'.[10]

In the published memoirs of Bensusan-Butt and Coombs we find three elements of the Keynesian revolution as myth: (1) reasoned iconoclasm, taken up by (2) critical youth, and (3) applied to government in a far-reaching and ultimately effective shaking up of the system. I remind you that 'myth' does not necessarily mean 'untrue'; rather myth is storytelling conventionalised by pleasurable reiteration. Let me throw into relief this myth of youthful-reason-triumphant. I will do so in three ways. First I will give you an account of a paper 'Economic Theory and Economic Practice' read by John La Nauze before the Melbourne Branch of the Economic Society in May 1937.[11] In this paper we find a young economist, fresh from reading Keynes, in a highly pessimistic mood about the future relevance and public authority of economics. My second strategy for highlighting the mythical quality of the memoirs of Coombs and Bensusan-Butt will be to show alternative ways of narrating the taking up of Keynes' ideas in Australia. Finally, I will examine some policy contexts in which Coombs attempted to apply Keynesian ideas.

---

7   H.C. Coombs, *The Fragile Pattern: Institutions and Man* (Sydney: Australian Broadcasting Commission, 1970), 41–2.
8   H.C. Coombs, *Trial Balance* (Melbourne: Macmillan, 1980), 3.
9   Ibid.
10 Ibid., (emphasis added).
11 J. La Nauze, 'Economic Theory and Economic Practice', typescript, Governor Herbert Coombs files, Reserve Bank of Australia RBA GHC-50-I, (1937).

Dr H.C. (Nugget) Coombs, 1950

Source: National Archives of Australia, M2153, 4/33

La Nauze's pessimism

What could Economics as a discipline do to win the respect of politicians and the public?, La Nauze asked. Economists were unworldly and so lacked authority, he complained. Orthodox economists condemned 'protection' as inefficient, yet this had no impact on the politicians' and the public's enthusiasm for protection policies. La Nauze argued that economists would continue to suffer popular incredulity if they accepted Lionel Robbins' argument that economists were value-neutral analysts of the means to attain ends and had no competence or duty to discuss those ends. In this they deceived themselves, argued La Nauze, for economists did, in fact, employ a conception of human welfare – one that equated welfare with monetary income. Such economists supported free trade because their theory told them that this would maximise income. They failed to realise that people and politicians had other aspirations for their nations: security, and safety in war through industrial strength. Economists had developed a concept of 'welfare' when international peace and prosperity could be assumed, and they had failed to adapt their notion of 'welfare' to more insecure times.

La Nauze offered further explanations of economists' lack of authority in public debate. To the extent that economists spoke in the language of everyday affairs, it was possible for every person to hold an opinion about the matters on which economists expressed themselves – there was nothing special about what economists said. Another problem was that economists devoted their efforts to improving existing institutions, but 'a growing section of the intelligent minority … are not interested in the proposals of economists for the better working of existing institutions'. Neither of these problems was the fault of economists, La Nauze conceded. The problem to which La Nauze gave emphasis, however, was in his opinion of economists' own making. Economists persisted in making simplifying free market assumptions and in postulating narrow monetary conceptions of 'welfare'.

La Nauze then raised a second obstacle to economists' authority: their inability to promote, from outside political debate, a consensual view. Keynes was his main example. La Nauze disputed not the substance of Keynes' arguments in *The General Theory* but his polemical manner of expression. By denouncing theoretical orthodoxy Keynes risked discrediting, in the mind of the lay public, 'all economic theorizing, including that of Mr. Keynes'. In calling for greater decorum among economists, La Nauze seemed close to making the opposite complaint to that with which his talk had begun – economists were perhaps too worldly. Economists were unlikely ever to speak with one voice because they held too great a variety of opinions about the good society. As well, Australian politicians publicly endorsed the authority of economists whose advice suited their politics and then ridiculed the same economists when they found their advice unacceptable. In this politicised atmosphere economists competitively solicited support, to the detriment of their 'true impartiality and detachment'.

After canvassing these explanations for economists' lack of authority, without assigning priority to any one of them, La Nauze was unable to point out any way forward in theoretical, methodological, epistemological or ethical terms. Rather, his dismal paper led the reader towards the conclusion that economists' authority was ever fragile. Would the demands of the looming war lead to a better economics or to better standing for economists? La Nauze doubted it. Indeed, 'I do not think that there is likely to be any revolution by which the world will turn from its irrationality to the comparative rationality of economic theory'. It is most likely, he thought, that 'we will be driven to escape into the worlds of elegant equilibria, or the history of doctrine, where we know we are safe'.

La Nauze was wrong in his prognosis – the Second World War was the making of economists, because it forced them into a relatively unified policy stance favouring a popular program – full employment – and because governments hired economists in order to run the war economy and to project a peace that inspired hard-pressed citizens. Nonetheless, La Nauze's forgotten paper is of historical interest because it is a contrary instance to the impression – gained from Coombs and Bensusan-Butt – that at the end of the 1930s, early career economists were seized with joyous optimism upon reading *The General Theory*.

Coombs' unpublished letters, 1936–38

Coombs and La Nauze were good friends in the late 1930s. Since Coombs was ambivalent about the Bank and missed the academic life, correspondence with La Nauze (then teaching economics at the University of Adelaide) was important to him. In his letters to La Nauze he could air – more in jest than in earnest – his worries that the bank ethos was eroding his political integrity and intellectual vitality. In February 1936 Coombs reported to his friend that he and Jock Phillips

> lunch together each week and join in a chorus of abuse of Fascists and Conservatives. I enjoy meeting him exceedingly – as that is one aspect of this job which is less satisfactory than it might be. Apart from discussions with Melville on theory – I find it very hard to meet people with whom I can talk about things other than Banking. After Universities where one's

contacts are so varied and made automatically, it is hard to have to take thought to prevent one's interests being narrowed. Work at the Bank is pretty varied and interesting.[12]

In Coombs' letters at this time are scattered references to a number of economists he was reading: Bohm-Bawerk, Cassel, Durbin, Hayek. Then, in March 1936:

> Have you seen Keynes' new book? Judging by the summary of it Walker used to damn the Commonwealth Bank with recently – it must be somewhat iconoclastic.[13]

Followed by:

> A group of us, including Walker, Black, Butlin, Melville and I are to meet once a week to chew this book over. So I am reading it with some attention – the more particularly since its practical implications are important. At the moment I am not impressed – but am trying to keep an open mind on the question. It is useful to try and put one's impressions on paper.[14]

Coombs evidently attached some notes to this letter, but they have not survived. Later, he wrote again on Keynes:

> I hear from Phillips that you have been wrestling with Keynes and find him a pain in the neck. I am struggling with him too … so far I am more irritated than anything. His habit of having half a chapter of close and difficult analyses and then slipping into general criticism of the system which does not follow from the analysis is damned annoying. Of course the crux of the business is the theory of interest and there I think he's about half wrong.

And later in this letter:

> By the way don't you think Keynes puts things into the mouths of Malthus and others when he seeks for his intellectual ancestors?[15]

In two subsequent letters, Coombs outlined his doubts and dissatisfactions with *The General Theory*. One was to do with Keynes' ideas about the rate of interest:

> I have been trying to make sense of the theory of interest. Keynes' work I found unsatisfying and yet it seemed to me to have one aspect of truth

---

12   H.C. Coombs to J. La Nauze, 12 February 1936, La Nauze Papers, National Library of Australia (NLA) MS 5248.
13   Coombs to La Nauze, 18 March 1936, La Nauze Papers, NLA MS 5248. He was referring to Walker's recent appearance before the Royal Commission on Money and Banking.
14   Coombs to La Nauze, 22 June 1936, La Nauze Papers, NLA MS 5248.
15   Coombs to La Nauze, n.d., La Nauze Papers, NLA MS 5248.

> – that interest is predominantly a monetary phenomenon. He goes wrong in confining the influence of the quantity of money to the yield on fixed money claims. The idea that I have been trying to follow up is that money is one form of property – the others being fixed money claims, equities, durable consumption goods and goods for immediate consumption and that a person at any time distributes his available wealth between those different forms in the way which gives him the maximum net satisfaction from the point of view of liquidity, income, immediate satisfaction, etc. So that the rate of interest will not (as Keynes suggests) merely be the rate which will make it worthwhile for people to hold money balances equal in aggregate to the quantity of money but that rate which establishes a relationship of relative attractiveness of the various forms of property as a result of which people will hold money balances equal in aggregate to the quantity of money. What this means is:
>
> 1. that the changes in the quantity of money affect the attractiveness of all forms of property
>
> 2. that equilibrium in money holdings is restored not by changes in the rate of interest only but by a reshuffling of all the forms of property
>
> 3. that the effects of any change in the quantity of money will be different according to where they come into the economy.[16]

In this passage we see Coombs pursuing a line of thought that would later be developed by Milton Friedman.[17] The theoretical background against which he was reading Keynes was certainly eclectic, 'the result as far as I can trace it of reading Cannan, von Mises and Melville'.[18]

Coombs' second substantive criticism of *The General Theory* concerned the problem of conceptualising and measuring the propensity to consume – a point on which he had published a short article in the *Economic Record*:[19]

> Since writing the note I have come to doubt whether it is possible to speak of the propensity to consume for the community as a whole at all. It is clearly possible to compile for an individual a schedule of consumption for given levels of income which would be reasonably valid for a short range of income on either side of the actual income. It is clearly impossible, however, to aggregate schedules of individuals

---

16 Coombs to La Nauze, 9 September [1936?], La Nauze Papers, NLA MS 5248.
17 M. Friedman, *Studies in the Quantity Theory of Money* (Chicago: Chicago University Press, 1956). I would like to thank Sean Turnell, Michael White and Roy Weintraub for helping me to place this line of thought within the history of economic theory.
18 Coombs to La Nauze, 9 September [1936?], La Nauze Papers, NLA MS 5248.
19 H.C. Coombs, 'A Propensity to Consume, a Comment on the Note by Dr. Smithies', *Economic Record*, 13 (June 1937), 250–5.

whose actual incomes are widely different, since the range of income for which their respective schedules would be valid would not coincide. At best it may be possible to talk of the propensity to consume of a representative individual – a very doubtful concept.[20]

In Coombs' letters to La Nauze there is not only evidence that Coombs was working his way critically and thoughtfully through Keynes' *General Theory;* there are also passages of writing which suggest that Coombs found Keynes, for all his critique of classical economics, limited by the framework of a discredited liberalism. This scepticism about Keynes' liberalism emerged in two further letters from Coombs to La Nauze. The first is a comment on La Nauze's gloomy paper on economics' lack of authority, in which Coombs put the problem in historical terms. Economists' credibility had been high when their laissez-faire assumptions and convictions had expressed the interests of 'the rising small capitalist class … the most dynamic section of the community', he suggested. Now capitalists were bent on maintaining 'large scale monopolistic units', and they no longer welcomed liberal economists' strictures against market-distorting political privilege. And if Laski was right in seeing the state as the instrument of 'predominant groups in the community' then economists could expect no better hearing from governments. Because there could be no return to capitalism's earlier laissez-faire stage, Coombs concluded, it was futile for economists to 'cry for the moon of free competition'. Either economists could cease to make any critique of capitalism and simply describe, without judgment, its contemporary dynamics; or economists could develop a critical conception of 'welfare' and throw themselves into the political process. As a bank employee, Coombs was clearly inhibited from choosing the second option. In a postscript mentioning the possibility of escaping from the Bank to a university job he asked: 'In view of the above can I remain in a bank and retain my integrity?'[21]

A sequel to this letter, one year later, survives in the La Nauze papers. Coombs again wrote down his thoughts about what economics and economists could hope to do. He and La Nauze had been reading Barbara Wootton's recent *Lament for Economics,* and Coombs found that book's argument 'hard to answer.' If there were hope for Economics, it lay in:

1. the adoption of a theory of the state

2. the willingness to consider people making economic decisions in statistical groups about which it would be possible to make judgments as to behaviour which would have [hold?] true for the group but not necessarily for the individual

---

20   Coombs to La Nauze, 20 September 1937, La Nauze Papers, NLA MS 5248. In this comment, Coombs parallels such post-Keynesian writers as Kalecki who introduce the complicating factors of class and income level into any attempt to measure and predict changes in the propensity to consume.
21   Coombs to La Nauze, 9 June 1937, La Nauze Papers, NLA MS 5248.

> 3. the willingness to abandon the search for certainty and to base economics consciously upon probabilities.
>
> Of course if Economists will do this – they will reject equally the fictions of liberal economics and the limited interventions of Keynes, Meade, Harrod and co.[22]

This is neither as reasoned nor as clear a comment as one might wish to read, but it supports my impression that Coombs' dissatisfactions with economics in June 1938 were those of a critical (if not Marxist) realist. As well as a theory of the state, a sociology of differentiated economic motivation would be required to give economists a purchase on social reality, and even then economists could hope only to rest their analysis on 'probabilities'. If the comment on Keynes, Harrod and Meade is a *non sequitur,* it nonetheless demonstrates that Coombs' restless intellect had yet not found what it sought in Keynes' liberalism. This mid-1938 letter does not sit well with Coombs' recollections of his Keynesian hierophany in *Trial Balance,* and with Melville's recollection that 'Coombs ... went the whole way with Keynes.'[23]

If Coombs was going the whole way with anyone in 1938, it was with Barbara Wootton. Wootton's survey of the discipline made a particular target of Lionel Robbins' *The Nature and Significance of Economic Science*. She began by dismissing the assumptions dominant within economics: 'every encroachment of monopoly upon a competitive system narrows the field in which the economist's tools can ever be applied at all.'[24] Increasing state intervention similarly attenuated economics' pertinence. A world structured by monopoly and by state intervention was less and less amenable to economists' theory. Declining to suggest new theoretical paths for economics, Wootton cited Keynes only sparingly, but to good effect. By pointing out the possibility of equilibria in the midst of unused resources Keynes questioned economic theory's assumption of scarcity. Sometimes economic analysis could rest on the assumption of a prevailing scarcity, but in other situations, the opposite assumption was necessary. Keynesians were

> at least trying to define the respective spheres in which each of the two mutually contradictory assumptions now offered as the basis of economic analysis is valid. But until this job has been satisfactorily completed, it is not to be wondered at if the economists stand helpless before urgent practical problems. Until they know which assumption it is appropriate to apply, they cannot even answer such an elementary

---

22   Coombs to La Nauze, 4 June 1938, La Nauze Papers, NLA MS 5248.
23   S. Cornish, 'Sir Leslie Melville: An Interview', *ANU Working Papers in Economic History,* 173 (1993), 19.
24   B. Wootton, *Lament for Economics* (London: Jonathan Cape, 1938), 82.

question as whether an increase in the total volume of employment is more likely to be brought about by increasing or by diminishing the general level of wages.[25]

In her third and fourth chapters, Wootton declared herself unconvinced by arguments that economics is a science. Rather she sought to expose economists' unreasoned faith that free markets optimised welfare. In her fifth chapter, she found fault with the idea that the economic system is shaped by the choices made by all those within it; some peoples' choices, she pointed out, powerfully determined the options which the rest of us confront. Finally Wootton outlined a charter for economic studies that would require of economists:

> a ruthless disregard of present boundaries and definitions. If anything substantial is to come out of the economists' work, he must be allowed to poke his nose into questions of the quality of social ends, and of the means by which these are formulated. He must retain his freedom to be as sceptical as he thinks proper about market optima, and to suggest alternative standards by which these may be checked.[26]

She concluded by stating a research program for the reform-minded economist, a program whose breadth would not have shamed a school of social sciences, a program as broad as the range of research projects commissioned by the Department of Post-War Reconstruction after 1943.

Some policy contexts of *The General Theory*

My second approach to the question of Coombs as exemplar of the Keynesian revolution takes us away from intellectual biography in order to emphasise the continuity in Australian economists' policy advice before and after the publication of Keynes' 'seminal' book.

Such continuity is Neville Cain's point. Cain casts Ronald Walker as a leading advocate of Keynes to Australian economists, climaxing in his presentation of the gist of *The General Theory* to the Royal Commission on Money and Banking in 1936. However, Cain warns not to exaggerate the policy benightedness of Australian economists prior to the publication of *The General Theory*. 'By 1933 most of them had abandoned wage-cutting and warmed to treasury-bill financing of deficits and "minimal" public works (one or two indeed had pressed for a bolder line on works outlays).' The significance of Walker's work, Cain argues, was in 'giving intellectual credibility to the policy stance of an emerging group

---
25 Ibid., 98.
26 Ibid., 261.

of expansionists whose political strength was concentrated in Sydney.' Cain's footnote then lists Bertram Stevens, Alfred Davidson, Torliev Hytten, supported by L.F. Giblin and D.B. Copland – all urging the federal government and the Commonwealth Bank to loosen expenditure and exchange policies.[27]

It would be consistent with Cain's point to emphasise the way that wartime circumstances forced governments to behave *as if* they were converts to Keynesian ideas. Recall Walker's observation in 1943:

> In the library of the Australian parliament in Canberra there is a copy of the *General Theory*. The first three hundred pages, in which theory is worked out, are of virgin whiteness; the last eighty pages, with the practical applications, are well thumbed and heavily scored.[28]

Sir Leslie Melville, interviewed by Selwyn Cornish, also drew a line between those attracted by Keynes' policy prescriptions and those agreeing with his theoretical arguments; the former were not necessarily 'Keynesian'. Thus, Sir Leslie was able to recollect which Australian economists were 'Keynesian', and to what degree they were 'Keynesian', by the Second World War.[29] Another economist who looked back, after the Second World War, on the Australian inception of expansionary economics, Douglas Copland, also seemed to distinguish theory from policy:

> At the January 1939 meeting of ANZAAS Giblin and I put forward a resolution advocating the diversion of public works expenditure to strategic defence needs, and although it was received rather timidly it was not long before events themselves forced action along the lines we had been suggesting.[30]

Copland went on to caution advocates of 'full employment' against placing 'too much emphasis on the Keynesian doctrines in circumstances in which it is difficult to apply them':

> Full employment during and since the war has been inevitable and has not been due to any overt act on the part of economists *or* governments, so that there is no particular justification for self-satisfaction in that direction. If one thing is certain, it is this: when full employment ceases to be a reality there will be nothing straightforward about the measures needed to correct the situation.[31]

---

27 N. Cain, 'Australian Keynesian: The Writings of E.R. Walker 1933–36', *ANU Working Papers in Economic History*, 13 (1983): 17–18.
28 R.E. Walker, *From Economic Theory to Policy* (Chicago: University of Chicago Press, 1943), 72.
29 S. Cornish, 'Sir Leslie Melville: An Interview', 18–19.
30 D. Copland, *Expansion and Inflation* (Melbourne: Cheshire, 1951), 24.
31 Ibid., 25–6.

Copland doubted, in 1950, that the lay public who believed in full employment had any understanding of the Keynesian measures: 'We have already seen him object when orthodox Keynesian theory, namely high taxation in a boom, hurts him.'[32]

This alternative way of narrating the Keynesian revolution differentiates the theoretical conversion of economists from their endorsement, under well-defined circumstances, of certain policy prescriptions. Coombs' doubts about *The General Theory* were thus no obstacle to his pragmatic support, from 1939 onwards, for macroeconomic policies that managed effective demand in order to employ all available resources.

Further insights based on the theory/policy distinction can be found in a study of the Labour Movement. Kuhn argues that Labour intellectuals were strongly disposed to welcome any theory of the capitalist economy that laid emphasis on the problem of effective demand.[33] Labour leaders looked not to Marx but to the economists of 'underconsumption' such as J.A. Hobson. In mapping this theoretical tradition Kuhn casts Hobson in the 'real school' of underconsumption theory – concerned with income distribution – and Keynes in the 'monetary school' – concerned more with monetary policies. One might argue with such a classification of the mercurial Keynes, but Kuhn's underlying point is that Labour Movement intellectuals argued both versions of 'underconsumption' theory and, in doing so, found convergence with the populist economics that depicted the evils of 'Money Power'.[34]

Though Labour Movement leaders in the 1930s could have cited Keynes in support of the expansionary policies that they favoured, they rarely did so until after the publication of *The General Theory,* argues Kuhn. He cites 'the suspicion of the profession that had been engendered by its behaviour during the Depression, and the participation of some of its foremost representatives in the preparation of the Premiers' Plan'.[35] A number of events helped to reconcile the 'Laborites' to the academic economist: the publication of *The General Theory* gave theoretical respectability to the advocates of expansion – Laborites and others; the Report of the Royal Commission on Money and Banking endorsed Keynes' and others' arguments for greater political accountability of finance capital (though there remained significant differences as to how to effect that accountability); and W.B. Reddaway's Keynesian analysis led him to advise the Arbitration Court in 1937 to grant a basic wage increase in order to dampen employers' inflationary optimism. Kuhn confines his story to the opinions and

---
32   Ibid., 26.
33   R. Kuhn, 'Labour Movement Economic Thought in the 1930s: Underconsumptionism and Keynesian Economics', *Australian Economic History Review,* 28 (September 1988).
34   Ibid., 59.
35   Ibid., 64–5.

actions of the leaders of the Labour Movement. Thus, he tells us nothing about the reception of Keynesian ideas in the non-Labor governments led by Lyons and then Menzies. However, Kuhn does note that Labor and non-Labor were converging around a Keynesian centre – at which point stood such figures as Bertram Stevens and Ronald Walker.[36] From the point of view of moderate Labor leaders, this was a welcome development – the tensions between Capital and Labour seemed to be eased by Keynes' theory and policy prescription. Kuhn's narrative of the Keynesian revolution thus brings us back to the mythical resonances of the phrase 'Keynesian revolution'. That is, Kuhn's account makes it clear that Keynes was read as addressing the political anxieties of Labour Movement leaders who were struggling against a popular economics still saturated with Douglas Credit theory and concerns about 'Money Power'. The phrase 'Keynesian revolution' persists as shorthand for an ideological conjuncture, when Capital and Labour seemed to be finding a new formula for peaceful coexistence. In *Trial Balance,* Coombs gave expression to such a memory – Keynesian analysis 'seemed to bypass the most divisive issues within our society'.[37]

The war economy and the 'Keynesian revolution'

In a policy-focused telling of the story of the Keynesian revolution, the point is to define 'Keynesian' contextually. One way to do this is to pay attention to Keynes' 1940 pamphlet, *How to Pay for the War*. Keynes' preface sensitises us to the political issues of the Australian government's war-inspired policies of economic expansion.

Coombs' publishers cut from the draft of *Trial Balance* words that illuminate the politics of war finance. For example, when Coombs wrote that the F and E Committee 'progressively gave the economic planning of the war an essentially Keynesian character', he had added the words 'but success in establishing this character was not immediately or easily won'.[38] What did he mean? One possible answer to that question can be found in Maddock and Penny's study of the F and E Committee, which draws attention to the issue of how to distribute the burden of financing a larger government budget.[39] In neither the published nor the draft version of *Trial Balance* did Coombs comment on the redistributive impact of the Menzies and Curtin governments' approach to the war economy.

---

36   Ibid., 70.
37   H.C. Coombs, *Trial Balance* (Melbourne: Macmillan, 1981), 146.
38   H.C. Coombs, *Trial Balance,* unpublished typescript in the author's possession.
39   R. Maddock and J. Penny, 'Economists at War: The Financial and Economic Committee 1939–44', *Australian Economic History Review,* 23 (March 1983).

From the point of view of any historian who wishes to trace the 'Keynesian' character of both policy advice and policy this was a significant omission, because in *How to Pay for the War* (1940) Keynes had given prominence to his recommendations' consideration of distributive social justice.[40]

Keynes argued for an explicit political pitch for the British population's consent to the privations of war. 'In peace time … the size of the cake depends on the amount of work done. But in war time the size of the cake is fixed. If we work harder, we can fight better. But we must not consume more.'[41] How to get the public to swallow this inescapable economic truth? Keynes admitted that in his first thoughts on the war economy – three articles in *The Times* in November 1939 – he had ignored this issue, for he had been

> mainly concerned with questions of financial technique and did not secure the full gain in social justice for which this technique opened the way. In this revision … I have endeavoured to snatch from the exigency of war positive social improvements. The complete scheme now proposed, including universal family allowances in cash, the accumulation of working-class wealth under working class control, a cheap ration of necessaries, and a capital levy (or tax) after the war, embodies an advance towards economic equality greater than any which we have made in recent times.[42]

The concern for social justice was not at the forefront of Australian economists' public consideration of war finance issues. When four Australian economists – Butlin, Critchley, McMillan and Tange – reviewed the first 20 months of the war economy in 1941, they took little interest in the political question that had impressed its importance on Keynes – whether a program of social justice was essential to winning popular consent to the war economy. Butlin and his colleagues decided to leave to others a study of the distributional effects of wartime taxes. They could not ignore completely the political challenges of wartime economics, but where Keynes laid out a program that might woo the masses, Butlin and his colleagues evinced a fear and loathing of the public. Not for them Keynes' confident appeal to the public's interest in what he called 'social justice'. Such a phrase was not in the four authors' vocabulary. Rather, they expressed fear of the public's irrationality:

> [M]ost are ready to be carried away by muddled catch-cries. The economic superstition which passes for theory about the mysterious

---

40   For British discussion of the social justice issues of Keynes' pamphlet see B. Littleboy, 'The Wider Significance of *How to Pay for the War*', *History of Economics Review*, 25 (Winter–Summer, 1996); and J. King, 'Oxford versus Cambridge on *How to Pay for the War*: A Comment on Littleboy', *History of Economics Review*, 27 (Winter, 1998).
41   J.M. Keynes, *How to Pay for the War* (London: MacMillan, 1940), 4.
42   Ibid., iii–iv.

virtues of the Commonwealth Bank, the sedulously cultivated doctrine of 'maintain private spending', and the indestructible faith in unlimited idle resources, make it extremely difficult for any uncourageous government to avoid inflationary finance. Reinforcing the faith in witch words are the natural disinclination to face unpleasant readjustments of living habits, and the equally natural tendency to identify the interest of one's class with those of the community.[43]

Butlin and his colleagues favoured taxation as a method of war finance, but they did not declare support for any particular mix of taxes and so, unlike Keynes, they declined to let the problem of political consent to the war economy shape their consideration of that economy's fiscal techniques. When they turned, unavoidably, to the question of how to win popular consent to restrictions on consumption, the four Australian economists could only appeal in the most general terms to the necessity for government 'propaganda'[44] — a term whose lame centrality to their discourse passed unnoticed by whoever compiled the book's index.

Australia Foots the Bill thus departed significantly from its Keynesian precedent — *How to Pay for the War* — in the paucity of its political and social vision, and in its effective refusal to consider the psychological and ideological underpinning of a war economy. We might say that in being so apolitical, these economists were 'essentially unKeynesian'. That is, until the last few pages of their book. There, Butlin and his colleagues *did* express an opinion about the Menzies Government's taxes — they were too regressive, and this was 'inefficient'. More money could be raised if the government would target the better off. As well, the economists were critical of the risk of inflation courted by the Menzies Government's decision to use loans from the Commonwealth Bank. To counter the inflationary effects of this increase in the money supply, Australians should be required to set aside some of their money until after the war. Less well off consumers could be invited to divert their expenditure into 'contributory unemployment and old-age insurance and similar social services'. Whatever was done to siphon off the public's money, its impact should be progressive: 'Any scheme of finance which does not conform to these principles is not a Keynes Plan.'[45]

If progressiveness in taxation and in compulsory levies was the essence of Keynesian fiscal policy at this time, then we are in a position to mark one of the

---

43   S. Butlin, T. Critchley, R. McMillan and A. Tange, *Australia Foots the Bill* (Sydney: Angus and Robertson, 1941), 10.
44   Ibid., 71.
45   Ibid., 122.

7. Coombs the Keynesian

limits of Keynesian influence in Australia. According to Maddock and Penny, the F and E Committee's 'commitment to equity was never really transferred into policy' by the Menzies Government:

> Suggestions for income taxation increases made considerably less progress than the Committee had hoped, with indirect taxes assuming a correspondingly more important role. Schemes for a national minimum income or unemployment insurance also made little headway.[46]

Whether Australian fiscal policy during the war ever became as 'progressive' as Keynes hoped is a matter that could be debated. Butlin and Schedvin made no explicit evaluation of this point in their *War Economy 1942–5*. They note merely that the Curtin Government lowered the taxation threshold to encompass low and middle income earners, while gathering a higher proportion of net company income as well.[47] Rob Watts' negative evaluation of the Curtin Government's approach to social equity is based on the former fact.[48]

Once again, our judgment of the reality and thoroughness of the 'Keynesian revolution' in wartime economic policy is dependent on our definition of 'Keynesian'.

Post-war blueprints

Finally, the theme of Coombs as Keynesian exemplar can be filled out by referring to the Keynesian provenance of some of Coombs' (among others) schemes to reconstruct capitalism along more socially equitable lines, chiefly by committing governments to practicable policies of 'full employment'. I make two kinds of criticism of this theme: we should not ignore Coombs' essays on future possibilities, which owe nothing to Keynes; and in the politics of the 'full employment' crusade, there is no clear Keynesian line.

Coombs did not enlarge, in any document that I have seen, on his remark that Wootton's 'lament for economics' was 'unanswerable'. However, I see a resonance with Wootton in Coombs' 1942 paper to a meeting of the Economic Society of Australia and New Zealand. His experience of being director of Rationing, since the beginning of 1942, deepened his sympathy for the thought

---

46   Maddock and Penny, 'Economists at War', 39. W. Coleman, S. Cornish and A. Hagger, *Giblin's Platoon: The Trials and Triumph of the Economist in Australian Public Life* (Canberra: ANU E Press, 2006) discusses the politics of economic policy at this moment, commenting that 'the inability to implement a politically acceptable policy of war finance was the principal reason for the failure of the Menzies and Fadden governments … Labor attacked the Menzies and Fadden Governments unmercifully on the grounds that their financial and economic policies – including the compulsory loan – were inequitable' (p. 193).
47   S.J. Butlin and C.B. Schedvin, *War Economy: 1942–45* (Canberra: Australian War Memorial, 1977), 578.
48   R. Watts, *The Foundations of the National Welfare State* (Sydney: Allen and Unwin, 1987).

that 'experts' might determine more rationally than markets the allocation of society's resources. Just as *Lament for Economics* had argued that economists made far too much of the sovereignty of the utility-maximising consumer, so too had Coombs witnessed and indeed brought about the practical attenuation of consumer choice under wartime rationing. Wootton had written that

> the really fundamental choices are made by those who decide what options to put before us. We never knew that we wanted cars and gramophones and cellophane wrappings until these things were actually produced, and we found ourselves buying them.[49]

In her view, 'the right of choice can be an affliction just as much as a privilege'.[50] Coombs applauded the way that rationing relieved consumers from that affliction. Was it not possible, Coombs asked, that wartime arrangements demonstrated a better way for allocative decisions to be made – the expert estimation of people's needs? 'The economist has always tended to discount the value of expert opinion as a proper basis for action in economic fields', he suggested. He put it to his audience that consumers' sense of value was, to a significant degree, artificially constructed by advertising. It was time that economists dethroned the consumer from his/her bogus sovereignty and considered a more rational mechanism for the allocation of resources. Wartime management of the economy was already demoting those unreliable and irrational figures, the private investors; now rationing had begun to rationalise consumer behaviour. He asked: 'Will we have a place for the estimation of people's needs, of objective standards by appeal to experts, and will we find that production can be guided, with the maximum social benefits, by objective standards rather than by the private motive?' Leaving that provocative question unanswered, Coombs nonetheless hailed rationing as 'the application to the social problem of cooperative principles'.[51]

Such opinions are not easy to contain within a formula which characterises Coombs as a leading figure in the Keynesian revolution. We might rather call this the Fabian Coombs. In contrast, there can be no doubt of the Keynesian inspiration of Coombs' 'positive approach' to the international discussions about trade liberalisation. Coombs set out to persuade political leaders in Australia and abroad that dependent economies such as Australia could accept the United States' wish for free trade if the United States would, in turn, commit to domestic policies of full employment. If global 'effective demand' was sustained by American imports, then all trading nations could be 'positive' about protecting their domestic markets less.

---

49 Wootton, *Lament For Economics*, 203.
50 Ibid., 234.
51 'The Economic Implications of Rationing', n.d., Coombs Papers, National Archives of Australia (NAA) CRS M448/1/179.

7. Coombs the Keynesian

What, in Keynes' view, was the relationship between trade policies and full employment? When nations afflicted by the Depression had got together in London in 1933, Keynes had dismissed as a 'waste of time' the 'pious resolutions concerning the abatement of tariffs, quotas and exchange restrictions'. Protection policies he saw as symptoms, not causes. Symptoms of what? Of popular economic insecurity. In *The General Theory* Keynes had argued that if policy-makers focused on maintaining effective demand they need not be so worried about keeping a favourable balance of payments. Keynes was highly critical of an economic orthodoxy – associated with Britain's dominance within the global economy – that, in order to keep the nation a net creditor in its financial dealings with the rest of the world, it was justified to allow internal interest rates to rise (attracting other nation's currencies) and to push wages (a major cost of production) down. High domestic interest rates and low wages enabled a nation to attract more currency than it spent. In pre-Keynesian orthodoxy this combination of policies had been thought 'financially sound'. Alternative ways to maintain a positive balance of payments, such as altering the value of the currency or restricting the flow of money in and out of the country were not so 'sound', according to orthodox opinion, because they compromised the sanctity of the pound sterling as a medium in which the value of other currencies was to be measured. To Keynes the folly of this high interest/low wages orthodoxy had been demonstrated in the economic stagnation of the 1920s and 1930s. Recovery from the Depression would have been quicker had interest rates been kept low (to encourage investment), had governments spent freely and had the value of wages been maintained (to encourage spending on the products from which investors hoped to profit). If such recovery policies caused a nation's balance of payments to fall into the negative, then either this was a short-term problem which should be tolerated, or, if the problem persisted, it was better to change the value of the currency or to intervene in the flow of money in and out of the nation.

Nations that refused to manipulate the value of their currency and that wished to avoid the social upheavals of a high interest/low wages strategy had only one option, Keynes pointed out in the penultimate chapter of *The General Theory* – aggressive trade policies. But aggressive trade policies required some nations to fail if others were to succeed, giving rise to 'increasingly internecine' international relations – war and/or increased protectionism. Keynes insisted that it was therefore a mistake for governments to define the national interest too much in terms of defending their balance of payments. Better to make it the primary objective of economic policy to set interest rates and government expenditure at levels that would encourage investment, employment and consumer spending consistent with full employment. While the resulting prosperity of the domestic market would stimulate imports, this would be balanced by the simultaneous stimulation of the export trade. In a brief and isolated remark on the possible future of international trade, Keynes foreshadowed, in very broad terms, Coombs' 'positive approach':

> And it is the *simultaneous pursuit* of these policies by all countries together which is capable of restoring economic health and strength internationally, whether we measure it by the level of domestic employment or by the volume of international trade.[52]

Though Coombs' positive approach was of Keynesian inspiration, Keynes' internationalism, during the war, was *tactically* at odds with that of Coombs. Preoccupied with arguing for his International Clearing Union, Keynes waited until after the war before he promoted his views about trade policy. His sympathy for American free trade proposals, according to Harrod,[53] did not crystallise until late in 1945, when Keynes heard American government officials explain the trade policies they would expect Britain to endorse if the American public was to support lending Britain billions of dollars for reconstruction. Coombs recalled that Keynes was known to be rather contemptuous of economists who took a great interest in trade policy.[54] For Keynes, the paramount issue for those designing the post-war global economy was currency. Britain had damaged the social fabric of capitalism, thought Keynes, by trying to maintain sterling as the currency in which much of the world's trading bills were paid. It was not necessary, he argued during the war, for any one nation's currency to be the pre-eminent medium of post-war international exchange. Keynes' proposed International Clearing Union would have created a genuinely international currency, and it would have set up mechanisms by which no single country could hold so much of that unit of exchange that other nations had insufficient for their own buying and selling. His scheme can be interpreted as recognising the impossibility of Britain maintaining hegemony over the global economy, while attempting to make it unnecessary (and indeed impossible) for the United States to succeed to that hegemonic position.

Keynes' diplomatic endeavours in this cause failed, but his pursuit of them determined his immediate response to Coombs' 'positive' approach to trade policy. Coombs met Keynes in London in June 1943, dining in a restaurant off Piccadilly and finding him 'stimulating and charming'. But a subsequent exchange of letters did not produce agreement about how Britain and her Dominions should approach the foreseeable agenda of international discussions

---

52 J.M. Keynes, *The General Theory of Employment, Interest and Money* (London: Macmillan, 1936), 349 (emphasis added).
53 R. Harrod, *The Life of John Maynard Keynes* (London: Pelican, 1972), 721–2.
54 H.C. Coombs, conversation with the author, 2 September 1995.

on currency, trade and employment.[55] On 3 September 1943, Keynes assured Coombs that although 'we do not differ about the importance of the subject [of employment]', they differed in their tactics:

> [A]t this stage more is likely to be achieved by tackling the problem of unemployment indirectly than by calling an international conference, which might find itself overmuch concerned with what were little better than pious resolutions … though it is quite possible that at some later stage, when the ground has been more fully prepared, a conference of this kind, or possibly one of even wider scope, might be of help both in educating public opinion in the various countries and in facilitating the international acceptance of whatever plans may ultimately be agreed upon in the monetary, commodity, commercial and investment fields.[56]

Keynes' sympathy for Coombs' 'positive approach' never made him their wartime advocate. Keynes' focus was on how to modify the American proposals for a Stabilisation Fund so that they did not recreate the constraints, on governments facing unemployment, of the old gold standard. To advocate an international commitment to full employment, to a New Deal administration on the political defensive for its leanings towards 'socialism', would have seemed to him an additional burden on British diplomacy. Indeed, the Australian emphasis on 'full employment' as a condition of free trade was seen by some North Atlantic officials as Australia's ingenious, but disingenuous, way to avoid the challenge of free trade. British officials such as Keynes could not afford to be seen to be obdurate on trade policy if they were to bargain successfully with the Americans on the design of post-war currency arrangements.

My final comparison of Coombs' and Keynes' 'blueprints' concerns wages. In drafting the White Paper on Full Employment in 1944–45, Keynes' followers in the Department of Post-War Reconstruction, including Coombs, were attempting to solve one of the unsolvable mysteries of Keynesian economics: in an economy in which the demand for labour slightly exceeds supply, how would governments limit trade unions' pursuit of higher money-wages? Without an answer to that question, 'full employment' would probably bring with it both inflation and crises in the balance of payments.

Lord Kahn, Keynes' colleague, has stalked this issue through Keynes' published and unpublished writings, concluding that Keynes' thoughts on the money-wage problem were 'unsystematic and unsatisfactory'. As Kahn pointed out, wage discipline had hardly been threatened by Depression levels of employment, when Keynes was writing *The General Theory*; when war made labour scarce, it

---

55   Ibid. I am grateful to Sean Turnell for sharing with me his copies of these letters, which are to be found in British Treasury records, Public Records Office (London) T 247/84 15587.
56   Keynes to Coombs, 3 September 1943, NAA CP 43/114311324/1.

also supplied extraordinary political instruments for labour discipline. In a 1943 debate with Friedrich von Hayek, Keynes acknowledged that it 'remains to be seen' whether 'a capitalist country is doomed to failure because it will be found impossible in conditions of full employment to prevent a progressive increase in wages.' In correspondence in 1943 and 1944, he suggested that the problem was not one for economic theory but for politicians to solve.[57] When the Australian White Paper on Full Employment appeared in 1945, Keynes remarked to S.G. McFarlane, secretary to the Australian Treasury: 'One is also, simply because one knows no solution, inclined to turn a blind eye to the wages problem in a full employment economy.'[58]

Coombs and his colleagues did not turn a blind eye. Stimulated by another of Keynes' Cambridge colleagues, Joan Robinson, their early drafts of the White Paper explored the political economy of wage earnings in the new social order. However, the political sensitivities of the Labor Cabinet forbade all but cursory mention of full employment capitalism's most important problem – the abandonment of capitalism's discipline over the working class, the threat of unemployment.[59] Perhaps this omission is what helps to make the White Paper Keynesian – just as Keynes had nothing constructive to say about wage and work discipline, so did the Curtin Government, unlike Coombs and his colleagues, prefer silence on an issue so provocative to Labor's constituency. Thus, Coombs' comment in *Trial Balance* that Keynesian analysis 'seemed to by-pass the most divisive issues within our society'[60] takes on a more ironic and even critical meaning.[61]

Conclusion

I began by suggesting that autobiographical accounts of the impact of *The General Theory* can be understood as myths of youthful, critical and relevant Reason. I then reviewed some other ways of telling the story of *The General Theory*'s reception, and I suggested that the adjective 'Keynesian' begged the distinction between

---

57 For references to Keynes see R. Kahn, 'On Re-reading Keynes', *Proceedings of the British Academy*, 60 (1974), 387–8.
58 J.M. Keynes, *The Collected Writings of John Maynard Keynes Vol XXVII* (London: Macmillan, 1980); Keynes to S.G. McFarlane, 5 June 1945.
59 S. Cornish, *Full Employment in Australia: The Genesis of a White Paper*, Research Paper in Economic History, No. 1 (Canberra: Department of Economic History, ANU, 1971).
60 Coombs, *Trial Balance*, 146.
61 I have examined the Labor Government's consideration of this issue in the context of the drafting of the White Paper in T. Rowse, 'Full Employment and the Discipline of Labour: A Chapter in the History of Australian Social Democracy', *The Drawing Board: An Australian Review of Public Affairs*, 1, no. 1 (July 2000), 1–13, www.australianreview.net/journal/v1/n1/rowse.html; 'Curtin and Labor's Full Employment Promise'. Seminar Paper, 'From Curtin to Coombs: War and Peace in Australia', 25 March 2003, Curtin University of Technology, john.curtin.edu.au/events/seminar2003_rowse.html.

supporting Keynes' theoretical innovations and being attracted to his policy solutions. To what extent was Coombs 'Keynesian' by theoretical conviction, and to what extent 'Keynesian' by force of policy circumstances and opportunities? The evidence from the correspondence is admittedly fragmentary, but it does not support a story of Coombs' rapid theoretical conversion to an economics of hope, reason and joy. I have noted, with some sympathy, a way of telling the story of the 'Keynesian revolution' that puts the emphasis less on theoretical conversion than on force of circumstances: the war demanded expansionary policies. Recall Wootton's point that economists had been deprived by Keynes' arguments of any firm theoretical conviction about the postulate of scarcity. Could we not say that the war economy compelled governments and economists to decide that 'scarcity' was farther away than anyone had dared, in peacetime, to suppose? The phrase, 'Keynesian revolution', implies a rationalist view of history, raising theory over circumstance and understating the Second World War's contribution to resolving (or perhaps deferring) economists' doubts about the cogency, relevance and authority of their discipline.

I would like to differentiate my approach to 'the Keynesian revolution' from that of Selwyn Cornish.[62] Cornish proposes a tension in the making of public policy between adherence to Keynesian theory and susceptibility to political exigencies. Thus 'as with the Labor government, so with the Coalition, political dogma and election priorities, rather than Keynesian economics, exercised the minds of policy makers'.[63] For this to be a sustainable framework, however, Cornish would have to be able to specify the 'Keynesian' prescription for each of the policy conjunctures which he analyses. He is unable to do so because, as Cornish points out, in neither his definition of the objectives of good policy – full employment without inflation – nor his indication of possible means to determine aggregate demand was Keynes clearly prescriptive, though it is plausible to argue that for Keynes 'full employment' usually meant unemployment of 3 per cent. The burden of demonstrating that a policy is/was *not* 'Keynesian' tends to fall, in Cornish's analysis, on adducing two kinds of evidence: material showing that politicians took notice of sectional interests when making policy; and quotes from reputable economists (Meade, Perkins, Arndt, Coombs) complaining that such policies strayed from what they understood to be Keynesian orthodoxy. In the post-war years, up to the mid-1950s, such economists characteristically complained that more fiscal and monetary *restraint* was needed to curb the inflationary tendencies evident in high levels of demand. Cornish is unable to show – only to assert – that these economists were truly 'Keynesian' in their identification of the trade-off between inflation and unemployment. The precise definitions of 'full employment' and of 'inflation' are essentially political;

---

62 S. Cornish, 'The Keynesian Revolution in Australia: Fact or Fiction?', *Australian Economic History Review*, 33, no. 2 (1993), 64.
63 Ibid., 64.

equally, our notion of a successfully managed employment-inflation trade-off is essentially contestable. Economists' opinions about these matters are of great historical interest, but they do not bind us to any view about what policy instruments, rates of inflation and rates of unemployment are truly Keynesian and what are not. In the absence of clear prescriptions by Keynes, we are entitled to be sceptical before any invocation of the great economist as an arbiter of the degree to which a specific policy is 'Keynesian'.

My understanding of the relationship between 'politics' and 'economics' thus differs from Cornish's in that I see no basis to judge the former from the standpoint of the latter. To judge policy from the standpoint of its fidelity to a theory or a theorist is a way of thinking which arouses my curiosity as an historian, but I see no good reason why, as an historian, I should see in the contingencies of 'politics' betrayal of the purity of 'economics'.

Let me further illustrate my point. I differ from Cornish in my reading of Coombs' paper 'Australia's Ability to Avoid Booms and Depressions'.[64] We agree that Coombs was arguing that the experience of post-war economic management had revealed the practical weakness and/or political unavailability of some instruments of macroeconomic policy foreshadowed in the White Paper (such as large public works and schemes for the stabilisation of export incomes). However, Cornish does not point out that Coombs was equally concerned to show that other instruments remained, in his opinion, effective and politically available. He pointed to 'automatic' stabilisers, such as consumer spending. 'So long as people get incomes they tend to spend approximately the same proportion of it.' Social security and taxation policies could also be aimed at further stabilising consumption, he hoped. Governments' spending on consumption goods (such as health and education) was another stabilising factor. Though private investment was volatile, its gyrations were becoming more predictable, with new government surveys of business intentions, and the joint stock company was a form of private capital capable of longer-term development planning. Could not private investment be encouraged by tax incentives? The government, for social reasons unlikely to be challenged, was committed to a certain volume of house construction. Finally, the spending by governments' nationalised industries was a factor for stability.

This list indicates a Keynesianism seasoned in the practicalities of politics and administration. Its author celebrated progress – 'we are certainly better equipped than ever before to deal with economic fluctuations.' Coombs' survey of practicable policy concluded that 'the difficulties are primarily political and social rather than economic and technical'. When Cornish quotes this conclusion – 'It is not always politically practicable to do things which economically appear

---

64 H.C. Coombs, 'Australia's Ability to Avoid Booms and Depressions', *Economic Papers*, 8 (1948).

necessary'[65] — we should not understand it as Coombs endorsing Cornish's generalised tension between the 'economic' and the 'political'. For it is quite clear that for Coombs the possibility of doing 'economically necessary' things was *no less an effect of politics* than the impossibility or difficulty of doing other things. Politics never presents economic rationality with an open and unlimited palate of options, but nor do any useable options in economic management exist outside of political circumstances. It is not a matter of getting politics out of the way of economics, as Cornish's antithesis implies, but of working out politically appropriate instruments of economic management. This essay has suggested that there is no theoretical formula which can predictively encompass the contingencies of *Keynesian politics*.

It is therefore fitting to close a paper on the contextual political meanings of the phrase 'Keynesian revolution' by quoting the most ironical Australian Keynesian of all, Trevor Swan. In 'The Economic Interpretation of J M Keynes',[66] he delighted in distinguishing Keynes' theoretical acuity from his political banality:

> the fact is that the heretical doctrines of *The General Theory of Employment, Interest and Money* are even more revolutionary than their author conceives them to be … it is in the direction of revolution that a realistic interpretation of the arguments of *The General Theory* points.[67]

War took all participant nations 'in the direction of revolution'. War necessitated the rapid introduction of a new politics of the economy; a reconsideration of the social contract, and new controls over investment and consumption, approaching a condition which Keynes called — in a teasing adjective — 'socialisation'. The outcomes of such experiments were not predictable in any economic theory. If I had to make a case that Coombs was an exemplary Keynesian, I would point not to any theoretical conviction nor to any policy preference but to Coombs' willingness — like Keynes in *How to Pay for the War* — to make political innovation integral to his conceptions of economic rationality.

---

65   Coombs cited by Cornish, 'The Keynesian Revolution in Australia: Fact or Fiction?', 50.
66   T. Swan, 'The Economic Interpretation of J M Keynes', *The Australian Quarterly*, 11, no. 1 (March 1939), 62–70.
67   Ibid., 70.

8

Sir John Crawford and Agriculture and Trade

David Lee

Sir John Grenfell Crawford was one of the most significant of the seven dwarfs — the group of diminutive senior Commonwealth public servants active in the period from the 1940s to the 1960s. Agriculture and trade, the two issues with which Crawford engaged as a Commonwealth public servant, were closely connected. In 1948–49, immediately before Crawford was appointed secretary of the Department of Commerce and Agriculture, agricultural commodities still amounted to 85 per cent of Australia's exports. Moreover, wool alone made up between 40 and 50 per cent of the total in the 1940s and 1950s. Until the Second World War the domestic aspects of Australian agriculture were matters within the exclusive concern of the states, while the marketing of agricultural exports was a matter for the Commonwealth. But during the Second World War, when it acquired a monopoly of income taxes under the *Uniform Taxation Act* and with the aid of the defence power, the Commonwealth became much more active and interventionist on the domestic aspects of agriculture as well its trade aspects. As agricultural economist and policy-maker, Crawford's innovation was to integrate agricultural economics within public administration and policy making.

This chapter will discuss how Crawford's formative years equipped him for his leadership role in the Commonwealth Public Service and then examine how his contribution as a public servant to agricultural and trade policy qualified him to belong to the elite grouping of Australia's most powerful mandarins.

The formative years

John Crawford was born in Hurstville, Sydney, in 1910, the tenth of 12 children of Henry Crawford, a stationmaster.[1] The young Crawford was forced to leave school at the age of 16 when his father left his employment in the railways, failed in an effort to set up a commercial enterprise, and was forced to labour in a quarry. Returning to school in 1927, John Crawford gained the Leaving

---

1   R.M. Crawford, 'My Brother Jack: Background and Early Years', in L.T. Evans and J.D.B. Miller, eds, *Policy and Practice: Essays in Honour of Sir John Crawford* (Canberra: Australian National University Press, 1987), 1.

Certificate and was employed by day as a junior clerk in the New South Wales Public Service while studying at the University of Sydney for Bachelor's (1932) and Master's (1940) degrees in economics. Crawford taught in schools in Stanmore and Temora before holding a research fellowship and part-time lectureship in rural economics at the University of Sydney in the middle to late 1930s. The Depression left its mark on the young man – he was without a job for several months and sympathy for his stationmaster father having to work in a quarry left him with a 'broad sympathy with underdogs'.[2]

In Sydney in the 1930s Crawford was imbued with Keynesian economic ideas, a set of ideas which provided an intellectual framework for all of the dwarfs. In 1938 he wrote *The National Income of Australia* with Colin Clark.[3] In this book Crawford and Clark suggested:

> the framework of a policy which will mitigate or even overcome depression arising from the fall in export income. This is a planned expansion of public works to keep pace as far as possible with the decline in export income … it may be desirable that Commonwealth and State Governments should deliberately plan for budget deficits.[4]

A reviewer in the *Economic Journal* described the book as combining 'skilled research with something of the excitement of a detective novel and an occasional flavour of the political pamphlet'.[5]

Crawford's predisposition towards government intervention in rural affairs and in the broader economy was strengthened after 1938 when he won a Commonwealth Fund Fellowship to the United States. From 1938 to 1940, Crawford studied American agriculture intensively. He saw first hand the influence of active rural policies by the US Federal Government and was inspired to follow the American example by establishing a Bureau of Agricultural Economics as an agency of the Australian Government. J.D.B. Miller later commented on the importance of Crawford's American sojourn:

> It was the vitality of American society which excited him; and the fact that he had gone to the United States for postgraduate work, rather than Britain, as most Australian academics then did, influenced much of his thinking about the two countries.[6]

After the outbreak of the Pacific War, Crawford was appointed as rural adviser to the Commonwealth Department of War Organisation of Industry and in the next

---

2 Ibid., 14.
3 C. Clark and J.G. Crawford, *The National Income of Australia* (Sydney: Angus and Robertson, 1938).
4 Ibid., 107.
5 Review in *The Economic Journal*, 49, no. 193 (March 1939), 142.
6 J.D.B. Miller, 'The Man', in Evans and Miller, eds, *Policy and Practice*, 196.

year as Director of Research in the Department of Post-War Reconstruction. In 1945 he became founding director of the Bureau of Agricultural Economics (BAE), which was transferred to the Department of Commerce and Agriculture in 1946.

Sir John Crawford, 1967

Source: National Archives of Australia, A1200, L68147

Director of the Bureau of Agricultural Economics

Crawford's period in Post-War Reconstruction and the BAE coincided with publication of 10 separate reports by the Rural Reconstruction Commission (RRC), a commission established by the Curtin Government in 1943. The reports dealt with soldier settlement, land tenure and environmental issues, social amenities, rural credit and commerce. Although written in the last years of the Second World War, the reports were framed against the conditions of the 1930s rather than wartime developments.[7] Conveying the enthusiasm of the Hot Springs Conference of 1943 that established the Food and Agriculture Organization, they highlighted the government's obligations to raise the levels of nutrition and standards of living of its people, to improve the efficiency of agricultural production and distribution, and to foster international collaboration to achieve those ends. Crawford supported their clear assumption that government should intervene in rural affairs, particularly in marketing.

In a contemporaneous article, he had observed that 'the rural economy was not able, without assistance from the State, to maintain all our farmers and farm workers at a satisfactory living standard'.[8] Crawford was orthodox in the Second World War and early post-war years in believing in the necessity for state intervention at the domestic level. But he also urged that Australia should cooperate with other nations to create conditions internationally where states could improve the living standards of their citizens. In this sense he pursued, in a different way, what European officials such as Jean Monnet were trying to achieve (European economic collaboration to improve standards of living within European states). Later academics would describe the sorts of ideas supported by Crawford as 'embedded liberalism', namely the idea that the only way ahead for the post-war world was to construct the right blend of state, market, and democratic institutions to guarantee peace, inclusion, well-being and stability.[9]

Both the Chifley and Menzies governments, advised by broadly the same mandarins, subscribed to this view. The post-war Labor Government's White Paper on Full Employment had, as its main objective, the attainment of full employment for a growing Australian population with rising standards of living. These objectives required a much higher level of imports. Crawford identified increased agricultural production as a way of earning the export income to pay

---

7   A.W. Martin and J. Penny, 'The Rural Reconstruction Commission 1943–47', *Australian Journal of Politics and History*, 29 (1983), 218–36; T. Whitford and D. Boadle, 'Australia's Rural Reconstruction Commission, 1943–46: A Reassessment', *Australian Journal of Politics and History*, 54, no. 34 (December 2008), 525–45.
8   J.G. Crawford, 'Rural Reconstruction', *Australian Journal of Science*, 5 (October 1943), 37.
9   For example, J.G. Ruggie, 'International Regimes, Transactions and Change: Embedded Liberalism in the Postwar Economic Order', *International Organization*, 36, no. 2 (1982), 379–415.

for these imports. As director of the BAE he recommended to the government ways of achieving this expansion through acceleration of land clearing and land settlement; better stock watering facilities; development of irrigation; improved pest control; more flexible credit facilities; and more orderly marketing arrangements domestically and internationally.

Crawford's framework was accepted not only by the Chifley Labor Government but also by the Country Party. In the immediate post-war period up to 1950, despite the Chifley Government's best efforts, agricultural exports stagnated and markets for Australian exports were secured by bilateral inter-governmental contracts with the United Kingdom, which would be Australia's best customer until the late 1960s.

Permanent secretary

When the Liberal and Country parties came to office in December 1949 under the prime minister, R.G. Menzies, the deputy leader of the Country Party, John McEwen, became minister for Commerce and Agriculture. Crawford was appointed secretary in 1950, an office he held until 1956 when, after a major reorganisation, he came to McEwen's new Department of Trade. Crawford formed a constructive relationship with McEwen and with his department. In doing so, Crawford conducted himself according to the dictum of Sir Paul Hasluck that if any attempt was made by a minister 'to exercise close control over a department in such a way as to make a department the acquiescent echo of a Minister's will, the Service is being debased'. On the other hand, wrote Crawford,

> the Permanent Head has the obligation of the security he enjoys to maintain his intellectual integrity and to make sure that his Minister's policy views are subjected to critical but friendly and constructive analysis. On the other hand, having done his best to persuade his Minister that a proposed line of action is wrong, a Permanent Head must carry out that policy loyally and as efficiently as possible. If he cannot do this a difficult situation can arise, one which might well lead to a change of position, preferably by agreement.[10]

When Crawford took up his position as secretary of the Department of Commerce and Agriculture, administrative responsibility for trade was divided between a protectionist Department of Trade and Customs and a more liberal Department of Commerce and Agriculture, which was responsible for securing

---

10   J.G. Crawford, 'Relations Between Civil Servants and Ministers in Policy Making', *Public Administration*, 19, no. 2 (June 1960), 104.

markets abroad.[11] The Korean War was sparking a worldwide boom in the prices of commodities. A particularly dramatic increase in the price of Australian wool in 1950 and 1951 sparked an import and inflationary boom, which later engendered a significant balance of payments crisis in 1952 when the price of wool and Australia's export income collapsed.

Crawford helped the Menzies Government in two respects, first by representing the Australian delegation at a (British) Commonwealth–United States wool conference in London in September 1950. At this conference he successfully resisted American pressure to abandon the auction system for wool and to purchase Australian wool at ceiling prices. He later described the issue as a policy problem 'out of the blue' and one that imposed a great strain on the department and its permanent head. As he elaborated:

> The auction system for wool is almost certainly the golden calf of the Australian economy, and certainly of the wool industry. Yet there were pressing questions to be answered. They mostly boiled down to this: Was it practicable – politically, legally and economically – to suspend auctions wholly or in part, and were requests for a price ceiling practicable or justified? Who caused the price boom anyhow – the buyer or seller? In all this there was a conflict of known policies: the economic and political importance of maintaining our wool marketing system versus the desire to co-operate internationally if important allies needed our help.[12]

In that same year, Ronald Walker, executive member of the National Security Resources Board (NSRB), invited Crawford to advise the board on how the anticipated outbreak of a major world war might affect Australia's agricultural industries.[13] Menzies had established the NSRB in December 1950 to advise the government on how to rebalance the civil and military economies. As a result of extensive examination, Crawford concluded that, in the event of war, Australia would be called on to supply additional food to India and the countries of South East Asia, whose food supply would be affected. He added that Australia would probably be asked also to fill the gap caused by reduced exports of food from Western Europe to the United Kingdom. Later in the year Crawford visited Britain and the United States to investigate the defence aspects of Australian food production.[14]

---

11   R.P. Deane, *The Establishment of the Department of Trade: A Case Study in Administrative Reorganization* (Canberra: Australian National University Press, 1963).
12   J.G. Crawford, 'The Role of the Permanent Head', *Public Administration*, 13, no. 3 (1954), 161.
13   D. Lee, 'The National Security Planning and Defence Preparations of the Menzies Government, 1950–1953', *War & Society*, 10, no. 2 (October 1992), 123.
14   Savingram no. 28 Crawford to McEwen, 19 July 1951, National Archives of Australia (NAA) A1604/1, 5164 part 1; 'Report on Overseas Discussions – Defence Aspects of Food and Agricultural Policy by J.G. Crawford', n.d. [1951], NAA A1604.1, 51/64 part 2.

On returning to Australia he advised the Menzies Government to urgently develop a concrete program of expanded agricultural production on the basis of complete understanding between the Commonwealth Government, leaders of primary industries and the states. On 26 April 1952, McEwen submitted a five-year plan that was hoped to add £A100,000,000 – or nearly a tenth – to Australia's income and to save £A7,000,000 of imports, particularly of tobacco, cotton and linseed.[15] McEwen's general aim was achieved well before 1957–58. While some of the subsequent increase in agricultural production was attributable to good seasons, the various policy measures recommended by Crawford and administered by the Department of Commerce and Agriculture stimulated enlarged investment in improved farming. Crawford wrote in 1968 that: 'All told the policies of 1952 did contribute to expansion without which the balance of payments situation would undoubtedly have proved even more serious than it has been on occasions in the last fifteen years.'[16]

In 1952, Crawford helped the government to frame a system that established a regime of import licensing which would last until 1960. One anecdote pertaining to Crawford's role in the administration of the import licensing system well illustrates his authority with ministers and his determination to protect his department. In 1957 Crawford was attending a meeting with Prime Minister Menzies, ministers and senior public servants. At this meeting Menzies attacked a deputy secretary from Trade for taking action that had previously been approved by Menzies. Crawford answered the criticism by pointing out that there had been agreement beforehand with Menzies based on a Cabinet decision that Crawford as secretary of the Department of Trade had opposed and then accepted after it had been made. Crawford told Menzies that he was 'fed up' with attacks on his officers for implementing decisions made by ministers. He was prepared to resign and make public his reasons unless the prime minister apologised to the deputy. Menzies did apologise and this ended Menzies' attacks on Crawford's department and its head in that area of policy.[17]

The shift from bilateralism to multilateralism

Crawford's greatest achievement as a senior official in Commerce and Agriculture and, then, Trade was to help both Labor and Liberal–Country party governments manage the transition from a bilateral to a multilateral framework in Australian trade policy. It is first necessary to sketch the historical background in order to put this achievement in context.

---

15 'Australia Sets the Sights', *The Economist*, 26 April 1952, cited in J.G. Crawford, ed., *Australian Trade Policy: 1942–1966* (Canberra: Australian National University Press, 1968), 450.
16 Crawford, ed., *Australian Trade Policy*, 438.
17 D.B. Williams, 'Contributions to Agricultural Economics', in Evans and Miller, eds, *Policy and Practice*, 18.

In reaction to the Depression, Australia in 1932 had signed a trade agreement with the United Kingdom at Ottawa. The Ottawa Agreement was based on the exchange of tariff preferences between Empire (later Commonwealth) countries. The Depression years also saw the emergence of a currency area, the sterling area, to which Australia belonged. Members of the sterling area conducted their trade in sterling, pegged their currencies to the pound, maintained sterling reserves in London and collectively rationed their use of hard currencies such as the US dollar.

When, in 1942, both Britain and Australia signed the Mutual Aid Agreement with the United States (in return for Lend-Lease aid), they both agreed to participate in long-term arrangements under Article VII of the agreement for the reduction of barriers to world trade. Crawford later wrote that '[a]ll major developments in Australian post-war trade policy, at least up to the late 1950s, can be traced back to the commitment in Article VII'.[18]

The Article VII commitments led in due course to the establishment of the General Agreement of Tariffs and Trade (GATT) as a provisional instrument to provide rules for international trade based on the principle of non-discrimination. The GATT was immediately successful in framing rules for, and helping reduce, tariffs on manufactured goods. But agriculture was largely exempted from its rules and, in the early 1950s, this situation was exacerbated when the United States received a waiver from what disciplines there were on agriculture. Doubly irksome for Australia as an agricultural exporting country was the GATT's decision to limit Australia's benefits from imperial preference by a 'no-new preference' rule.[19]

In 1953, the prime minister (Menzies) announced that Australia would be seeking major changes in the GATT to secure flexibility to make changes to the tariff; to gain some relaxation of the GATT's no-new preference rule; and to remedy the imbalance in the GATT by addressing such issues as protection of agricultural subsidies, surplus disposal and state trading. Crawford was successful in gaining some flexibility for the operation of Australia's tariff system with its independent Tariff Board; was unsuccessful in modifying the no-new preference rule; but made some progress in improving the effectiveness of the GATT.[20]

---

18 Crawford, *Australian Trade Policy*, 8. Crawford modified the statement by acknowledging that 'Australia's propensity for fairly high tariffs for some industries [was] not altogether consistent with the spirit of Article VII, although it [was] quite within the framework of tariff-making machinery allowed by GATT'.
19 Under the General Agreement of Tariffs and Trade's (GATT) rules no new preferences could be extended where none existed before and existing preferences could not be widened beyond their October 1946 absolute level.
20 S. Harris, 'Managing Australia's Shift to Multilateralism', in Evans and Miller, eds, *Policy and Practice*, 58–61.

Indeed, Crawford was the driving force in persuading the GATT to adopt a more specific approach against subsidies insofar as his general criticism of agricultural protection culminated in the 1957 Haberler Report. The Haberler Committee was appointed as a result of an Australian initiative in the GATT to review agricultural protectionism as it affected exporters of primary products. This report vindicated what Crawford and others had been saying about agricultural protection by noting how domestic attempts to create price stability created a greater degree of price instability in international markets.[21]

Crawford helped to persuade the Menzies Government to remain supportive of the GATT despite its imperfection and its imbalance as far as Australia's trade interests were concerned. Previously, in 1952, the Menzies Government had debated whether Australia should be looking for some more tightly integrated British Commonwealth economic bloc or moving towards more rapid convertibility of sterling with the US dollar. Crawford advised the government that autarky was impossible for the (British) Commonwealth. Many of the Commonwealth's members, including Australia, were dependent on non-Commonwealth markets for important exports, in Australia's case for wool, wheat and minerals. Crawford later wrote,

> [the] 1952 conference really turned its back on the hopes of some (including those held by the Australian Prime Minister) that the Ottawa road would be further explored, turning the Commonwealth into a more tightly integrated economic unit. The debate was not difficult nor was it prolonged, but it was decisive … simply because the case against was overwhelming.[22]

This advice influenced his attitude to the 1956 review of the Ottawa Agreement. The Commonwealth Prime Ministers' Conference of 1952 had made it clear that adding to the mutual preference structure was not an acceptable option for the Commonwealth as a whole. Moreover, the 1955 GATT Review had decisively rejected Australia's attempt to gain even minor latitude in its enjoyment of preferences. The Menzies Government and its advisers therefore looked at all options in expanding its overseas trade, including the Ottawa Agreement.

Crawford had formed the view by that time that the agreement was imbalanced in Britain's favour. British exports to Australia were expanding much faster than Australian exports to the United Kingdom. Put another way, the market in the United Kingdom for Australian goods was a declining one.[23] Accordingly, on 24 May 1956, Menzies announced that trade discussions would take place with

---

21 Crawford, *Australian Trade Policy*, 133–4.
22 Ibid., 101.
23 Ibid., 321.

British ministers to review the Ottawa Agreement.[24] Crawford and McEwen adopted a clear-eyed bargaining position to these negotiations by being willing to have no agreement at all rather than one in which Britain accepted little or no revision to an agreement deemed to be out of balance. The result was an agreement under which Britain used its best endeavours to maintain imports of Australian wheat and flour to no less than 28 million bushels a year and to reduce the preferential margins granted to British imports.[25] The latter concession was significant in forming part of Crawford's plan to gain negotiating coin in trade negotiations with Japan. Crawford emphasised the symbolic importance of the renegotiation of Ottawa as a signal of Australia's retreat from Empire in the post-war period.

Crawford had always been prescient about Australia's long-term trading interests – in foreseeing the opportunity for Asia to compensate for limited markets in Europe. This was exemplified in a chapter he wrote in a book published in 1938 in which he called for 'economic appeasement' of Japan.[26] The article was written at a time when orthodox opinion was that Australian security would be secured by cooperating with Britain in the Singapore strategy and when Australia was just recovering from a disastrous attempt to shift purchases of imported textiles away from Japan towards the United Kingdom. In the 1938 article, Crawford argued that Australia stood to gain from Japan's peaceful economic expansion and that Japan was already becoming as a trading partner for Australia, what Japan, China and the rest of East Asia might in the future collectively become. The young economist argued for a system of 'collective agreements' to take the place of 'power politics'. By collective agreements he envisaged an acknowledgement of trading rights and freedoms within accepted rules.[27]

In the 1950s, Crawford followed on his earlier thoughts by pressing for a trade agreement with Japan at a time when powerful interest groups in the community and within the bureaucracy were opposed to such a course. Under Article 12 of the Peace Treaty signed by Japan in 1952, Japan was obliged to accord Allied Nations, including Australia, most-favoured-nation status with respect to trade. What would happen in four years time touched a real difficulty for Australia which not only did not accord Japan most-favoured-nation treatment with regard to the tariff but, in addition, extensively discriminated against Japan in its licensing of imports.

---

24 Press statement by R.G. Menzies, 24 May 1956; Crawford, *Australian Trade Policy*, 336–7.
25 Harris, 'Managing Australia's Shift to Multilateralism', 55–8.
26 J.G. Crawford, 'Australia as a Pacific Power', in W.G.K. Duncan, ed., *Australia's Foreign Policy* (Sydney: Angus and Robertson, 1938), 69–121.
27 P. Drysdale, 'The Relationship with Japan: Despite the Vicissitudes', in Evans and Miller, eds, *Policy and Practice*, 66–71.

Crawford was concerned by an outcome after 1956 in which Japan retaliated, as it had during the Trade Diversion dispute of the 1930s, by restricting access of Australian primary products to the Japanese market. At the same time, Crawford well appreciated that the objective of reaching a trade agreement with Japan was affected by powerful currents in Australia, including the bitter legacy of the Pacific War and the concern by Australian manufacturers at having to compete against cheap Japanese imports. As a *Sydney Morning Herald* leading article commented on 17 August 1955, 'Japanese trade is associated in the minds of Australians with cheap labour, price undercutting, shoddy goods and "dumping", just as Japanese "defence policy" still tends to be envisaged in terms of brutal militarism'.[28]

Crawford discounted the idea that Australia could continue to enjoy the advantages of an expanding market in Japan while denying benefits to the Japanese in the Australian market. For one thing, the United States was able to sell Japan wheat from production and surplus stocks; for another, Crawford feared that Japan might give strong preference to synthetics over purchasing wool from Australia.[29] In June 1953, Crawford participated in a meeting of the permanent heads of Commerce and Agriculture, Trade and Customs, External Affairs and the Treasury to prepare a document for the Cabinet Committee on Overseas Commercial Relations being held on 23 June, a document that would be submitted to full Cabinet on 2 July.

Crawford regarded the statement emerging from the heads of department meeting, which urged an easing of the highly restrictive import licensing of Japanese goods, as the 'important document' in the process leading up to trade talks with Japan.[30] The recommended course of action led to a significant increase in Japan's access to the Australian trade market but not towards trade talks with Japan on the basis of non-discriminatory treatment. This was because of the reservation of Frank Meere, comptroller-general of Customs, who argued that further liberalisation was 'impracticable at this stage'; Meere was an ardent advocate of tariff protection.[31]

Cabinet did not respond to a further request for trade talks with Japan made strongly by McEwen and Crawford in January 1954 (elections were scheduled for May 1954). By November of that year, however, Cabinet had agreed to

---

28   *Sydney Morning Herald*, 17 August 1955.
29   Crawford, *Australian Trade Policy*, 352–3.
30   Drysdale, 'The Relationship with Japan', 75; 'Note for Ministers agreed by Departments of Commerce & Agriculture, External Affairs, Trade & Customs and Treasury', 23 June 1953, in Wendy Way, ed., *The Australia–Japan Agreement on Commerce 1957* (Canberra: Australian Government Publishing Service, 1997), 54–8.
31   Drysdale, 'The Relationship with Japan', 75.

proceed to trade talks with Japan. In October 1955, Crawford wrote to Meere with an outline of what he hoped could be achieved in trade negotiations with Japan and commenting:

> I believe that there is some importance in our being amongst the first to initiate talks with the Japanese and also being able to say at G.A.T.T. that we are, in fact, both willing and currently undertaking talks with the Japanese, and I wonder if you could give me a call when you have a chance to look at this.[32]

Crawford hoped that Australia would be able to negotiate fair and reasonable access to the Japanese market in the form of most-favoured-nation treatment on the tariff and non-discriminatory treatment in regard to import licensing.

Crawford's campaign to conclude a trade agreement with Japan was greatly assisted when the Department of Trade and Customs and the Department of Commerce and Agriculture merged in 1956 into a single Department of Trade with Crawford as secretary; customs administration was assigned to a Department of Customs and Excise and the Department of Primary Industry was created at the same time. On 25 October 1956, the acting Trade minister, William McMahon, announced that trade negotiations between Australia and Japan would commence. A year later, a satisfactory outcome was reached. It encompassed non-discriminatory access to Australian markets for Japanese exports; guaranteed access to Japanese markets for Australian primary products and assured safeguards for Australian industry.

The Australia–Japan Agreement on Commerce was a landmark agreement under which, within a decade, Japan would overtake Britain as Australia's major trading partner. The agreement, however, was concluded in the face of hostility from sectional interests who subjected Crawford personally 'to what he has described as the worst personal attack he experienced during his public career'.[33]

Conclusion

In 1960 Crawford left the public service to become in due course vice-chancellor and chancellor of The Australian National University. He built a career as an academic and university administrator which was as successful and influential as his career as a mandarin from 1945 to 1960. J.D.B. Miller has described his essential character in both his bureaucratic and academic careers:

---

32 Crawford to Meere, 14 October 1955, Crawford Papers, National Library of Australia, MS 4514/9/33.
33 Drysdale, 'The Relationship with Japan', 77.

He endeared himself to those with whom he worked because he seemed moderate in opinion though extreme in concentration; because he was essentially fair-minded in his approach to problems; because he liked to help lame dogs over stiles; and because, when roused, he could speak boldly and with much effect.[34]

As public servant and mandarin, his loyal and dispassionate approach to serving government had made him equally valued by both Labor and Liberal–Country party governments, and the ministers he admired most, J.B. Chifley and John McEwen, came from both sides of politics. While he continually searched for agreed principles in politics, his success as a public servant also came from his recognition that politics was the art of the possible. 'He was', as Miller put it,

> A natural politician who knew, almost by instinct, what would work and what would not, whether it was a ploy at a meeting, a resolution which required acceptance, or an overall policy which had to satisfy various groups which normally would not agree with one another.[35]

---

34 Miller, 'The Man', 192.
35 Ibid., 193.

9

Sir Allen Brown: An Exemplary Public Servant

Sir Peter Lawler

Allen Brown was described – I suspect by Fin Crisp – as Nugget Coombs' Vicar-General. This is an insightful and appropriate ecclesial analogy. Allen's appointment as Vicar-General marked the beginning of a 16-year career as one of the key players at the centre of Commonwealth Government administration. This was a watershed time of change in the reach of federal government and the nature of its administrative arrangements. When Coombs was commissioned to create the Department of Post-War Reconstruction, he already knew Allen Brown as a staff member and colleague in the wartime Rationing Commission. He had evidence of Allen's strength as an administrator – just the man to get the machinery of Coombs' ad hoc enterprise up and running for the effective discharge of the varied and nationwide activities assigned to it. Nugget also knew that his Vicar-General could and would as necessary fill the director-general's shoes. He knew Allen was a top-class policy thinker with remarkable vision and a sure sense of the department's specific mission – someone who could help identify and set in motion major initiatives and projects in the service of that mission.

Brown did not meet all the canonical requirements for Vicar-General. He did not have the tonsure and he was not celibate – he had a wife, Hilda, and three children to whom he was devoted. But he was over 25 years of age (33 in fact) and was certainly commendable for the probity of his life, for his prudence, and for his knowledge of the law. He had an excellent academic pedigree: Caulfield Grammar, Wesley College, and Queen's College at the University of Melbourne, from where he gained a Master's degree in law. Better still, he had had the best part of a decade in the real world as a practising, successful and well-liked solicitor in country Victoria. In Post-War Reconstruction and the Prime Minister's Department, Allen Stanley Brown's staff knew him affectionately as ASB. Menzies came quite quickly to refer to him, also affectionately, as Bruno ('Where's Bruno?') or, less frequently, as 'le brun'. Menzies was fond of such tags: 'Black Jack' McEwen was 'le noir'.

Sir Allen Brown, 1958

Source: National Archives of Australia, A1200, L27006

9. Sir Allen Brown

There were two segments of ASB's 16-year career at the centre of Commonwealth administration and political affairs: first, from 1944, some five-and-a-half years as deputy director-general and a few final months as director-general of Post-War Reconstruction; and, second, his 10 crucial years from 1949 to 1959 as permanent head of the Prime Minister's Department. In each of these career segments ASB faced a similar administrative challenge – to create a Department of State. In the one case the department was a temporary creation set apart from regular Commonwealth departments. Few of the staff in Post-War Reconstruction had started their public service careers as telegraph messengers. It was an exciting, vibrant and constantly changing enterprise of young men (and some women), with a mission to promote ways and means for a better Australia. By early 1950, its work was over and it was abolished. In the second case, an existing central department was to be created anew to serve the prime minister and cabinet as one of the key departments at the top level of the departmental hierarchy. As it was, the Prime Minister's Department had been allowed to become something of a non-entity – a mere handful of staff tucked away in a few rooms in West Block. It needed to be thoroughly and permanently transformed. Brown was highly successful in each of these two career segments, but it is for his re-creation of the Prime Minister's Department that he best deserves to be remembered. In this he is a standout amongst the seven dwarfs – whichever seven is identified.

What sort of man was ASB? What was he like to know? Menzies is quoted as saying of Brown, 'He can see further through a brick wall than anyone else I know'. I would add that ASB could also see through people. He has been characterised as a naturally taciturn man with a laconic style of communication. I found him a cheerful, warm, caring, rather unassuming and humble person. He had a nice sense of humour. He was quick to see the droll side of things and would sometimes exploit it to defuse awkward situations. He had a protective amount of cynical streak. Here was a quiet man with great strength of character.

His personal secretary from the early days, Nalda Richards, remembers Brown as a man who never lost his temper and who, when he came as secretary to Prime Minister's in West Block in 1949, would take his turn in preparing morning and afternoon tea for the total staff – gathered in one room. I remember how, as deputy director-general in 1944, ASB batched with three decent but lower-level young public servants in a scruffy flat in Civic. This accommodation was above Charlie Thompson's Chemist Shop; it was known simply but ominously as The Flat. Some thought the deputy director-general should have booked into Beauchamp House or Acton Hotel but others saw the flat as a nice democratic touch.

It was said of one of the dwarfs that he had a tongue barbed with fishhooks and no respect for anybody – an uncharitable caricature surely, but it could apply to more than one of them. But it certainly did not apply to Allen Brown. He was courteous and respectful – and at ease – whether with prime ministers and royals or with the lowliest clerk. I recall how ASB used to joke that when making his final notes after the Cabinet meeting, alone at his little side table in the Cabinet Room, with ministers tucking into food and pouring drinks in the Ante-Room, he would write down 'what he thinks they thought they ought to have said'.

At times ASB was known to indulge in doggerel or word play as, indeed, was Menzies. Researchers in the archives of the Prime Minister's Department will likely come across examples. When the Queen Mother came to Australia in 1958, ASB found favour with her and her entourage. Somehow the Queen Mother must have encountered some of ASB's doggerel and enjoyed it. Later, when calamity struck and the Queen Mother found herself marooned in Mauritius – the cowling having fallen off the engine of the Qantas plane taking her home via South Africa – she called for the solace of some of Sir Allen's 'poetry'. And, solemnly, over the airwaves, went ASB doggerel of doubtful quality. It began: 'A cowling is a piece of tin, To keep an aircraft engine in'; it later featured something about 'When you're in Mauritius, And you're feeling rather vicious'. These anecdotes illustrate something of what ASB was like to know.

Allen Brown deserves great credit for his essential share in the successes of Post-War Reconstruction; not only the large administrative successes such as the Commonwealth Reconstruction Training Scheme, but project and policy successes as with The Australian National University; or in the department's economic section and its White Paper on Full Employment; or in the 'missionaries' that Post-War sent out into various parts of Commonwealth administration.

ASB was decisively involved in two notable projects. Sir William Hudson's name comes to mind when the Snowy Scheme is mentioned, and rightly so, but ASB in Post-War and later as secretary of Prime Minister's played a decisive part in making the scheme happen. He identified its huge possibilities and was an advocate from the very beginning. He then worked with Commissioner Tom Lang to lock in vital United States expertise, and, finally, he was a persuasive adviser with the 1950s Coalition Government to ensure that the Snowy Scheme continued to completion as planned.

The other project I want to underline is of more than passing interest but perhaps less well known. This is Post-War's studies and discussions about the administrative arrangements that ought to be developed to service government at the centre – that is the Prime Minister, the Cabinet and the committees of Cabinet. Chifley, prime minister and treasurer in 1945, felt both the administrative and the political need for an efficient Cabinet Office system and for quality alternative sources of advice in his own department. Allen Brown turned to the British Cabinet Office as a model and to the Cabinet secretary, Sir Norman Brook, for ideas and staff exchanges. So when Chifley appointed ASB in mid-1949 to be secretary of Prime Minister's Department, it was not exactly without preamble or out of a clear blue sky.

When the Coalition Government under Menzies came to power in December 1949, Allen Brown had been secretary of Prime Minister's for only six months. He had already begun to build up staff numbers by transfers from Post-War and especially from its Economic Section. The Coalition had believed, not without reason, that Post-War had harboured a nest of Labor Party supporters. Now they were similarly suspicious of Prime Minister's. This presented a problem with which ASB had to deal.

Brown might have had another problem – old Frank McKenna, the deputy secretary he inherited in Prime Minister's. McKenna had firmly believed that Chifley was going to appoint him as the secretary, so Brown might have had a disaffected deputy secretary on his hands. McKenna had lived through many trials in the Prime Minister's Department – a period of banishment to the Defence Department when the Prime Minister, William Morris Hughes, had purged Catholics from his department in 1917, and various heads of department of indifferent quality.

McKenna had begun his career as a telegraph messenger. He had no academic qualifications, yet he had progressed on-the-job to be an eminent public servant of the old school: dignified; of great courtesy; careful about due process and detail; deploying abundant common sense; shrewd and capable in the cut and thrust of debate; accurate and candid in his assessment of personalities. McKenna's disappointment, when told by Chifley that young Mr Brown from Post-War Reconstruction was to head up Prime Minister's Department, was something ASB could feel with him. ASB told me that Frank had every reason to expect to succeed Strahan and could have filled the position with credit.

The outcome speaks for the human quality of each of these two men. They developed the warmest regard for each other. McKenna saw that young Brown could make the department what it ought to be and what he, McKenna, wanted it to be. McKenna welcomed that and gave ASB whole-hearted support. Brown was always ready to recount with gratitude how Frank had insisted when the election results in December 1949 were clear, that ASB must not, as he was proposing, wait until the new prime minister called him, but should go to the Canberra Airport to welcome his new prime minister. Brown went. Menzies was appreciative. Allen Brown was off to a good start with his prime minister.

The Coalition would have known that amongst the staff already transferred from Post-War was the active president of the ACT Branch of the Labor Party. It might have been this knowledge that prompted Menzies to ask Brown, somewhat diffidently, whether Brown was a member of the Labor Party. Brown replied, 'I wouldn't be seen dead in the Labor Party.' As Menzies expressed relief, Brown added, 'And I wouldn't be seen dead in the Liberal Party either.' This reply captured Menzies' fancy. It also accorded with the position Menzies felt a public servant should take. It fortified his acceptance of ASB and of the plans ASB had to develop the Prime Minister's Department.

Menzies accepted Bruno as a perfected public servant who had taken the oath of office and set store by its meaning. He could tell that ASB studied deeply, gave advice freely, and accepted responsibility cheerfully. As with any perfected public servant, these criteria existed within an envelope of vocation and mission; Bruno was the trusty custodian of the conventions and due process required by tradition, the Constitution and the rule of law. I remember an episode where, exceptionally, one of the Cabinet decisions recorded and issued by Brown was challenged. Brown had no doubt that the decision accurately reflected the Cabinet discussion and conclusion. However, the prime minister – as chairman of Cabinet – on being consulted had his own reasons for thinking otherwise. This did not present a problem for ASB. He simply signed off a decision that read: 'The Prime Minister has directed me to issue a decision in the following terms Quote … Unquote'. Researchers looking over Cabinet decisions when the archives are released can find at least one other case where this format is invoked; there may be more.

ASB proceeded as quickly as he could to develop the Secretariat for Cabinet and its committees and to build up the department's advising capability. He had instituted the practice of Cabinet Notebooks from about the mid-1950s. Using his contact with Sir Norman Brook, ASB sent Ken Herde to the British Cabinet Office to get experience of the workings of their Secretariat. Cedric Cliffe came on short-term secondment from that Secretariat to Prime Minister's. I myself was sent for a somewhat longer posting to be under Robert Hall in the separate Economic Section of the British Cabinet Office. I saw Brown and Brook together in London at a foursome lunch hosted by ASB at Pruniers. They discussed the wine list. Brown selected a red – it may have been a Bordeaux 45. Brook thought the wine excellent but the price exorbitant. Brown quelled Brook's concern with 'Norman, we don't do this very often'.

I must mention one inspired intervention by McKenna, which Brown was pleased to support, and which paid huge dividends. This was the appointment of Jim Scholtens, later Sir James, KCVO, to fill a vacancy as Head of Ceremonial and Hospitality. McKenna said, 'Young Jim Scholtens could do that job.' ASB said, 'Frank, he's only an accountant, but if you think he can head CERHOS, we'll give him a trial.' It happened that Scholty had a remarkable likeness to Danny Kaye. Brown had occasion to chuckle some years later when on a visit to Japan the Japanese Major Domo made the famous introduction, 'The Prime Minister of Australia, Sir Robert Menzies, Dame Pattie Menzies and Mr Danny Kaye.'

The early 1950s were turbulent times politically with the Communist Party Dissolution Bill and its surrounds. Allen Brown negotiated this terrain with care. He had a keen sense of the proper role of a permanent public servant under a system of constitutional monarchy, democratic government and the rule of law. He had his counsels of perfection but also knew the real world. His first duty, consonant with his oath and pledge of office, was to provide honest, efficient, impartial administration and some assurance for the community of continuity in such administration. ASB recoiled from any politicisation of the public service. He stood ready to serve to the best of his ability, responsively and loyally, whatever political party might be in government. He would master the facts of an initiative or an issue and their analysis. He would ensure that his minister, in this case the prime minister, was fully informed on that basis – pointing out alternative courses of action and their consequences, not neglecting political consequences. He would present matters as they were with firm advocacy of courses of action but with this advocacy not pressed beyond the point where, aware of consequences, the minister takes a different view. Nevertheless, he was vigilant to identify where, by law or convention, matters fell within his responsibility and where they fell within the minister's. He would never usurp or intrude on the minister's responsibility or allow the minister or the minister's office to intrude on his.

By July 1955 Brown was sufficiently satisfied with the department's progress to marshal virtually its whole staff for a photo opportunity on the steps of Parliament House. I know of no other occasion when a secretary of a department arranged such a photograph. The assembly numbered 74, mostly young, and 26 of them women. The front row exquisitely reflects transition; it consists of ASB flanked by two old hands, Frank McKenna and Stan Temby, and on either side of them, the new generation, Jack (later Sir John) Bunting, whom Brown, in wise succession planning, was grooming to follow him, and Bob Durie who, but for his untimely death in the midst of a posting to Australia House, would have been returning to Australia to be Bunting's deputy.

In 1959, Brown decided on a career change. He became deputy high commissioner at Australia House. I had, and have, difficulty in understanding this move – exceptional talent diverted to lesser purposes. He was only 48 years of age. Allen Stanley Brown was the most exemplary public servant I encountered in all my 42 years in the Commonwealth Public Service.

10

Sir Frederick Wheeler: Public Servant

Ian Hancock

On 16 July 1975, Sir Frederick Wheeler, secretary to the Treasury, was summoned before the bar of the Senate to be questioned about the Loans Affair. Asked to state his name and occupation, he replied: 'Frederick Henry Wheeler, public servant.' Four years later he attended the magistrate's court in Queanbeyan to give evidence in a private prosecution brought against four former ministers of the Whitlam Government. Asked to state his name and occupation, he replied: 'Frederick Wheeler. Superannuated public servant.' On both occasions Wheeler was not merely identifying himself, he was asserting his identity. His career, his perspective, everything about him, spelt 'public servant'.

Frederick Henry Wheeler was born on 9 January 1914 and attended Scotch College, Melbourne. Cyrus Lenox Hewitt was a junior boy at the same school; in time they were to become, in the words of Patricia Hewitt, 'the best of enemies'.[1] After taking a Bachelor of Commerce degree, part-time at the University of Melbourne, Wheeler worked for 10 years at the State Savings Bank of Victoria (1929–39) before joining the Treasury as a research officer. He was promoted to assistant secretary in 1946 and to first assistant secretary in 1949. Wheeler was a member of the Australian delegation to the Bretton Woods Monetary Conference, attended several conferences of British Commonwealth finance ministers between 1944 and 1951, and played a key role in preparing the Labor Government's banking legislation and its White Paper on *Full Employment in Australia*. As Fin Crisp has pointed out, he had 'a very special place in Chifley's confidence'.[2] Wheeler expected, and was expected, to succeed Norman Watt as Treasury secretary in 1951 but the Menzies Government preferred Roland Wilson for the post. Wheeler subsequently left the public service to become treasurer of the International Labour Organization (ILO) in Geneva. Returning to Canberra he was, in succession, chairman of the Public Service Board (1960–71) and secretary to the Treasury (1971–79). Appointed OBE in 1952 and CBE in

---

1 Patricia Hewitt, personal communication through Philip Wheeler, 1 September 2007.
2 L.F. Crisp, *Ben Chifley: A Biography* (Croydon: Longmans, 1961), 258.

1962, knighted in 1967 and appointed AC in the year of his retirement, Wheeler was suitably rewarded as befitted a leading and respected member of the mandarinate.

When Wheeler first went to Canberra he was one of the 30 or more young officers who formed the 'kindergarten' of the 'official family' in the 1940s. Many of them held economics degrees and were committed Keynesians whose task was to help shape wartime and post-war Australia.[3] Employed or advising in various official bodies, they socialised as well as worked together and established personal relationships that proved important in promoting and protecting their careers in the public service. Among them, and among those above them, Wheeler acquired a reputation as a principled yet shrewd operator, endowed with a powerful mind and an acute sense of what was possible, ever-ready to defend Treasury's territory but always measured in approach and well prepared in detail.

Wheeler exhibited many of these characteristics when he became involved in preparing the White Paper on Full Employment. The paper was intended to be a bold statement of the Labor Government's commitment to full employment in the post-war world, accompanied by a detailed account of how this objective would be achieved. H.C. 'Nugget' Coombs, the director-general of the Department of Post-War Reconstruction, was its principal promoter.[4] Copies of an amended draft reached the Treasury in February 1945 and, believing the paper to be 'of the greatest importance' to the department, Wheeler wanted 'the greatest possible amount of work' to be done on it immediately. He feared that the Treasury's maturing role in providing economic advice to the government would be diminished, and he harnessed the Financial and Economic Committee, where he was assistant secretary, along with sympathetic outsiders, to resist interlopers. During the following month he also queried or successfully removed some of the paper's 'bold futurism', its 'cure-all' mentality and the 'unnecessary provocation' of its language. Wheeler won agreement not to publish the proposed appendix of statistics on the grounds it would mean nothing to the majority and would be misused by a minority. Above all, perhaps, he focused attention on the more limited exercise of outlining general government policy and dealing with the practical problems of a transition to peacetime. He could claim that the next draft was a 'very great improvement' and met 'a large number of Treasury objections', but continued to argue against premature publication and to apply a critical and pragmatic approach to policies he thought would arouse opposition in the community. Significantly, while the 'kindergarten' concentrated on

---

3   N. Brown, *Richard Downing: Economics, Advocacy and Social Reform in Australia* (Carlton South: Melbourne University Press, 2001), ch. 3.
4   S. Cornish, *Full Employment in Australia: The Genesis of a White Paper*, Research Paper in Economic History, No. 1 (Canberra: Department of Economic History, ANU, 1971), 1ff.

what government might do, he called for more emphasis on private rather than public investment because the Australian economy was still based on private enterprise. Overall, as Coombs recognised, 'Wheeler's contribution was especially important' in ensuring that the published version was a compromise expressing what could be supported by consensus and avoiding issues which would cause controversy.[5]

It is unclear whether or how far Wheeler's closeness to Chifley explains Menzies' preference for Wilson as secretary to the Treasury. The certainty is that Wheeler almost immediately began looking for alternative employment. He briefly considered private enterprise, but told his parents he did not want 'to break entirely with Governmental work and the sort of people you find in that field'. At the ILO, when approached by the Vickers Company, Wheeler said he was 'not interested in anything which was wholly or primarily based on lobbying and general contact'. Although he regarded 'the Geneva venture' as 'a great success', he was determined it would be 'an interlude and not a permanency'. He did not want to become an expatriate. At the same time he had a good idea of his own strengths: an ability 'to make good use of staff for substantive work in association with a lot of negotiating and committee work'. His reputation, he thought, 'is not based on any great ability to impress in general, but on steady work in a substantial field which brought a wide range of associations in its train without my seeking them out'. Wheeler liked the excitement and importance of what he called 'negotiating and representational work', though both had to be undertaken on 'a firm base of substantive work and responsibility'. Without spelling it out, his understanding of his own abilities pointed to a senior position in public service.[6]

Wheeler's friends and former colleagues in Canberra – they included Sir William Dunk, the chairman of the Public Service Board (PSB), Sir John Crawford, secretary of the Department of Trade, and John Bunting, the recently appointed secretary of the Prime Minister's Department – wanted to reclaim the man they felt had been wrongly turned away. Frederick Wheeler was, after all, one of them. Dunk approached Wheeler as early as 1957 to ask if he would consider succeeding him at the PSB, while Crawford wanted Wheeler to become chairman of the Tariff Board. Despite receiving offers from industry, Wheeler could tell Dunk he preferred 'to remain a civil servant'.[7] He would be pleased to accept either the PSB or the Tariff Board.

---

5 For Wheeler's many interventions and comments, see esp. National Archives of Australia (NAA) A571, 1945/574, Part 1, and A981, 1945/638. See also, H.C. Coombs, *Trial Balance: Issues of My Working Life* (South Melbourne: Sun Books, 1981), 52.
6 For the above paragraph, see Wheeler's private correspondence in Wheeler Papers, National Library of Australia (NLA) MS 8096/2/3.
7 Wheeler to Dunk, 20 December 1957, Wheeler Papers, NLA MS 8096/2/3.

Frederick Wheeler, 1959

Source: State Library of Victoria, H38849/4871

Dunk proceeded to work on Prime Minister Menzies. He described Wheeler as 'one of the bright boys' picked out by Stuart McFarlane (secretary to the Treasury, 1938–48), and 'no-one in my very extensive experience of war administration came through with the sureness and ability of this young man'. Six years at the ILO 'does not usually provide a good atmosphere for development', and the organisation may have left a mark on him, but 'it has not destroyed his perception, his penetration or his keenness'. Crawford and Dunk both thought he was 'still first class material'.[8] They continued to work hard on his behalf, seemingly untroubled by what Henry Bland, the secretary for Labour and National Service since 1952, who had his own claims for the post, saw as 'the hanky-panky that is going on about F.W.'.[9] According to Dunk, Wheeler passed the test of 'acceptability' because his 'very sound reputation, while he was in the Public Service, is built around the personal attributes of a keen intelligence, reliability, following government policy, co-operation with his associates, and a natural as well as proven integrity'. Bland was not 'acceptable' because he had a reputation for being 'something of an intriguer'; he had a 'quick intellect' but was 'slick' and talked too much. His only lead over Wheeler was his current knowledge of the public service.[10] Dunk advised Menzies to tell his Cabinet colleagues that a panel had produced three names – Wheeler, Bland and Keith Grainger (one of the two other serving commissioners on the Board) – and gave Menzies career notes on each so fashioned that Wheeler looked the obvious, indeed the only, choice.[11] In the event, Menzies and John McEwen, the Trade minister and Country Party leader, carried the day in Cabinet over three very senior ministers who had their reservations.

Frederick Wheeler's subsequent career in the public service followed two paths: the one, creative; the other, defensive. It is tempting to relate the one to his time at the Public Service Board and the other to his years at the Treasury. It is also tempting to equate the creative years to the period when Menzies, Holt and McEwen held prime ministerial office and to associate the defensive period with the Gorton, McMahon, Whitlam and Fraser years. There were, however, too many instances of overlap to adopt such hard-and-fast distinctions. It remains, however, that he did have two quite different experiences.

Wheeler began work as chairman of the Public Service Board on the morning of 2 January 1961. Although the board had seemingly wide powers and responsibilities – the supervision of personnel administration, the determination of pay and of conditions of employment, and the pursuit of

---

8   Dunk to Prime Minister, February 1959, Wheeler Papers, NLA MS 8096/2/3, 4.
9   George Sutcliffe (a Board commissioner) to Chairman, PSB, 21 August 1959, Wheeler Papers, NLA MS 8096/2/3.
10 Dunk to Prime Minister, 31 August 1959, Wheeler Papers, NLA MS 8096/2/3.
11 Ibid., 10 September 1959.

economy and efficiency — it was a free agent only in the case of the first.[12] The board's jurisdiction was to an extent circumscribed by statute and convention. In practice, it relied heavily on conciliation and persuasion, especially in its dealings with the permanent heads who were responsible for the management of their departments. The board also had to bend to the government's will over pay and conditions of employment, take account of the Determinations of the Public Service Arbitrator and of the Awards handed down by the Conciliation and Arbitration Court (or Commission as it became in 1956), and deal with a myriad of staff associations.

Whereas Dunk had settled for expedient compromises, Wheeler approached his inheritance 'attached to first principles'.[13] He was about to enter the most constructive period of his life for which he was prepared to put in the long hours and to pursue every detail, while bringing with him the necessary administrative and 'political' skills and the staying power to win through.

Napoleon Bonaparte would have approved of Frederick Wheeler. He was a lucky general. His creative period began with two strokes of good fortune, and he exploited both to the full. First, in 1960 the Menzies Government amended the *Public Service Act* to implement those parts of the Report of the Committee of Inquiry into Public Service Recruitment (the Boyer Report) that the government and the PSB could accept. Two changes were critical: henceforth, the Leaving Certificate or its equivalent was required for entry into the third division, and modern selection techniques replaced the exclusive reliance on examination marks. In November 1961, Wheeler's board introduced the Commonwealth Selection Test constructed by the Australian Council for Educational Research. This test measured abilities appropriate to routine clerical duties and to higher-level positions in the public service. All applicants within the prescribed age limit were required to take it, and offers of employment were made on an order of merit determined by the results achieved.

Wheeler believed the new system would improve the quality of recruits who would now be better placed according to their abilities. It would also enhance the principle of open competition and ensure greater accuracy and consistency in setting minimum standards. Thereafter, Wheeler and his fellow commissioners regularly provided commentary and statistics to bear out claims that the selection tests, being constantly updated and revised, were proving to be what the board's 1966–67 Annual Report called 'a satisfactory instrument'. But Wheeler remained circumspect. He was well aware that the success of the tests could not be established until the chosen ones had reached the middle and

---

12 G.E. Caiden, *Career Service: An Introduction to the History of Personnel Administration in Commonwealth Public Service of Australia 1901–1961* (Carlton, VIC: Melbourne University Press, 1965), 433.
13 S. Encel, *Equality and Authority: A Study of Class, Status and Power in Australia* (Melbourne: F.W. Cheshire, 1970), 271.

senior levels of the public service. In the meantime, however, Wheeler could go armed into an increasingly competitive market to attract a decent share of the post-war baby boom, provided he could also match some of the salaries and promotion opportunities of private enterprise.

In June 1961, in what became Wheeler's second piece of good fortune, the Commonwealth Conciliation and Arbitration Commission (CCAC) handed down its long-awaited decision on the Engineers' classification structures of the public service.

The public service at the time consisted of a highly varied and technically complex workforce, but its pay and classification structures were rightly described as 'monolithic'.[14] The cumulative effect of policy decisions, industrial pressures and arbitral decisions meant that the remuneration of all staff moved more or less in lock step. There was little scope for adjustment of particular occupations based on rates of pay in comparable outside labour markets. In addition, the many salary classification levels within occupational groups – 14 for the engineers – were complicated by overlapping and extended pay ranges. Relatively lowly paid classifications were included in the second division management group while others, which should have been, were not. The excessive layering and fine distinctions in classification may have increased the need for promotion but promotions did not necessarily mean significant pay increases. Wheeler, therefore, inherited a pay-fixing system that was rigid and a classification structure that hampered efficiency. He also faced the problems of recruitment and retention, particularly in the specialist occupations where the private sector was offering better opportunities and remuneration.[15]

The decision in the Engineers' case became the circuit breaker. The CCAC raised the annual salary range for a recruitment-grade engineer and replaced the table of uniform incremental steps with one varying from £140 to £180pa.[16] Its stated assumption was that the engineers constituted 'a special case'. Wheeler's strategy in response was twofold: the board would use the 'special case' argument to oppose an automatic flow-on of the engineers' pay increases to other occupational categories; and it would compress and simplify the salary classifications in the second and third divisions. Ever the careful planner, Wheeler held a series of meetings with the interested parties in the CPS to find out what they were thinking and, in part, to implicate them in moves the PSB might later make. His memos to the prime minister during the following year record his successful attempts to reclassify and reduce salary grades, to ensure the doubters among the permanent heads 'were not hostile', and to stand

---

14 I am grateful to Paddy Gourley for his assistance in preparing the following paragraphs.
15 For a typical statement of the problem, see *Thirty-Seventh Report of the Public Service Board, 1959–60*, 16.
16 For Wheeler's reaction and the immediate aftermath of the Engineers' Determination, see Wheeler Papers, NLA MS 8096/4/3.

firm against staff association demands for automatic adjustments. Wheeler had the perfect riposte for staff association objections: the board had 'no option' but to follow the commission's line 'to reject any notion of automatic or semi-automatic lateral flow-on'. The commission's 'status and authority' meant that its 'clear policy guidance' should be followed unless there were compelling reasons not to do so. Besides, Wheeler's political instincts told him that 'broad community considerations' militated against a sudden and substantial increase in public service salaries. Patient negotiations and 'sniffing the air' would carry the day. Following the CCAC's second Determination in the Engineers' case of June 1962, Wheeler could tell Menzies that the permanent heads regarded the reclassifications already undertaken as 'a genuine improvement', while some union representatives privately agreed even though they publicly attacked the board for attempting to defeat 'salary justice'.

The CCAC's decisions had important unintended consequences. The board ensured that a number of occupational groups, especially the engineers, became more professionalised through introduction of precise and externally certified educational prerequisites provided by the universities. The Commonwealth, as a result, became an exemplar for the rest of the community in graduate recruitment and became more competitive in the market place. The PSB itself became what Wheeler liked to call 'a primary wage fixing authority'. It now made decisions without direction from the government and, on occasions, caused the government some discomfort in doing so. Furthermore, Wheeler utilised the board's enhanced role as a primary wage-fixing authority, and other unrelated mechanisms, to advance his own power and influence within the public service, extending his reach into the more distant areas of Commonwealth employment where the board had no legal standing.

Throughout his career as a public servant, Sir Frederick Wheeler espoused a number of clear and generally consistent views about the role of public servants, especially of those in the first and second divisions. Definitions used in the *Public Service Act* were invoked to support his central assumptions. For example, officers in the second division 'are required to exercise *executive or professional* functions in the more important offices of the Service'. He noted how this definition adopted the 'modern view' where 'top management and policy formation is a distinctive and integrated function and ... even where a top management job does have technical content the choice of appointees should primarily be on the basis of managerial and administrative abilities'. Wheeler was not interested in specialists becoming permanent heads unless they had proven experience. Youthful appointments (that is, men below the age of 45) should be made only where they were clearly outstanding and a more mature alternative was lacking. Five requirements for appointment had to be met – integrity, judgment, maturity, leadership and experience – of which the first four came within the meaning of 'men of affairs'.[17] With these principles in mind, he was often direct in his confidential minutes to the prime minister and ministers. One minister's nomination to head his department (he was aged 42) 'was not yet ready' and 'would be badly received, both in the Service and in relevant circles in the community'.[18] Wheeler kept his best, however, for another contender: 'Able and ambitious but inflexible in approach; penetrating and hardworking but aggressively self-assertive and personal relations very abrasive over a wide field; has not shown up well as a leader or developer of his team; not suitable for [Secretary of Defence] position'.[19] Wheeler's view prevailed in both the above cases.

One of his working rules was that 'the maintenance of the tradition of loyalty to the Government of the day is vital'. Accordingly, he secured the demotion of the director of the Commonwealth Serum Laboratories (CSL), a popular hero for his work on the Salk anti-polio vaccine. Dr Bazeley had campaigned publicly against the Commonwealth Government's decision to hand over the administration of the CSL to a five-member statutory commission.[20] As Wheeler explained in a later minute to Harold Holt, the then prime minister, in 1967, 'senior public servants should maintain a proper reticence in matters of public and political controversy, and … should not normally take an active part in a matter which is, or could be, one of public and political controversy'.[21] Wheeler regarded entry into senior management as the equivalent of joining a monastic order, carrying with it a vow of silence. Public servants should be politically neutral and officially anonymous.

Loyalty to a government in public did not preclude giving 'frank and fearless' advice in private. Wheeler had few problems in his dealings with prime ministers Menzies, Holt and, briefly, McEwen. But he had a host of difficulties with the maverick John Gorton (1968–71) who had little respect for public service conventions and who could be so unpredictable. The two men clashed repeatedly over issues ranging from handling postal disputes to making appointments. Wheeler was particularly upset when the prime minister sought to remove Bunting as secretary of the Prime Minister's Department. Gorton believed that Bunting had exposed Harold Holt to political danger and ridicule during the 'VIP affair' in 1967.[22] Wheeler fought hard for his friend but lost. Worse, Gorton insisted on installing Lenox Hewitt as secretary of the Prime Minister's Department. The prime minister also overrode Wheeler's repeated

---

17 Wheeler to Prime Minister, 4 March 1963, Wheeler Papers, NLA, MS 8096/4/6 (original emphasis).
18 Ibid., 12 December 1966.
19 Ibid., 29 November 1967, 7.
20 Ibid., Wheeler's participation in this case can be followed in 4/3-4.
21 Ibid., Wheeler to Prime Minister, 15 May 1967, 7 (original emphasis).
22 See I.R. Hancock, 'The VIP Affair 1966–67: The Causes, Course and Consequences of a Ministerial and Public Service Cover-Up', *Australian Parliamentary Review*, 18, no. 2 (2004), vi–xiii, 1–106.

advice and appointed A.B. 'Tich' McFarlane, the secretary of Air, who had assisted Gorton over the VIP affair, to a vacant commissionership on the board. Wheeler had earlier dismissed the idea of McFarlane becoming secretary of Defence with the brusque comment: 'Relatively narrow experience; lacks the stature for a position of this type.'[23]

Despite some disappointments during his later years at the Board, Wheeler's record placed him next to the outstanding Duncan McLachlan, 'the Father of the Commonwealth Public Service',[24] as a reformer. He saw his task as one of preparing the Service to lead the Commonwealth through the final decades of the twentieth century. To this end, he improved the quality of the Service through the active encouragement of graduates, staff development and trainee schemes, he modernised the pay and classification structures, promoted the leadership roles of senior management, eliminated unnecessary regulations, and played a leading role in removing the bar that prevented married women from being appointed or retained as permanent officers.

At the behest of William McMahon, Gorton's successor, Wheeler moved to the Treasury in 1971. Clyde Cameron, the Labor frontbencher and hardened warrior, greeted his appointment with approbation. Cameron imagined the pleasure it would give 'Old Chif', and thought Wheeler would be 'the greatest asset the next (Labor) Government will have'.[25] Whitlam and many of his ministers soon demonised the 'greatest asset' as 'obstructionist'. Overshadowed as an economist by John Stone, whose appointment he secured in Treasury as a third deputy secretary, and by others he had appointed and encouraged, Wheeler spent much of his time mentoring the brightest of the incoming generation and defending the department from its critics both in Cabinet and in the public service.

Wheeler had to fight on several fronts in protecting his fiefdom and maintaining the Treasury's role as principal economic adviser to the government. The Whitlam Government brought in all manner of advisers and staffers some of whom saw themselves as Treasury's rivals. More seriously, the Treasury and the big spenders of the Whitlam Government were soon at loggerheads over strategies for dealing with inflation. During the budget discussions of 1973 Wheeler and two other Treasury officials attended a meeting of economic ministers 'to be', in Stone's words, 'dressed down', in part because they kept urging expenditure cuts.[26] Wheeler probably tested the credulity and patience of ministers by insisting that Treasury's officials were merely technicians who were asking for the clear and consistent policy direction they were not receiving. The 1974–75 budget discussions were even more fraught because the economic

---

23 Wheeler to Prime Minister, 29 November 1967, Wheeler Papers, NLA MS 8096/4/6.
24 Caiden, *Career Service*, 15.
25 Cameron to Wheeler, 15 September 1971, Wheeler Papers, NLA MS 8096/5/2.
26 NAA A5931, CL740; Stone to Secretary, 28 April 1975, Wheeler Papers, NLA MS 8096/5/8.

ministers and Caucus, fearing widespread unemployment, rejected the Treasury line of fighting inflation first and cutting government expenditure. After initially supporting Wheeler, Whitlam joined the growing band of 'Treasury bashers' and presided over a nominal increase of 32 per cent in budget outlays (Treasury had recommended a figure of 27 per cent). Wheeler and the Treasury were subsequently, if briefly, consigned to the margins for refusing to provide the advice the government wanted.

At a meeting of the Executive Council on 13–14 December 1974 four ministers – Whitlam, Dr Cairns (deputy prime minister and treasurer), Rex Connor (Minerals and Energy) and Lionel Murphy (Attorney-General) – agreed to borrow US$4 billion 'for temporary purposes'. The mid-1974 fall-out between the Treasury and the government and continuing suspicions between the two, as well as bureaucratic and personal rivalries (Hewitt was secretary to Connor's department), were important components in the bizarre, secretive excursion into the world of Tirath Khemlani, 'carpet-baggers' and 'funny money'.

Wheeler and the Treasury were deliberately excluded from the loan discussions until shortly before the Executive Council meeting. When apprised of what was in progress, and realising that it was designed to avoid 'due process' – by circumventing the Loan Council and parliament – Wheeler orchestrated a series of moves over an intense few days. He ordered enquiries to be made of the Bank of England and Scotland Yard about Khemlani. John Stone was assigned to raise questions about the wisdom and legality of the whole enterprise.[27] But Wheeler could not stop or divert Connor, who had Whitlam's backing if not his full attention – the prime minister had overseas travel plans in mind – while Murphy was probably as much attracted by the unconventional proceedings and Cairns was otherwise preoccupied. Challenged by Wheeler's persistent objections during the drawn-out, intense meetings of 13 December, Connor at one stage declared: 'I am a Minister of the Crown.' To which Wheeler replied: 'Yes, Minister, and I am the Permanent Secretary to the Treasury.' The Treasury secretary also upset the prime minister. Wheeler had observed how the proposed borrowing was far in excess of the remaining statutory authority, which stood at $610 million. Whitlam accused the secretary of sitting quietly for an hour-and-a-half before revealing this information. An angry prime minister turned on him: 'Fred, you are on the skids.' Wheeler's reply was prescient: 'Prime Minister, I simply wish to inform you of facts your ignorance of which will bring you down.'[28]

---

27 A copy of Stone's minute was published in A. Reid, *The Whitlam Venture* (Melbourne: Hill of Content, 1976), 9–11.
28 D. Rose, 'Transcript', *Sankey v Whitlam and others*, January–February 1979, 671.

Although the government would not be restrained, Wheeler did achieve some victories. He 'protected' Cairns by persuading him not to sign the Executive Council minute as treasurer, and campaigned successfully between 14 and 21 December to have Connor's authority rescinded. Two commentators later depicted Wheeler as 'a master of guerrilla warfare' for his marathon telephone efforts on 20 December where, fuelled by drams of whisky and operating inside clouds of cigarette smoke, he proffered 'a remarkable picture of a bureaucratic virtuoso at work'.[29] Connor did obtain a second Executive Council minute on 28 January, albeit for just US$2 billion, so Wheeler, the Treasury and the Reserve Bank had to keep up the pressure to expose the dangers of dealing with Khemlani. They pointed out how the 'funny money' had never materialised and how Connor's activities and the very existence of the Executive Council minute were jeopardising a much-needed American loan and other future borrowings by the treasurer. When the Executive Council finally revoked the minute on 20 May, the secretary thought he had achieved his dual purpose: the restoration of the Treasury as the focal point of overseas borrowing; and elimination of Khemlani and his associated carpetbaggers as intermediaries. He did not know – nor did anyone in the government know – that, once again, Rex Connor did not accept 'No' for an answer.

Even so, Wheeler was about to have an enduring victory. Earlier in 1975, Cairns had secured the approval of the Labor Party Conference to form a separate Department of Economic Planning to advise the government on medium and long-term priorities. Wheeler and the Treasury were profoundly disturbed by the implications. On 31 March the secretary handed Cairns a Treasury memorandum.[30] It was a clever document, fulfilling the duty of public servants to implement, or showing how to implement, government or ruling party policy, while making the task of implementation look well nigh impossible and even faintly preposterous. Wheeler's fear was that Treasury might be split and challenged, if not displaced, as the government's source of advice on economic and financial matters. To defeat the scheme, he adopted three strategies. First, he argued that the new 'Department' should be just a 'Unit' or 'Office' separated from Treasury but located within the treasurer's portfolio. This done, a substantial part of Treasury would not be transferred to the new body while the Treasury's traditional short-term planning role would be separated from any pie-in-the-sky long-term projects. Secondly, Wheeler highlighted the practical problems arising from the sheer complexity of the exercise. The Office would have to cover social as well as economic issues, cooperate with many departments, agencies and community groups, and 'would need experts from a

---

29   B. Toohey and J. Longstreet, *National Times*, 14 November 1982.
30   Wheeler to N. Hyden, 1 April 1975, Wheeler Papers, NLA MS 8096/5/3.

wide range of disciplines'. To achieve cooperative and unified action from such a multitude of egos, organisations and disciplines would require the resurrection of both Solomon and Job.

Thirdly, Wheeler applied his trademark tactic of delay. Just as he had done in 1945, he set about extending the boundaries of consultation, building a respectable and respected opposition, and uncovering further impediments. By early June 1975 he had successfully obfuscated the issue and slowed down the decision-making. When, in that month, the treasurer was dismissed over his separate participation in the Loans Affair, Cairns remained the lone senior advocate of his proposed new department.

Yet as one threat to the Treasury was removed another emerged. Following the double dissolution of May 1974 Whitlam announced the establishment of the Royal Commission on Australian Government Administration (RCAGA) to conduct a wide-ranging examination of Australian government administration. Many Labor ministers and members of Caucus believed that Labor's reform program was being stymied by a public service either unaccustomed to carrying out rapid change or unwilling to do so.

The Treasury submission to the commission of 17 November, which Wheeler signed, sought to establish three central points: the Treasury 'has become the primary economic policy adviser to the Government'; 'all the activities of the Treasury are closely inter-related and inter-woven'; and the Treasury did not exist to make policy but to administer existing policy and to offer advice on possible new policy.[31] Characteristically, Wheeler adopted a tone of reasonableness during his day-long appearance before the commission and the questioning by its chairman, H.C. 'Nugget' Coombs. He tactfully deflected criticisms of his domain and gently lauded the Treasury's achievements. Wheeler stressed, correctly, how the Treasury maintained a non-hierarchical structure and actively encouraged younger talent. Not surprisingly, he rejected Coombs' proposal of a formally established board, to include heads of statutory bodies and academics, to advise the treasurer. It was necessary in management terms 'to have a focus of authority'; a board would slow everything up and 'not add anything'. Just as Wheeler had expressed doubts about 'bold futurism' in 1945, he questioned the emphasis on long-term objectives when governments had to deal with the 'volatility' of policy on a day-to-day basis. It was the 'worst thing' for officials to advise on macro-economic management 'from an ivory tower divorced from grass roots realities'. Wheeler sensibly sidestepped the issue of advisers. Ministers, he said, should decide what they wanted. He was forthright, however, about claims of a 'Treasury line' on economic theory and

---

31   NLA MS 8096/5/3; The Treasury, *Submission to the Royal Commission on Australian Government Administration*, November 1974, 8.

principles; the notion was 'nonsense'. There was a diversity of opinion within the Treasury, and it was made known to treasurers. But there was a doctrine of another kind: 'all issues should be looked at on the basis of hard work … really turning propositions over, collecting the relevant data, and testing them rather than merely tossing them about at a high level of generality unalloyed by hard detailed examination.'[32] The secretary, as in 1945, probably had Dr Coombs in mind.

The Treasury's defence of the *status quo* was constantly questioned in the course of the commission's hearings and, not least, by Lenox Hewitt. Classified now as 'an enduring problem', Wheeler's Treasury looked to be in trouble, most of all for its centralised control mechanisms, which were deemed to hinder efficiency. But the passing of the Whitlam Government meant that most of the commission's findings and proposals would be left well alone.

Nevertheless, the Fraser Government delivered a sharp blow. On 18 November 1976, the prime minister announced that the Treasury would be divided into two departments.[33] A new Department of Finance would take over the financial management and control activities of the Treasury whose responsibilities were now centred on broad economic policy analysis including taxation matters and on giving advice to the government. Fraser claimed that the objective was to provide for more effective management of the business of government, and to strengthen the government's decision-making processes. Very few believed his explanation. The prime minister was furious about the Treasury's delay in providing advice, about the quality of advice received, and about an alleged leak over Fraser's support for the devaluation of the Australian dollar.

Wheeler was not caught unawares. As early as mid-1973 he had asked for some 'boy scout' work to be done after learning of a senior adviser's interest in a split and, a year later, with the Coombs Commission in mind, he asked for the relevant papers to be retrieved.[34] Soon after the dismissal of the Whitlam Government, Wheeler sought evidence from within the Treasury to show how the work was closely interwoven and how it was both necessary and desirable for such work to be interwoven. The secretary wanted to highlight the problems at the ministerial as well as the departmental level should the Treasury be split.[35] Wheeler did not know, however, of the prime minister's specific intentions until Sir Alan Cooley, the chairman of the Public Service Board, contacted him two days prior to Fraser's announcement.

---

32   RCAGA, Transcript of Proceedings, 28 November 1974.
33   *Commonwealth Parliamentary Debates*, House of Representatives, 18 November 1976, 2898–99.
34   See NAA A6385/236.
35   Cole to McBurney and others, 3 November 1975, NAA A6385/236.

Cooley was a surprise appointment as Wheeler's successor. He owed his elevation almost entirely to Wheeler's patronage, and Cooley worked hard on his benefactor's behalf. The prime minister had sought the chairman's advice on possible changes and, though directed not to consult Treasury beforehand, he made the Treasury's case for doing little or nothing.[36] If the prime minister felt he could not achieve his requirements within the present framework, then 'various steps can be taken to improve matters'. After listing several options, Cooley delivered a clear message: do not divide what is, and should remain, indivisible. At the very least, before making a decision, Fraser should talk to Wheeler.

After Cooley advised Wheeler of his exchanges with the prime minister, the secretary sent Phillip Lynch, the treasurer, four separate minutes on 17 November in a last ditch effort to avert the split.[37] Judiciously, he agreed that a split would have advantages as well as disadvantages at both the ministerial and public service levels. Yet, in his 'considered judgement', splitting Treasury 'would produce very substantial confusion and inefficiencies in the period immediately ahead and continuing inefficiencies in the longer term'. Wheeler canvassed every possible objection and looked everywhere for alternatives. He envisaged several problems: two 'sectional advisings' would not constitute 'two "overview" options'; the speed of communication and consultation between the areas would be diminished and 'would increasingly tend to produce "ivory-towerism" in the economic areas and "narrowness of thinking" in the expenditure areas'; any restructuring would disrupt ongoing work and there would be longer-term implications; the 'short and long effects on staff morale would be serious'; and there would be a need for more staff of the kind that is 'very scarce'. Wheeler also invoked, as he often did, broader political considerations: the media might fasten onto the failure to pursue the avowed aim of 'slim government'. To avoid controversy and catastrophe, therefore, the government might agree to the appointment of a fourth deputy secretary in Treasury.

If Fraser even saw these minutes there was no chance of him changing his mind. Wheeler's one victory was the appointment of a favoured Treasury official, Bill Cole, the Australian statistician, to head the new Department of Finance. Yet, typically, in defeat he worked diligently over the following weeks grappling with the technical details involved in formally dividing up the department. Moreover, on 6 December, the day before the split was to come into effect, he wrote the following in a staff notice:

---

36   A. Cooley to Prime Minister, 12 November 1976, NAA A6385/238, Part 5.
37   Wheeler to Treasurer, 17 November 1975, NAA A6385/238, Part 5.

> In the sense in which I have used that expression in the past, the splitting of the Treasury, while certainly meaning a different order of things for the future, is not in my view to be taken as signifying an end of the underlying concept. The two Departments will be working, under a common Minister, the Treasurer, in close collaboration with each other.

The sanguine underpinnings of this note left open at least two possibilities: either the Treasury secretary was deluding himself or, more probably, he was typically making the best of a situation he did not like, while hoping it would not get worse.[38]

As Wheeler fought to protect Treasury he had, on occasions, to protect himself, particularly during 1975. His own position came under scrutiny after Cairns was dismissed as treasurer. Before that, Whitlam had tried to shift him from the Treasury to the governorship of the Reserve Bank. Determined to remain where he was until reaching retiring age, Wheeler once again relied on holding up the decision-making process while projecting Lenox Hewitt's name to the forefront of any discussions of a successor at Treasury. He soon discovered that Whitlam's desire to remove him was not matched by the will to act. Further, he knew he could rely on fellow mandarins and respected figures outside the public service to say how inappropriate 'King Cyrus' would be as secretary. Peter Karmel, the chairman of the Australian Universities Commission, probably expressed the prevailing view among the well informed in declaring the 'obnoxious' Hewitt would be a disaster in Treasury. 'There must', he said, 'be something wrong with a man who is so universally disliked.'[39] It was soon evident to Whitlam that Wheeler was not going to move of his own volition, and that the secretary's intense lobbying – assisted by his friends – had rendered a Hewitt appointment impossible and of anyone else improbable. In the absence of an unanswerable case for shifting him, the prime minister simply folded.

Sir Frederick Wheeler was both a survivor and a survival. His value system belonged to an era preceding the one where advisers, consultants, and staffers, short-term contracts, performance bonuses, impermanent heads and media-conscious officials, would become the norm. Since 1961, Wheeler had nurtured and promoted the next generation but his perspective remained that of an older public service where powerful men – whatever their height – were used to getting their way and staying where they were, while insisting they were there only to serve. As they genuflected in the direction of their ministerial masters, the best of them, and Wheeler was among the best of the best, practised politics with a skill and know-how which many professionals admired.[40] No doubt,

---

38 NAA A6385/238, Part 5. For the last days before the split see parts 3 and 4.
39 Trevor Swan to Wheeler c. 3 April 1975. Swan was reporting his conversation over lunch with Karmel.
40 Sir John Carrick, interview with author, 31 January 2009.

Wheeler tested his own ethics in going beyond the role of adviser. Yet he could always claim that, throughout his career, he never abandoned nor compromised his core belief: public servants and ministers and prime ministers should all, and always, observe 'due process'.

11

Paul Hasluck with Dr Evatt at the United Nations

Geoffrey Bolton

Assessments of Dr H.V. Evatt's performance in the formative years of the United Nations from 1945 to 1947 have drawn on the critical comments voiced by Paul Hasluck in several publications.[1] Hasluck wrote with the authority of one who served in the Department of External Affairs with Evatt for more than five years, and had a justified reputation as a scrupulous historian whose judgments tried to avoid political bias. This essay, drawing on unpublished material in the Hasluck family archives, will show that for much of their association at External Affairs, Hasluck's outlook on foreign policy was closer to Evatt's than his subsequent writings might suggest.[2]

A successful Western Australian journalist, poet, drama critic and historian, Paul Hasluck was recruited to the Department of External Affairs in February 1941 on a temporary basis. He found his early months in Canberra undemanding and disappointing, but allowed himself to hope for improvement in October 1941 when the Curtin Labor Government took office and Dr Evatt was appointed minister for External Affairs. A former judge of the High Court, Evatt was known to be an intellectual with broad cultural sympathies. Disillusion came soon. A fortnight after Evatt's appointment Hasluck wrote in his diary: 'He has not come near us yet, has upset the Department on several matters and generally shows a disposition to try and find something to reform or "squash" rather than to understand.'[3]

Hasluck thought seriously of returning to Perth, but all changed in December when Japan entered the war and he saw it as his duty to stay at his post. During 1942 he became officer-in-charge of a new section of the Department of External Affairs on post-war policy and came to be seen as the department's authority in the field. He was good at his job, though he often fretted about bureaucratic

---

1   P. Hasluck, *Workshop of Security* (Melbourne: F.W. Cheshire, 1948); 'Australia and the formation of the United Nations', *Royal Australian Historical Society, Journal and Proceedings*, xl, no. iii (1954), 133–78; *Diplomatic Witness: Australian Foreign Affairs 1941–1947* (Carlton: Melbourne University Press, 1977).
2   Some of the material covered in this chapter is also addressed in G. Bolton, *Paul Hasluck: A Life* (Crawley, WA: UWA Publishing, 2014).
3   P. Hasluck, Diary 1941–42, 20 October 1941, Hasluck MSS, Claremont.

in-fighting.⁴ When Evatt went to the Food and Agriculture Conference at Hot Springs in Virginia in April 1943, instead of taking Hasluck with him, he borrowed Hasluck's friend, Dr H.C. Coombs, from the Department of Labour and National Service. At the conference Coombs distinguished himself by his advocacy of full employment as a post-war objective. To represent External Affairs, Evatt took with him his recently appointed private secretary, Dr John Burton.

With Hasluck, like himself an appointee from outside the departmental cadre, Burton was at first on friendly terms to the extent of suggesting that during his absence abroad Hasluck might escort his wife Cecily to the cinema. They shared little jokes about Evatt: 'I find the Minister rarely has much idea of the line he wants to follow,' Burton wrote to Hasluck, 'and he will accept a draft quite easily. I have not had so many ideas put over for a long time! The boss has behaved quite well and everyone is commenting that he is much less difficult this time than last.'⁵ But, Burton reported, Evatt wanted him to report to him personally: 'in other words, he refuses to allow me to be an officer of the Department.'⁶ Burton was soon colluding with Evatt's tendency to work outside official channels of communication and keep his permanent officials in the dark, and this was to cause friction.

Hasluck shared to the full Evatt's mistrust of American ambitions for post-war hegemony in the South Pacific, especially after the Cairo Conference of November 1943 when the United States, Britain and Nationalist China took decisions about the future of Japan's colonies without consulting Australia and New Zealand.⁷ To protect their interests, Evatt convened a conference between the two governments at Canberra on 21 January 1944. Hasluck was put in charge of the arrangements and appointed secretary to the conference.

The result was an unprecedented formal treaty in which Australia and New Zealand agreed to consult regularly about regional foreign policy, defence, commerce and the fostering of full employment. They claimed a place at any peace-making conference table and a voice in deciding the future sovereignty of any of the Pacific islands.⁸ Although Hasluck later commented that the calling of the conference reflected Evatt's 'almost psychological antipathy to any power that was greater than Australia',⁹ he described his own standpoint as 'offensively Australian'¹⁰ and fully shared Evatt's view that Australia should shape its own foreign policy in accordance with its own regional interests. The United States should not be encouraged to seek hegemony in the South-West

---

4   P. Hasluck to H.C. Coombs, 29 April 1943, National Archives of Australia (NAA) M1942 [36].
5   J.W. Burton to P. Hasluck, n.d. [May 1943], NAA M1942 [36].
6   Burton to Hasluck, 16 June 1943, NAA M1942 [36].
7   Hasluck to Watt, 30 July 1943; Hasluck to Brigden, 29 November 1943, NAA CRS M1942 [36].
8   P. Hasluck, *The Government and the People, 1942-1945* (Canberra: Australian War Memorial, 1970), 479–85, 495–99.
9   Hasluck, 'Australia and the Formation of the United Nations', 154.
10 Hasluck to Brigden, 28 November 1943, NAA CRS M1942 [36].

Pacific but need not be provoked unnecessarily. Here he differed from Evatt in tone rather than substance. Hasluck was already aware that, in an international community shaped first and foremost by power relationships, Australia must use judgment in achieving effect while working within its limitations.

Paul Hasluck, 1954

Source: National Archives of Australia, A1200, L16892

Hasluck's great contribution to the Canberra conference lay in his skill as a draftsman, finding forms of words that would reconcile differing points of view. In such exercises he found some of the same intellectual pleasure as he did in writing poetry, especially when he was teamed with an expert jurist in Kenneth Bailey. He was formidably hardworking, at least once working throughout the entire night. His colleague, Patrick Shaw, wrote: 'Everyone attributes a large part of the speedy agreement to the preparatory work, and that means you and your section.'[11] In old age John Burton commented that Hasluck was a very good bureaucrat with no sign of an underlying philosophy.[12] As Peter Edwards has suggested, Hasluck and Burton supplied different needs for Evatt, 'the one relatively orthodox, the other more idealistic and adventurous'.[13]

The rivalry between Hasluck and Burton grew during 1944, as it was never made clear whether the Economic Relations section of External Affairs headed by Burton was separate from Hasluck's Post-War Hostilities Division or subordinate to it. Ric Throssell, then a diplomatic cadet, recalled:

> And you had this ludicrous situation going on, with Hasluck writing on cables, 'Dr Burton, please advise', and Burton would screw 'em up and throw 'em into the waste paper basket and then go down and get another clean copy for himself ... There was a huge rivalry between them.[14]

In September 1944, fed up with the wrangling, Hasluck submitted his resignation, but Evatt persuaded him to withdraw it. Hasluck was still a temporary appointee to the Department of External Affairs, expecting to serve until 1947 when he would start work on writing the home front section of the official history of Australia in the Second World War.[15] For the present he was in Evatt's good books, and Evatt placed increasing reliance on him.

When the Great Powers met at Dumbarton Oaks in August–September 1944 to plan the structure of the United Nations, the British delegation took care to consult Australia. Evatt concerned himself mostly with broad principles and left the detailed submissions to be drafted by Hasluck and Bailey.[16] At the Wellington conference between Australia and New Zealand in November 1944, Evatt was ill and it was left to the departmental officers, Hasluck, Burton

---

11   P. Shaw to P. Hasluck, 26 January 1944, NAA CRS M1942 [36].
12   J.W. Burton interview with author, 26 May 2004.
13   P.G. Edwards, *Prime Ministers and Diplomats: The Making of Australian Foreign Policy 1901–1949* (Melbourne: Oxford University Press, 1983), 147.
14   Don Baker oral history interview, 30 January – 3 March 1992 (National Library of Australia).
15   For the attempt at resignation Hasluck to Dunk, 25 March 1947, NAA CRS M1943 [16]; for his appointment to the Official War History, Long to Hasluck, 27 August 1943; Hancock to Long, 3 September 1943; Long to Hasluck, 13 October 1944; official contract, Hasluck MSS, Claremont.
16   Hasluck, *Diplomatic Witness*, 145.

and W.D. Forsyth, to exercise their own discretion; Hasluck thought that this made for greater precision in the conference's statements about international organisation, trusteeship and colonial policy.[17]

For the San Francisco conference setting up the United Nations, Curtin decided to send the deputy prime minister, Francis Forde, together with Evatt, but never clearly spelt out which of the two should lead the delegation. With both men out of the way the ailing Curtin could give the treasurer, Ben Chifley, a clear run to establish his credentials as acting prime minister and likely successor. Evatt's response was to mobilise the strongest possible support team, including Hasluck, Burton, Bailey, Watt and Forsyth.

Before the San Francisco conference the Australian delegation went to London between 4 and 13 April. It was meant to be 'a rather mild family talk, at which the United Kingdom ... would give information and explanations to the Dominions and answer their questions in order to assist their preparations'.[18] Evatt changed that. Comprehensively briefed by Hasluck and Bailey and working with furious concentration, he soon made it clear that he controlled Australia's policy and that Australia would not always comply with Britain. The patriot in Hasluck was not unhappy with this state of affairs, though he disagreed with Evatt's thinking on colonial issues. To his wife Hasluck wrote: 'Australia took quite a prominent part ... and in this case I think it can be fairly stated that Australia was Evatt, Bailey and myself.'[19]

The San Francisco conference began on 25 April and was scheduled to close at the end of May; in the event it was prolonged until 15 June. Very quickly Evatt and his officials, augmented by Bailey, established themselves as the makers of Australian policy. The work of the conference was divided between four commissions. Evatt ensured that one of his officers was appointed secretary and executive officer of each of the Australian delegations to these commissions. Hasluck's duties included the daily coordination of committee meetings and the briefing of Australia's representatives. In the eyes of an observer who saw much of the action at this time:

> Hasluck, I think, more than anybody, was responsible for framing the policies that Evatt followed in the post-war world. From the time in 1943 when Evatt fastened his attention to what the post-war world would be like – what Australia's role should be in it – Hasluck was the principal guide that fed the ideas into him. There were others such as Bill Forsyth, Ken Bailey, etc. etc. but Hasluck was the main one, the main architect of policies. And he worked like a Trojan for Evatt ...[20]

---

17   Ibid., 148; Edwards, *Prime Ministers and Diplomats*, 164.
18   Ibid., 193 and ch. 17 generally.
19   P. Hasluck to A. Hasluck, 17 April 1945, Hasluck MSS, Claremont.
20   Alan Renouf, oral history interview, 23 November 1993, National Library of Australia (NLA) TRC 2981/6.

Early in the San Francisco discussions Hasluck succumbed to a mood of disenchantment. He told his wife: 'I become more and more cynical watching this crowd at work and less certain that truth is ever to be found from the lips of man.'[21] From this abyss of pessimism he soon raised himself by a growing realisation that all the desperately hard work by Evatt and his team was producing positive results. In a later letter describing the delegates as 'a collection of monomaniacs all trying to put something across their neighbours', he also wrote, 'the Australian delegation is going pretty well and is getting a great number of things it wants, so although the spiritual climate is not very exhilarating there is a certain amount of good humour around the place'.[22] Under the intensive pressure of working for a common goal, the Australian delegation suspended most of their office jealousies. Hasluck found himself praising Evatt's tremendous capacity for work, forming close alliances with Bailey and Watt, and even writing about Burton in complimentary terms.[23]

When the time came to set up a 14-nation committee to integrate the findings of the working parties into the text of the United Nations charter Hasluck and Bailey were nominated to membership. Evatt told them: 'Go ahead and use your own judgment.'[24] The task was completed after days of intense pressure. Hasluck's mood was one of relief and elation. Evatt, he wrote, 'has certainly made his mark in this conference and established Australia as, next to the Great Powers, one of the most important and influential delegations at the conference'.[25] 'The effort has been worth it … [Evatt] has made me proud to be an Australian and particularly to be one of the same team. He really has fought magnificently and with great judgment in very difficult circumstances.'[26]

These comments made to his wife in the immediate aftermath of the San Francisco conference contrast with Hasluck's verdict in later years:

> [Evatt] was working for a success at San Francisco rather than addressing himself to the continuing tasks of good international relations. He was eager to play a leading role in making the Charter and of being the champion of small powers. His ambition was clearer than his policy.[27]

For the present, the halcyon mood continued. On the voyage home across the Pacific the Evatts, Hasluck, Burton and Sam Atyeo and his wife settled down to a peaceful existence of relaxation and reading, the greatest antagonisms arising from that most competitive of shipboard games, deck quoits. Never previously close,

---

21   P. Hasluck to A. Hasluck, 9 May 1945, Hasluck MSS, Claremont.
22   P. Hasluck to A. Hasluck, 26 May 1945.
23   P. Hasluck to A. Hasluck, 5 May 1945 and 1 June 1945.
24   P. Hasluck to A. Hasluck, 1 June 1945 and 18 June 1945.
25   P. Hasluck to A. Hasluck, 13 June 1945.
26   P. Hasluck to A. Hasluck, 25 June 1945.
27   Hasluck, 'Australia and the Formation of the United Nations', 177.

Hasluck and Sam Atyeo discovered a common enthusiasm for jazz. Even the news that Curtin had died and that Chifley had been elected leader by a substantial margin over Forde did not long disturb the tranquillity of the voyage.[28]

During the next 18 months, relations soured between Hasluck and Evatt. It is not necessary to seek an explanation by casting Burton as an Iago figure fanning suspicion in Evatt's mind, although undeniably Burton's propensity for gossip was unhelpful.[29] But as Hasluck gained in experience and confidence his views were diverging from Evatt's. His idealism was giving way to a cold-eyed pragmatism. He questioned Evatt's attempts to limit the authority of the Great Powers, doubted the practicality of a commitment to full employment, and thought Australia was over-extending its interventions into other nations' affairs.[30]

Dr H.V. Evatt at the United Nations, 1949

Source: National Archives of Australia, A6180, 23/8/79/118

---

28 Hasluck, *Diplomatic Witness*, ch. 21.
29 I do not have space in this paper to give examples, but evidence may be found not only in Hasluck's writings but also in L.F. Crisp's San Francisco diary (NLA) and in Alan Renouf's correspondence (Renouf to Hasluck, 'Paris/Sunday' [August 1946], NAA CRS M1943 [12]).
30 Hasluck, *Workshop of Security*, 178.

These divergences did not surface while Hasluck was in London between August 1945 and February 1946 for the preliminary discussions setting up the United Nations. Hasluck shepherded Evatt's interests devotedly, pressing his claims for the first presidency of the General Assembly.[31] In the event, Paul-Henri Spaak of Belgium was chosen. Hasluck thought that British disapproval might have prejudiced Australia's chances.[32] The Australians were no more successful in the debate about the future site of the United Nations headquarters. Evatt was eager for San Francisco, a venue that he thought would ensure attention to the Pacific region. The Great Powers, the Europeans and the Latin Americans all preferred a site on the Atlantic coast of the United States. Hasluck found himself in a minority of one.[33] The choice soon went to New York. However, Australia gained one of the elected seats on the Security Council after Canada gracefully withdrew from contesting it.[34]

Hasluck's performance at London sufficiently commended itself to Evatt for his appointment as counsellor-in-charge of the Australian mission to the United Nations and acting representative on the Atomic Energy Commission. The leadership of the delegation went to Norman Makin, newly appointed ambassador to Washington, who found himself thrust into the chairmanship of the Security Council as the result of a decision that each delegation should hold the office for a month in turn in alphabetical order. Makin was a modest, decent old warhorse of the federal Labor Party who had been speaker of the House of Representatives when the Scullin Government held office and minister for the Navy under Curtin but had no more experience of foreign affairs than Forde. 'Makin thanked the Council effusively for being first chairman. While Hasluck's face preserved an oriental calm, Watt's constantly moving with nervous coughs, and Bailey's showed absolute disbelief, there was raucous comment and guffaws of laughter from Sam Atyeo.'[35] But Makin showed himself prepared to take advice and express appreciation, and the work of the Security Council proceeded smoothly. Colonel Hodgson, formerly secretary of External Affairs and now ambassador to France, was sent to New York to take over from Makin, but he returned to Paris because of his wife's serious illness, leaving Hasluck to head the delegation.

In May 1946, Australia was represented on two committees dealing with major issues of contention. One concerned the fitness of Spain, then under the Franco dictatorship, for admission to the United Nations. The other was examining an Iranian complaint about a perceived Soviet threat in the border region of

---

31   Hasluck to Evatt, 12 December 1945, NAA CRS M1942 [22]; also Hodgson to Evatt, 14 December 1945, NAA CRS M1774 [23].
32   Hasluck to Evatt, 12 December 1945, NAA CRS M1942 [22].
33   Ibid.; see also Evatt to Hodgson and Hasluck, 20 December 1945, NAA CRS M1774 [23].
34   Hasluck to Dunk, 19 January 1946, NAA CRS M1943 [1].
35   A. Renouf, *The Champagne Trail: Experiences of a Diplomat* (Melbourne: Sun Books, 1980), 19.

Azerbaijan. The Russians walked out of the Security Council in protest against the discussion of this topic. Evatt gave no instructions to the Australian delegation, and Hasluck used the debate to attack the Soviet Union for opting out of the processes of international peacemaking. His speech made a strong impact in the press; the evening papers in New York carried photographs of him with glowing references to him as a young diplomat.[36]

Evatt was not pleased. Renouf later reported: 'He maintains that this was a breach of instructions and Molotov was very incensed with it. I think the real reason, however, is the publicity you received for your work.'[37] Evatt asked Renouf to send him a weekly report on 'what Hasluck was up to', adding, 'I think he's building himself up, not me'. When Renouf refused, Evatt said: 'I'll fix you.' But there was no showdown when Evatt arrived in New York later in May. He concentrated on the Atomic Energy Commission, keeping Hasluck extremely hard at work as Evatt's draftsman, sometimes in all-night sessions. Hasluck was unimpressed with Evatt's performance as temporary chairman of the Atomic Energy Commission. He seemed 'hell bent' on securing a treaty creating an international atomic energy authority and a system of control without building up understanding between the United States and the Soviet Union. Evatt left at the end of June with the central issue unresolved, leaving Hasluck, assisted by Ralph Harry and two distinguished scientists, George Briggs and Mark Oliphant, to spend the rest of the year working on many technical problems.[38]

For the rest of 1946 Hasluck worked ceaselessly, took part in a busy social round, and gained more publicity, although he swore that he tried to deflect the media to Evatt.[39] In December it was once again Australia's turn to chair the Security Council. Evatt sent word that Makin, and not Hasluck, would fill the role. Hasluck snapped. In his eyes Makin's nomination undermined his standing and suggested that he lacked the government's confidence: 'If it signifies my replacement I would appreciate plain advice to that effect.'[40] Mainly because of Makin's tact the tensions subsided for a while. Hasluck refused an offer of appointment as head of the European section of the United Nations, with headquarters in London and a salary of US$10,000 a year. Trouble erupted again in February 1947 when word arrived that Burton would become the secretary of the Department of External Affairs.

Hasluck sent in his resignation, stating that he was not influenced by issues of salary or status, nor because of lack of promotion, nor because of the strain on his health, but because 'by Burton's appointment Cabinet set its approval

---

36 A. Hasluck to E. Darker, 22 May 1946, Hasluck MSS, Claremont.
37 Renouf to Hasluck, 'Paris/Saturday' [August 1946], NAA CRS M1943 [12].
38 Ibid., 279.
39 Ibid., 282.
40 Hasluck to Evatt, 14 December 1945, NAA CRS M1943 [16].

on a whole system of petty intrigue, talebearing, favouritism and personal attachment to the Minister which as an Australian citizen I consider contrary to public service principles.'[41] Evatt told Hasluck that his judgment was affected by personal feelings, and there was perhaps just enough truth in the comment to make it rankle. A journalist who observed Evatt closely remarked that 'he had a rough, sometimes precise insight into those who worked for him. He seemed to know the exact tactic or word likely to reduce them to size.'[42] But in his own family circle Evatt uttered no criticism of Hasluck harsher than that he was 'pernickety'.[43]

Hasluck's wife Alexandra, a dismayed spectator of her husband's treatment, thought of an elegant rejoinder. She told her mother that Paul should go into parliament and become minister for External Affairs. 'He is fed up with the diplomatic life … but I think he would like the running of foreign policy.'[44] From his previous stance as a middle-of-the-road agnostic in politics, Hasluck was now moving towards support of the Liberal Party under Robert Menzies. Eventually the scenario unfolded as Alexandra Hasluck had predicted, though it is debatable whether it benefited either her own personal happiness or her husband's sense of achievement. As the old Chinese proverb has it: 'Be careful what you wish for, as your wish may be granted.'

Hasluck was returned to the House of Representatives for the safe seat of Curtin in December 1949, taking his seat on the government back benches opposite Evatt in his new role as deputy leader of the Opposition. Parliamentary legend has it that whenever Hasluck was scheduled to speak Eddie Ward would tell Evatt that Hasluck was about to 'spill the beans' about his past experiences in External Affairs, and Evatt would rush into the House in a state of perturbation. But Clyde Cameron, that devoted historian of the federal Labor Party, told a kindlier story. Years later in the 1960s, when Evatt's powerful intellect had been brought low by illness, only two members of parliament came to visit him in his twilight world. One was Justin O'Byrne, a notably good-natured Tasmanian senator. The other, by now a busy Cabinet minister, was Paul Hasluck. Patiently he sat with Evatt yarning about their experiences in San Francisco and trying to rouse him with talk of men and events whom they both knew.[45] It was a graceful conclusion to a sometimes fraught relationship.

---

41   Hasluck to Dunk, 25 March 1947, NAA M1943 [16].
42   R. Donnington, 'Evatt at Large', *Observer*, 15 September 1958.
43   Interview with Mrs Rosemary Carrodus, 29 November 2009.
44   A. Hasluck to E. Darker, 17 February 1947 and 23 April 1947, Hasluck MSS, Claremont. John Burton (interview, 26 May 2004) thought that when Hasluck resigned he was aware that Menzies was interested in him as a possible recruit to parliament, but I have found no evidence for this.
45   Interview with Clyde Cameron, 12 November 2002.

12

John Burton: Forgotten Mandarin?

Adam Hughes Henry[1]

John Burton was part of a young generation of talented recruits into the Australian public service during and after the Second World War. This influx was mainly due to the manpower shortages caused by the strains of war. By late 1941 and certainly by 1942, the unfavourable strategic circumstances of the war encouraged the John Curtin Labor Government to seek more self-assertive and independent foreign policy relationships with Great Britain and the United States. This attitude would be continued after the war by the Chifley Labor Government. The new direction of Australian foreign policy and its brash spokesperson Dr H.V. Evatt (the minister for External Affairs) was not always well received by the British or the Americans. During this time Burton eventually found himself in the role of personal secretary to Evatt and was therefore well placed to observe the changing tide. Traditional reliance of Australian diplomacy on the British Foreign Office had been well established for decades, but as Burton noted, 'Evatt changed all that'.[2]

Yet Evatt clearly trusted Burton enough during his time as foreign minister to delegate responsibilities at certain times for such things as reading and responding to incoming diplomatic cables.[3] Evatt's approach to international affairs was thus compatible with Burton and no doubt encouraging of new perspectives. Burton's own support for this new independence of diplomatic thought was not an unusual trait among those who served throughout the war and into the post-war period. A similar attitude was shared by departmental colleagues such as Paul Hasluck, Arthur Tange and James Plimsoll, who all rose quickly through the ranks of the Commonwealth Public Service (CPS) during the

---

1   A version of this essay was first published in *ISAA Review*, 12, no. 1 (2013), 67–84. It is reproduced with the permission of the editor, Susan Steggall.
2   Dr J.W. Burton, interview with author, Canberra, 19 February 2009. I am grateful for the opportunity to interview Dr Burton. It is a lamentable and indeed puzzling shame that more academics writing about the period, and often based in Canberra, failed to take any opportunity to interview him. I take the opportunity also to thank the Burton family and the Independent Scholars Association of Australia for publishing this essay in an earlier form.
3   Ibid.

1940s. However, in their later attitudes towards communism, or more precisely Cold War anti-communism, a professional and political dividing line emerged during the 1950s.

Here we can make a brief, but important, comparison between Burton and Hasluck. Both men were quite similar in certain respects, but ultimately had very different experiences of Australian bureaucratic and political life. Differing attitudes towards anti-communism, war and the philosophical world of foreign policy led each to seek profoundly different careers and life experiences. By the early 1950s, Hasluck was already carving out what would prove to be a long career in federal politics as a member of the Liberal Party, while Tange and Plimsoll found themselves fast tracked into positions of pre-eminence within the Department of External Affairs, particularly after Tange became secretary in 1954. By the end of 1951, Burton had already failed in his attempt to move from the bureaucracy and into federal politics as a member of the Australian Labor Party (ALP), and his career with the Department of External Affairs was over.

Burton would later play an important role in the development of peace and conflict studies during his long overseas academic career. He certainly left a well-respected academic legacy in the United States and the United Kingdom in the disciplines of international relations and peace and conflict studies. While this is known in his homeland, it seems that he is primarily remembered in Australia as being a *controversial* former secretary of the Department of External Affairs. During his early post-diplomatic years, he took tentative steps towards an academic career, but continued to be engaged in Australian foreign policy debates. It was Burton's philosophical attitudes towards the nature of the Cold War and his ongoing questioning of strident anti-communism that made him memorable within the bitter ideological politics of the 1950s. For ardent anti-communists (particularly on the non-Labor side of Australian politics), Burton represented a controversial and troubling sort of intellectual liberalism towards South East Asia and the Cold War.

After leaving the department in 1951 nothing Burton undertook diminished this negative interpretation. For example, when his book *The Alternative* was published in 1954, he merely reinforced the attitudes of critics.[4] In this book Burton critiqued the philosophical and intellectual basis of the Menzies Government's approach to foreign policy (especially in South East Asia). Rather than seeing communism as being nothing more than subversion directed from Moscow or Peking, Burton linked the growth of communism in South East Asia with nationalist struggles against European colonialism and other

---

4 J.W. Burton, *The Alternative: A Dynamic Approach to our Relations with Asia* (Sydney: Morgans Publications, 1954).

forms of Western interference.[5] This was primarily an important intellectual argument about the assumptions guiding Australian security thinking towards South East Asia under the Menzies Government. That is, to ignore, reject or attempt to suppress legitimate Asian aspirations for freedom from Western domination (whatever forms it took), did little to enhance Australian security, in fact, this was more likely to promote continuing uncertainty. This was not the sort of analysis that was very popular with ardent anti-communists. Given the political context of the Cold War in Australia, the surveillance Burton (and his family) endured at the hands of the Australian Security Intelligence Organisation (ASIO) after he left the Department of External Affairs, and the saga of the Petrov Affair, *The Alternative* remains a fascinating book.

My own introduction to John Burton came during the course of my master of arts honours thesis where I examined cables from and to Burton regarding the situation in South East Asia; particularly the Netherlands East Indies during 1945 to 1947.[6] This was my introduction to Burton the bureaucrat, diplomat and so-called protégé of Evatt. In the course of my doctoral research examining Australian foreign policy in the 1950s and 1960s, I examined archival materials and media sources that have hinted, implied and indeed slandered men such as John Burton as left-wing sympathisers, or even secret communist traitors. These issues shall be dealt with in more detail towards the end of this chapter. This was my introduction to Burton, the public intellectual and Cold War political dissenter. During my doctoral research I interviewed Burton (then aged in his 90s) to discuss the late 1940s, Indonesia, communism, Evatt, Australia, and his concepts of conflict resolution for international affairs.[7] This was my introduction to John Burton, the reflective elder statesman.

The life story of Burton is intriguing, but as yet it has failed to be the subject of a major biographical study. He was born in Melbourne on 2 March 1915. His father was a noted Methodist minister unafraid to be controversial in pursuing ethical ideals in his own life. Burton rejected Methodism (and religion) as a basis for his own philosophical and ethical thinking and did not follow in his father's religious footsteps, yet it is difficult not to see something of a Methodist influence in him. For example, the characteristic of following through on one's ethical and intellectual convictions in spite of strident criticism.

---

5   Burton's general view was that growing Asian nationalism and anti-colonialism (communist or otherwise), was a legitimate phenomenon. For his views on the implications of a nationalist or communist China in 1948, see D. Lowe, *Menzies and the Great World Struggle 1948–1954* (Sydney: University of New South Wales Press, 1999), 35–36.
6   See A.H. Henry, *Independent Nation – Australia, the British Empire and the origins of Australian–Indonesian Relations 1901–1946* (Darwin: Charles Darwin University Press, 2010).
7   Dr J.W. Burton, interview with author, 19 February 2009.

Dr John Wear Burton, c1951

Source: Courtesy of Pamela Burton

Educated at Newington College (1924–32) and then at the University of Sydney, Burton entered the CPS in 1937. He was the first to be granted a Commonwealth Scholarship, through which he pursued a doctorate at the London School of Economics.[8] Burton entered the Department of External Affairs in 1941 in the role of private secretary to Dr Evatt. The relationship between Burton and Evatt would prove to be both significant and at times controversial. In 1947, Burton became secretary of the Department of External Affairs and he served in this capacity until mid-1950. His elevation by Dr Evatt to this position at such a young age angered senior diplomats such as Alan Watt. This might also be a significant source of the professional friction between Evatt, Burton and Hasluck. Burton admitted that his handling of the notoriously sensitive Hasluck as secretary might have been a tipping point for the latter's resignation from the department. He reflected that he should not have denied Hasluck a permanent posting to the United Nations. Yet he was surprised by Hasluck's decision to join the Liberal Party of Australia and enter federal politics – he had always assumed that Hasluck was 'a Labor man'.[9]

After the election of the Menzies Government in 1949, Burton worked well by all reports with the new minister, Percy Spender. Yet the new government was also quickly moving into Cold War foreign policy directions that would eventually be quite incompatible with his own views. He was also weary of the bureaucratic life.[10] In 1950 he left his role as secretary of the department and later briefly held the position of Australian High Commissioner to Ceylon during 1951. He would famously resign from this position to stand unsuccessfully for election in Australia as a Labor candidate. This failed attempt to enter federal politics confirmed for Burton's critics their negative perceptions of him, and Burton continued to be a particularly maligned figure among conservative figures within Australian politics.

Despite his brief flirtation with politics, after 1951 he began a journey of transition from politics and bureaucracy towards new intellectual pursuits, which pushed Burton towards an academic career. After failing to win a seat in the federal parliament, he continued with his farming enterprises, but it was during this time of introspection that Burton worked with the ideas that would become *The Alternative*. It is from the time of the publication of this book in 1954 that we really see Burton moving more towards academia. By 1960 he was a fellow at The Australian National University; in 1962 he received a Rockefeller

---

8   For this information I am indebted to John Nethercote (Adjunct Professor, Canberra Campus, The Australian National University), for his detailed knowledge of Australian bureaucratic history.
9   Dr J.W. Burton, interview with author, 19 February 2009.
10 Ibid. Burton indicated to me that after such frantic years of working in the Department, he had developed a growing weariness and fatigue with his bureaucratic life. The combination of weariness, his new role in distant Colombo as high commissioner, and the changing political environment in Australia after the election of Menzies obviously made 1951 a time of serious personal and professional reflection.

Foundation grant to study African neutralism; in 1963 he was a reader of international relations at University College London. It was also at this time that he established a centre for the analysis of international conflict. The emphasis on negotiation, discussion and peaceful resolution (instead of militaristic strategy) remained central to Burton's thinking. By 1965 he had published two original books: *Peace Theory* and *International Relations: A General Theory*.[11]

Later in his academic career Burton would leave the field of international relations to become a founding figure in the development of peace and conflict studies. He would help to establish centres for this new discipline in the United Kingdom and the United States. His 'human needs theory' also provided a non-militaristic framework for conflict resolution built on structured dialogues and negotiated settlements.[12] One of the best descriptions of the logic of the human needs concept was provided by Doug Cocks:

> [B]ullying people does not make them behave the way you want them to behave, at least not for long; bullying does not get rid of conflicts. Burton's second article of faith is that conflicts between individuals, or collectives of individuals, will often resolve themselves if the disputants, with or without some outside help, can come to see each other as having, and seeking to satisfy, similar fundamental needs ... if people's fundamental needs are being met, they will be less conflictual ... It is Burton's conclusion, after long observation, that people most commonly come into conflict because they feel that their identity is not being recognized, that they are not being treated with dignity and respect for who they are; even when the conflict appears to be about something much more material such as land or resources.[13]

In retrospect this style of thinking can also be seen in aspects of Burton's earlier role as secretary of the Department of External Affairs, particularly towards the question of Indonesian independence.

---

11   For examples of publications during Burton's engagement with international relations (prior to his involvement in peace and conflict studies) see *Peace Theory* (New York: Alfred Knopf, 1962); *International Relations: A General Theory* (Cambridge: Cambridge University Press, 1965); *Systems, States, Diplomacy and Rules* (Cambridge: Cambridge University Press, 1968); *Conflict and Communication* (London: Macmillan, 1969); *World Society* (Cambridge: Cambridge University Press, 1972); *Deviance, Terrorism and War* (Oxford: Martin Robertson, 1979). For an overview see D.J. Dunn, 'John Burton & The Study of International Relations: An Assessment', *The International Journal of Peace Studies*, 6, no. 1 (2001), www.gmu.edu/programs/icar/ijps/vol6_1/Dunn.htm.

12   For a detailed overview of Burton's work in the field of peace and conflict studies see D.J. Dunn, *From Power Politics to Conflict Resolution: The Work of John W Burton* (London: Palgrave Macmillan, 2004). Dunn highlights that Burton developed the 'needs' idea around the same period that psychologist Abraham Maslow was developing his own theory of 'human nature'.

13   D. Cocks, *Learning from John Burton*, www.labshop.com.au/dougcocks/BURTONREVIEW.htm. See also J.W. Burton, ed., *Conflict: Human Needs Theory* (New York: St. Martin's Press, 1990).

What then can we learn from Burton in the context of Australian diplomatic, political and administrative history of the late 1940s and early 1950s? First, he worked in a small and at times amateurish department; it lacked funds, skilled manpower and prestige. Yet the Second World War had done much to encourage new directions for Australian foreign policy and it was during the Chifley-Evatt-Burton period that the fledgling Department of External Affairs began its long process of professionalisation. Working closely with Evatt, Burton was actively involved in this revolutionary yet sometimes chaotic process.

It was with the Dutch–Indonesia dispute that Burton saw at first-hand the merits of adhering to peaceful negotiated settlements. He shared this vision with Chifley, the Australian prime minister. To the horror of non-Labor critics, by 1946–47 Australian diplomacy (guided by Chifley, Evatt and Burton) began to view Dutch colonialism and its propensity for violence with great negativity. There was also growing sympathy towards the aspirations of Indonesians for freedom. Such attitudes were motivated by strong ethical and strategic considerations. The experiences of Indonesia's war of independence against the Dutch (1945–50) were profound for Chifley, Evatt and Burton. These policies resulted in Australia and India defending Indonesian republicanism through the United Nations from 1947.[14]

As secretary, Burton wrestled with implementing what I would see as the 'Chifley-Evatt' line on international affairs. This was an Australian foreign policy energised by the more nationalist legacy of the Second World War, social justice, the economic development of post-war Australia, engagement with the Asia-Pacific region, the centrality of the United Nations Charter and peaceful negotiations. This approach viewed nationalistic and anti-colonial ferment in South East Asia as being a reaction to European colonialism and not Soviet or Chinese directed subversion. Evatt and Burton's 'open diplomacy' approach certainly sought to introduce circuit-breaking dialogues and relationships into Australia's foreign policy thinking. Diplomatic dialogues and discussions with Soviet diplomatic officials might be open to criticism, but they only appear sinister if this approach was not also applied to dealings with other nations. The Chifley-Evatt-Burton style of foreign policy did not automatically accept Anglo-American attitudes towards the Cold War, international economics, full employment, Asian nationalism, European colonies, China, or defence planning. This approach was not popular with the non-Labor side of politics, nor with the British or Americans. Such attitudes certainly caused Burton to clash with Sir Frederick Shedden (secretary of the Department of Defence) over their differing attitudes towards foreign policy. For example, a major source of tension with the Department of Defence had been that in 1948 Shedden accepted British

---

14 For an extensive examination of the genesis of such attitudes towards Indonesian independence see Hughes, *Independent Nation*.

assessments that Moscow was directing communist subversion in South East Asia.[15] Evatt, Chifley and Burton were far more circumspect. Yet this clash was also connected to a bureaucratic rivalry between Defence and External Affairs over the administration of Australian foreign policy itself. Burton's efforts to centralise all cable communications about Australian foreign affairs through the Department of External Affairs was an attempt not just to modernise, but to break a stranglehold long held by the Department of Defence under Shedden.[16] In short, Burton had begun transforming the robust independence of diplomatic action generated by the Second World War into new administrative reforms and this development was not always welcomed.

Returning now to *The Alternative*, I would like to highlight in more detail possible reasons why Burton's ideas were unable to find lasting traction within the Department of External Affairs, at The Australian National University where he had been a fellow in the Department of International Relations, or within the foreign affairs thinking of the Australian Labor Party. Why did this unique and talented man, who rose to the heights of bureaucratic power so rapidly and with such immediate impact for Australian public policy, eventually leave Australia to forge an academic career in the United Kingdom and United States?

In his second career, Burton was viewed internationally as a former high-ranking Australian diplomat who became a cutting-edge scholar of new thinking. This respected status within international circles was shown by the almost instant and heartfelt expressions of thanks and condolence from all over the world on the sad news of his passing. The reaction was no less heartfelt in some Australian circles, but was generally more muted in his homeland. To explain this contrast one must delve back into Cold War politics and the Australian political scene of the late 1940s and 1950s. Burton's ideas in *The Alternative* seem relatively tame to modern eyes, but they (like Burton himself) were considered unacceptable to men such as Robert Menzies (prime minister), Richard Casey (minister for External Affairs, 1951–60) or Charles Spry (second director-general of ASIO) during the 1950s. His less rigid attitude towards Asian communism and anti-colonialism was an affront to the strategic thinking of such Cold War warriors. Certain factors conspired to make Burton's liberal views little more than poison in the minds of his critics. First, there was the revelation in the late 1940s of information leaks to Moscow from Canberra uncovered by the Venona cryptology operation.[17] In response, the Americans cut off the flow of classified intelligence material from the United States to Australia. This was problematic for the British who were hopeful of cooperating with the Australians on the development of

---

15   See Lowe, *Menzies and the Great World Struggle*, 28.
16   Dr J.W. Burton, interview with author, 19 February 2009.
17   F. Cain, 'Venona in Australia and Its Long-Term Ramifications', *Journal of Contemporary History*, 35, no. 2 (April 2000): 231–48.

long-range weapons and testing. Due to the American intelligence ban, technical information from the United States that was highly advantageous to the future development of British weaponry was either being denied to the United Kingdom or could not be shared with the Australians when it was. The Venona operation highlighted that certain employees of the Department of External Affairs were possible sources of these leaks. In their book *Breaking the Codes*, Desmond Ball and David Horner have speculated that at least 10 individuals (not all in External Affairs) were involved in an operation that resulted in thousands of cables being sent to Moscow.[18] Despite the severity of the American reaction, there were actually only two classified British documents that have been cited in scholarly articles as being leaked to Moscow from Canberra in their entirety via sources in the Department of External Affairs.[19] The revelations about the leaks eventually led to the establishment of the Australian Security Intelligence Organisation (ASIO) in 1948; a counter-intelligence agency that initially operated under judicial oversight. The Moscow leaks, or 'The Case' as it was known, became something of a Holy Grail to men such as Richard Casey, Charles Spry and Robert Menzies.

In the 1950s, the saga of 'The Case' became publicly connected to the Petrov Affair in 1954. After the defection of Vladimir Petrov, third secretary at the Soviet Embassy, and his wife Evdokia, the Menzies Government utilised a very public royal commission to examine espionage issues effectively inspired by Venona-related intelligence. This was all designed to uncover communist traitors and they seemingly hoped to ensnare even Burton himself. It is in Burton's attitudes and responses to these smears and allegations that a less sensational picture emerges. Burton was highly contemptuous about the value of ASIO, sceptical of its potential role and dismissive of the alleged extent and damage caused by the known Moscow leaks. He was equally unimpressed by Petrov whom he thought 'too stupid' to be a master spy.[20] The use of smear and innuendo still connected to 'The Case' is also instructive of the political climate that faced Burton in the late 1940s and increasingly into the 1950s. Rumours about the troubled Australian relationship with US intelligence had certainly found their way to the Menzies' Opposition by the late 1940s.[21] In 1948, when Chifley

---

18   D. Ball and D. Horner, *Breaking the Codes: Australia's KGB Network* (St Leonards, NSW: Allen and Unwin, 1998).
19   In all the scholarly materials I have encountered on this topic these are the only two full documents cited: 'Security in the western Mediterranean and Eastern Atlantic', Public Records Office UK, CAB 79/34/8, PHP (45)6(0), 19 May 1945; 'Security in India and the Indian Ocean', PRO CAB 79/34/8, PHP (45)15(0). See also National Archives of Australia (NAA) A5954/1, Item 848/1.
20   Dr J.W. Burton, interview with author, 19 February 2009.
21   The issue of Venona (and the US intelligence embargo) certainly provided opportunities for domestic and international critics of the Chifley Government. There is intriguing circumstantial evidence that news about the intelligence embargo could have been passed to Menzies or the non-Labor Opposition by US, or most likely UK sources. For one, the British had already supplied classified information to Menzies in 1948 while he was still Opposition leader. Furthermore, the leaking of information to the Australian press suggesting that the Americans were refusing to share atomic secrets with Australia (see the *Sydney Morning Herald* in

attended the Commonwealth Prime Minister's Conference in London, Menzies also visited Europe. During his time in London classified British assessments about communism in South East Asia were shown to him.[22] These assessments (which saw the hand of Soviet subversion as the root cause of political ferment in South East Asia) were supported by the Attlee Labour Government. Such assessments diverged strongly with those of Chifley, Evatt and Burton, but were highly compatible with the views of Menzies.

While British intelligence informed Chifley of the leaks, they were initially under instructions from the Americans not to disclose the true origins of this information, that is, the cryptology operation named Venona. Intense American hostility towards Evatt and Burton and the Australian Labor Party meant that they, including Chifley, were initially provided with an MI5 cover story about the Moscow leaks. Once Chifley was in possession of the full story he embarked on the establishment of ASIO (if somewhat reluctantly) to restore American faith in the Australian Labor Government. Although sceptical of the true importance of British documents leaked to Moscow, Burton nonetheless approved a joint Commonwealth Investigation Service and MI5 counter-intelligence operation against a visiting Russian delegation during 1948.[23] He also appeared as a witness before the Petrov Royal Commission providing detailed evidence of his side of 'The Case' story. Burton's testimony was taken 'in camera' and therefore in complete secrecy from public scrutiny. His 'in camera' testimony did not appear in the published proceedings of the royal commission, nor were they publicly available for decades.[24]

There has also been something of a selective airbrushing of history in regards to 'The Case' and its 'nest of traitors'. When the National Archives of the United Kingdom released a large amount of material connected to 'The Case' in April 2011, this speculation re-emerged. Professor Desmond Ball (of The Australian National University) made an allegation, reported in a national newspaper, that either Burton or Evatt were 'agents of Soviet influence'.[25] Historians as diverse as Peter Edwards, Gregory Pemberton, Robert Manne, and even former New South Wales premier Bob Carr were unconvinced by Ball's speculations. Ball's allegations seem connected to revelations in the British documents that in 1958

July 1948), and subsequent questions raised in parliament (for example Arthur Fadden in September 1948), seem to indicate Opposition awareness of some of the issues. This was all highly embarrassing for the Chifley Government.

22   See 'Minutes of Defence Committee Meeting DO (48) Meeting 13 August 1948, Minute 3 Prem 8/1406 Part 1', PRO cited by Lowe, *Menzies and the Great World Struggle 1948–1954*, 192. Lowe also refers to the document 'Russian Interests, intentions and capabilities', 23 July 1948 J.I.C (48)9(0).

23   L. Maher, 'The Lapstone Experiment and the Beginnings of ASIO', *Labour History*, no. 64 (May, 1993): 103–118, available from www.jstor.org/stable/27509168.

24   See 'Extracts from the Official Transcript of Proceedings taken In Camera, 2 November 1954 – Dr Burton', NAA A6215, 10.

25   P. Wilson, 'Fearing Herbert Evatt's Soviet Ties, Robert Menzies Leaked Petrov Papers', *Australian*, 9 April 2011.

Spry had told the British that should Evatt win that year's federal election they should withhold classified intelligence, and that Menzies apparently handed over classified intelligence files connected to espionage in Australia to the British and the Americans in fear of Evatt.

> Spooked by signs that Evatt might win the November 22 election, Menzies secretly ordered ASIO to hand sets of top-secret documents to Britain and the US for safe-keeping because of his fear that Evatt would bury or destroy the material if he became Prime Minister. Until then the Australian government had refused for four years to give the British and US governments full access to the material, a pile of Russian documents handed over by former KGB man Vladimir Petrov when he defected in 1954.
>
> But two days before the election Menzies suddenly decreed that Britain's spy services MI5 and MI6 should each be given a complete copy of the documents and two more sets should go to the CIA. The originals were held in the PM's office. The copy given to MI5 filled nine envelopes and was among the material released on Monday by the spy service.[26]

The ironies of Menzies' extraordinary actions have seemingly been missed. Menzies had after all handed intelligence documents about Soviet espionage to MI5. According to a range of sources, including Peter Wright's *Spy Catcher*, MI5 was an organisation that had been spectacularly penetrated at very high levels by Soviet spies from the 1940s, throughout the 1950s, and into the 1960s. There were opportunities for Ball to have put forward these allegations in the book *Breaking the Codes* while Burton was still alive, but such allegations were removed from the original book draft after receiving 'legal advice'.[27]

Such controversy has tended to obscure Burton's thinking about foreign policy. There were of course others during the late 1940s and 1950s who, like Burton, considered Asia to be vital to Australia's future interests – men such as Richard Casey, Arthur Tange, Tom Critchley, MacMahon Ball, Richard Kirby, James Plimsoll or Alan Watt, but there are distinctions to be made. Casey's approach to Asia was built first and foremost on adoption of an anti-communism strongly connected to Anglo-American approaches towards the Soviets and later the Chinese. Australian diplomacy was therefore designed to build dialogues (often

---

26 Ibid.
27 Ibid. Wilson writes that: 'Dr. Ball said the only previous time he had expressed this view was in a draft of *Breaking the Codes*, which was published when Burton was still alive, but the reference was removed on legal advice.' It would appear that it was *wise* that this legal advice was heeded. For an examination of the merits of raising this issue again only *after* Burton passed away see G. Pemberton, 'Old Gossip, but No Evidence John Burton was a Spy', *Australian*, 18 January 2012. See also P. Burton, 'Burton Was a Patriotic Public Servant, not a Traitor', *Australian*, 30 April 2011. While researching *The Spy Catchers: The Official History of ASIO, 1949–1963* (Crows Nest, NSW: Allen & Unwin, 2014), David Horner did not seek an interview with Burton.

with non-communist regimes) in South East Asia against the hidden hand of Soviet-Chinese subversion. While Tange oversaw this process, he himself largely credited Casey with the expansion of Australian diplomatic missions into South East Asia. James Plimsoll was interested in aspects of Asia, particularly South Korea, but was very fearful of the Chinese. Crucially, Burton was highly critical of concepts and assumptions that placed military technology, military covenants and the threat of force at the heart of American, Soviet, and European (let alone Australian) foreign policy planning. This highly negative view of militarism can be seen in Burton's early work on international relations theory and later in his work on peace and conflict studies. Such attitudes are highly incompatible with military interventionism in Asia and by implication, covert interventions by either communist or Western powers against third world nations. These actions were unable to resolve the root cause of political and social conflicts and as such they would remain effectively unresolved. In retrospect, some of this style of thinking is present during his tenure as secretary of External Affairs.

Another reason that the Burton legacy in Australia is ambiguous is that after leaving the department he did not go off silently into the sunset; he continued his independent commentary on Australian foreign policy. This was an irritating trait from the perspective of his many enemies. His trip to China in 1952 as leader of a self-styled Australian peace delegation and public speaking engagements did little to soothe the tempers of the critics. A particular issue of contention in Australia was Burton's public questions regarding the possible use of germ warfare by the US military in the Korean War.[28] Another case in point was his attendance as an observer at the Bandung (or African-Asian) Conference in April 1955; the neutralist tendencies of the conference were viewed with great alarm by ardent anti-communists in Canberra, London and Washington. Burton was surprised by the Indonesian reception at Bandung and he recalled the hospitality and excellent accommodation he received. The Indonesians remembered Burton's diplomatic support during their struggles against the Dutch. He noted with some amusement that his warm welcome (and the excellent accommodation he enjoyed in Bandung) contrasted with Australia's official diplomatic representatives within Indonesia at that time.[29] Burton's liberal attitudes and the legacy of 'The Case' made him a continued high profile

---

[28] In 1952, these allegations found widespread currency. See T. Buchanan, 'The Courage of Galileo: Joseph Needham and the Germ Warfare Allegations in the Korean War', *History*, 86, no. 284 (October 2001): 503–22. Phillip Deery notes that we now seemingly have confirmation that these biological warfare allegations were part of a communist disinformation campaign. See 'New Evidence on the Korean War', *Cold War International History Project Bulletin*, no. 6-7 (Winter 1995/1996). See also P. Deery '"Behind Enemy Lines": Menzies, Evatt and Passports for Peking', vuir.vu.edu.au/571/1/Behind_Enemy_Lines'.pdf. It is possible that conditions suitable for the outbreak of contagious diseases existed at that time in various parts of Korea; see Shu Guang Zhang, *Mao's Military Romanticism: China and the Korean War, 1950–1953* (Lawrence: University Press of Kansas, 1995), 184–185.

[29] Dr J.W. Burton, interview with author, 19 February 2009.

target of ASIO well past any conceivably valid timeframe.[30] Yet Burton's approach to foreign policy, his attempt to implement ethical dimensions sympathetic to peaceful conflict resolution through the United Nations into the External Affairs culture, his rejection of strategic militarism (most often favoured by his critics as central to international affairs), is profound. This assessment is neither romantic nor uncritical. Burton made mistakes and was not afraid to admit shortcomings in his reflections of his period as secretary. Yet the loss of Burton to academia overseas was also a great loss to Australian public policy and ultimately to national knowledge. He was the mandarin that might have been, if only the shifting political sands of anti-communism in the late 1940s and 1950s had not moved with such ruthless and unforgiving speed.

---

30 For reactions to Burton's criticisms of Australian foreign policy after his resignation from the Department of External Affairs, see 'Chapter 12, The Nest of Traitors', in D. McKnight, *Australia's Spies and their Secrets* (St Leonards, NSW: Allen & Unwin, 1994), 51–5.

13

Sir Arthur Tange: Departmental Reformer

Peter Edwards

Sir Arthur Tange was remembered, especially in Canberra, long after his retirement, but very largely for his last position, as secretary of the Department of Defence throughout the 1970s. There are many in the military who have still not forgiven the author of 'the Tange report' and the instigator of 'the Tange reforms', which resulted not only in a fundamental reorganisation of the Defence group of departments but also in major changes to Australian strategic policies. Particularly among left-leaning journalists, there was a longstanding belief that Tange was the crucial link between the CIA and the Governor-General that led to the dismissal of the Whitlam Government in November 1975. Others long contended that he played a dishonourable role at the time of the deaths of five Australia-based journalists at Balibo, Portuguese Timor, in October 1975. Within the public service, anecdotes long endured of Tange's style, which would today be described as unacceptable bullying. Tange was capable of browbeating officers, even senior officers, in front of their subordinates, stopping just short of physical contact, throwing down files so that they disintegrated on the floor – and then, in a split second, turning to welcome a visiting dignitary with wit and charm. Ever conscious of the importance of his own time, he would insist that a lift was kept available for his use, and Heaven help anyone who encroached on his parking space, even at a weekend. Wits liked to describe the Chinese floor vases outside his office as 'Late Tang – slightly cracked'.

The focus and span of this volume offer an opportunity to look anew at Tange's career as if, as very nearly happened, it had come to an end in the late 1960s, before his appointment to Defence. A study of Tange's career in the 1940s, 1950s and 1960s adds further evidence and nuances to some of the themes under consideration. These include the importance of the new cohort of university graduates, especially in economics, in the Commonwealth Public Service; the dedication to institution-building, especially strong departments, as a mark of the professionalism of the public service; and the simultaneous adherence to both the concept of an independent public service, giving frank and fearless advice to governments of whatever party, and a broadly social democratic ethos, embodied in the great project of post-war reconstruction. If we, for the moment, leave aside Tange's work in Defence in the 1970s, he remains important and distinctive, albeit not unique, for his role in taking these themes into the relatively new area, for the Commonwealth Public Service, of foreign policy.

Tange was born in the fateful month of August 1914.[1] Although the youngest of seven siblings from his father's two marriages, Arthur was in many ways more like an only child than a member of a large family, and he long retained the psychological outlook of a loner. His grandfather, Anton Tange, migrated from Denmark in the 1850s and prospered as a tea merchant in Sydney; the next generation lost much of the family's fortune. Arthur's father, Charles, attended The King's School, Parramatta, and graduated from the University of Sydney, where he was a resident of St Paul's College, but discarded his promising practice as a lawyer in Sydney, with a house on the upper North Shore, to go on the land, establishing an orchard near Gosford on the Central Coast. This venture failed and Arthur's early years, when he attended Woy Woy Primary School and Gosford High School, were shaped by the impecunious circumstances. Tange was never close to his father, who was 54 when Arthur was born, but was always loyally supportive to his mother during her 40 years as a widow. The spur to Arthur's ambition was his determination not to fail his dependents in the way that his father had.

Despite good results in his matriculation examination, at the age of just 16, Arthur would have had little chance of following his father to university but for a stroke of fortune. His eldest sibling, his half-sister Dorothy, 22 years his senior, had married Alfred Davidson, who rose spectacularly in the 1920s to become general manager of the Bank of New South Wales, the position known today as the Chief Executive Officer of Westpac. Davidson, a dominant figure in Australian finance in the 1930s and early 1940s who did much to shape Australia's response to the Depression, became employer and mentor to his young brother-in-law. He gave Arthur a base-grade job in the bank, and then transferred him to the Perth branch so that he could attend the University of Western Australia, the only free university in Australia. Davidson was especially impressed with the dynamic professor of history and economics, E.O.G. (Ted) Shann.

In later life Tange liked to speak of the three great achievements of his time as a student in Perth. He gained post-graduate qualifications (as an honours degree was then regarded), gaining a Bachelor of Arts with first class honours in economics, with a thesis on the Australian capital market. (Essentially he argued that Australian banks were unduly conservative in lending to business; *plus ça change*.) Secondly, he became an outstanding rugby player, representing Western Australia against the visiting Springboks. Thirdly, he won the heart

---

1   For a fuller account of Tange than is provided here, see P. Edwards, *Arthur Tange: Last of the Mandarins* (Crows Nest, NSW: Allen & Unwin, 2006).

and, when he could afford it, the hand of Marjorie Shann, one of Professor Shann's three daughters. (Keith Shann, better known as Mick, was Marjorie's first cousin.)

After graduating, Arthur and Marjorie were both employed by Davidson in the bank's Economics Department, an in-house think tank established by Davidson with considerable influence from Ted Shann. Arthur was then posted to Fiji, where the bank had a profitable business in foreign exchange, and where Tange saw no reason to hold British colonial officials in high esteem. From there he was recruited to become what his employer and mentor, Davidson, had long held in low esteem – a Canberra public servant. Tange became a lowly research officer in that section of the Department of Labour and National Service, which was already looking at post-war policies. Later this became the Department of Post-War Reconstruction.

In Post-War Reconstruction, Tange became one of the team of officials working under senior economists such as Leslie Melville, L.F. Giblin and Douglas Copland. A principal focus was Article VII of the Lend-Lease agreement, which made American aid conditional upon working towards free trade. The Australians sought to reconcile this with their traditional policies of protectionism and imperial preference. In 1944 Tange, with Melville and his friend and contemporary Fred Wheeler, were the only three officials on the absurdly small and overworked delegation to Bretton Woods, which laid the foundations for the post-war international economic order. In all this work, Tange's admiration for the British and American officials fell short of being overawed. Neither then nor later would he be one who naturally genuflected before great and powerful friends and allies.

During the late 1930s and early 1940s, Australia had been developing the basis of a foreign office and diplomatic service, known as the Department of External Affairs. This was another channel through which bright young graduates – mostly men, in the days of the marriage bar – were recruited into the Commonwealth Public Service. That department was also giving attention to the problems of the post-war world, with Paul Hasluck the central figure. The two departments worked separately, but in the latter years of the war, when Evatt and his closest adviser, John Burton, became aware that the proposed United Nations Organization was likely to have an economic component, they realised that External Affairs needed to boost its economic capacity. For a time Arthur Tange was shared 50/50 between Post-War Reconstruction and External Affairs.

Immediately after the war, Tange was recruited full-time to a position in External Affairs at the diplomatic level of first secretary, then quite senior in the departmental hierarchy. He was promptly despatched to the Mission to the United Nations in New York. There, while Hasluck worked on Security Council and related matters, Tange worked not only on international economic questions but also on other fields. This was an era of international conferences establishing, and writing constitutions for, international organisations in a diverse range of fields. Tange rapidly developed expertise in these new aspects of international diplomacy, a new field for the Commonwealth Public Service.

Tange had thus joined the cohort of bright young graduates in External Affairs, but he was, from the start, a little apart from the rest. He had been laterally recruited, rather than coming up through the department's own cadet scheme, and his expertise was primarily in economics, unlike most of his new colleagues. He remained a little apart.

From New York, Tange returned to Canberra. Soon after the change of government in December 1949, the new minister for External Affairs, Percy Spender, recruited Tange as his principal adviser at the conference that devised what became the Colombo Plan. He was not, however, part of the official team who worked with Spender on what became the ANZUS Treaty, although he had some marginal involvement in those negotiations. Without over-emphasising the point, it is probably fair to say that, of the two pillars of Australian foreign policy that were erected during Spender's short but highly creative term, Tange remained closer to that which prescribed engagement with the region than to that of the US alliance.

Tange's next diplomatic posting, at an unusually senior level for someone of his years and experience, was as deputy head of mission at the embassy in Washington, where Spender had been made ambassador. Here his unwritten brief was to try to restrain Spender, who seemed (in the eyes of many in Canberra) to think that he was still minister rather than one of the new minister's official servants. In this exercise, Tange did not have much success, but the experience of working in Washington during the time of Senator Joe McCarthy did nothing to raise his estimation of American officialdom.

The age structure of External Affairs in the early 1950s was very unusual, with a tiny handful of diplomatic officers over the age of 40 and burgeoning numbers in their twenties and thirties. It was highly likely, therefore, that when one of the senior men, Alan Watt, retired as secretary in 1954, the baton would be passed to one of the junior men. In the event, the minister, R.G. Casey, evidently considered two of the senior men, Keith Officer and Alfred Stirling, but both wisely considered that they were not well suited to the post. Casey chose Tange, just ahead of Jim (later Sir Laurence) McIntyre and the three who would become Tange's principal lieutenants, Keith Waller, Pat Shaw and James Plimsoll. Others in the same cohort included Peter Heydon, Keith 'Mick' Shann and Ralph Harry, all of whom became departmental heads and/or senior ambassadors in the coming years. (Waller, Shaw, Plimsoll, Heydon and Shann were all later knighted; Harry was appointed AC.)

13. Sir Arthur Tange

Sir Arthur Tange, 1965

Source: National Archives of Australia, A8947, 45

Tange remained secretary of the Department of External Affairs for 11 years, starting with the Petrov Affair and the rupture of relations with the Soviet Union and ending just as Australia was about to commit combat troops to Vietnam. Typically, for a man who liked to work with the written word, Tange wrote two papers early in his tenure, one on administration and one on policy, which did much to establish the framework for his term as secretary.

Tange spent much of his time reorganising the department's structures and methods, with the aim of turning a group of more or less talented individuals into an effective and cohesive foreign office and diplomatic service. He initiated a wide range of major and minor reforms, some of which were remarkable largely for their previous absence – systems for appointments and promotions, performance appraisal, records of conversations, financial management and so on. Tange made it clear that he wanted the officers in External Affairs to put aside some of the pretensions to which ambitious diplomats were susceptible and to think of themselves first and foremost as public servants, competent and qualified in all the skills and responsibilities of good public servants, and then applying those skills and meeting those responsibilities in the field of foreign policy. At a time when the department was explicitly divided into Group A, the diplomatic officers, and Group B, the administrative and consular officers, this approach won the respect of the Group B officers but did not always endear Tange to the diplomats.

In establishing a professional foreign office and diplomatic service, Tange was obliged to accept three elements in the department that he thought did not properly belong there. In each case Tange's reservations, shared by his diplomatic colleagues, were overridden by Casey, a much admired and personally respected minister but one whose enthusiasms often frustrated his officers. These three elements were the Australian Secret Intelligence Service, the Antarctic Division, and the implementation of the Colombo Plan. Tange would doubtless approve of the current situation, under which ASIS is an autonomous agency, separate from the department but reporting to the same minister, while the Antarctic Division is placed in the Department of the Environment. It is less likely that he would have approved of the 2013 decision to re-integrate AusAID into the Department of Foreign Affairs and Trade.

Whatever setbacks he may have had, the department was certainly far more effective at the end of his 11 years as secretary than it had been at the beginning.

Tange's policy document was notable for the priority it gave to relations with Asia and the comparative downplaying of relations with the United Kingdom and the United States, at a time when Prime Minister Menzies and his government placed pronounced emphasis on these 'great and powerful friends'. In policy matters, Tange and the department experienced both success and failure.

13. Sir Arthur Tange

An early attempt to have the government reconsider its attitude towards the recognition of the People's Republic of China was clumsily handled by Casey and the department, setting back policy on this critical issue for many years. Perhaps the greatest achievement was the handling of Konfrontasi, the low-level conflict between Indonesia and the new federation of Malaysia between 1963 and 1966. The minister, Garfield Barwick, the department in Canberra, and the missions in Jakarta and Kuala Lumpur worked extremely effectively to shape and implement a policy that was by no means always consistent with the instincts and attitudes of the long-serving and dominant prime minister, Menzies.

Tange's ministers during his term as secretary were some of the most significant Liberals of their era – Casey, Menzies himself, Barwick and Hasluck. His relations with them ranged from cordial to frosty, illustrating the degree to which the relationship between departmental head and minister depended on matters quite separate from party. Tange and his officers, for example, found Barwick almost an ideal minister, whereas their relations with their former colleague, Hasluck, when he returned as minister, were highly strained. I have considered these relationships in some detail in *Arthur Tange: Last of the Mandarins*. The relationship between Tange and Hasluck over some four decades would make an interesting study in itself.

Tange's relations with other public servants covered in this volume also ranged widely, from emulation through admiration and friendly, or not so friendly, rivalry to hostility and even contempt. He greatly admired H.C. 'Nugget' Coombs from his first exposure to Nugget's persuasive ways with Wall Street bankers; he thought that Frederick Shedden by the 1950s was well past his wartime prime and a failure at running the post-war Defence Department; he clashed with Wilson and his deputy, Lenox Hewitt, over the Treasury's control of departmental finances; he had a complex friendship-cum-rivalry with Fred Wheeler and a more distant respectful rivalry with J.G. Crawford (Tange and Crawford were knighted on the same day); and he thought Ken Bailey was able but weak in standing up to ministers.

Tange had been highly regarded by Menzies in the late 1950s, but by the early 1960s the prime minister was clearly seeking to move him onwards. Tange resisted this pressure, as a permanent head could do in those days, but he finally agreed in 1965 to become high commissioner to India. For some years, he thought that his career might end there, as he was determined not to accept any position below what he thought appropriate. Then, in what reads like an episode of *Yes, Minister*, he was rapidly offered the embassy in Washington, a return to his position in External Affairs, and the secretaryship in Defence. He spent the last 10 years of his career in the last position, undoubtedly the most remarkable occupant of the position to that point – and perhaps ever, because the public service reforms of the 1980s were brought in precisely to ensure that no departmental secretaries would ever again have the clout that was held, in fact and even more in reputation, by Tange, Wheeler and a handful of their cronies. That is why my biography of Tange is subtitled *The Last of the Mandarins*; but it is timely to recall that he contributed much to the strengths and, indeed, the weaknesses, of the public service in the 1940s, 1950s and 1960s.

14

Sir James Plimsoll: Mandarin Abroad

Jeremy Hearder[1]

James Plimsoll's life and career had similarities with others featured in this volume, but also significant differences. The main difference was that for two-thirds of his time he was abroad. Dwarfs and mandarins succeeded in part because they had effective communication with the ministers for whom they worked; that is, mutual comprehension, trust and respect. For the mandarin based abroad this was more difficult, given distance, poor communications, and being less aware of the atmospherics at home. Provision of frank and fearless advice was hard from afar, when such advice clearly was not going to be well received and even harder when you do not personally know the minister or Snow White. So the ideal was for the ambassador to feel confident in knowing Snow White's mind, and for Snow White to have personal confidence in the ambassador.

Let me tell you a true fairy story. Once upon a time, in 1962, Snow White decided to go to New York without any of the dwarfs, because Snow White knew he would be well looked after by that mandarin over there, Plimsoll. In New York, Snow White found that Plimsoll kept on trying to bring up the subject of Rhodesia. An increasingly prominent and sensitive issue, it had been inscribed as an agenda item to be debated in the United Nations General Assembly in a few days time. Plimsoll was getting no guidance from officials in Canberra on what he should say. Snow White kept fobbing him off. Eventually, when Snow White was about to board a plane to return home, Plimsoll implored him once again for guidance about what he should say about Rhodesia. Snow White clapped him on the shoulder and said: 'My boy, I'm glad you're making [the speech], not me', and climbed aboard. Plimsoll took it that he could say what he wanted to.[2]

That sort of latitude extended to a diplomat abroad is rare. Menzies knew what he was doing. Plimsoll was someone whose judgment he had come to respect during Plimsoll's earlier six years in Canberra. Menzies knew that during the

---
1   The following is based on the author's research for his book *Jim Plim Ambassador Extraordinary: A Biography of Sir James Plimsoll* (Ballarat, VIC: Connor Court Publishing, 2015).
2   James Plimsoll in conversation with Clyde R. Cameron (1984), National Library of Australia, nla.oh-vn677900, transcript, Vol. ii, 6–7.

past three years Plimsoll's duties had taken him on three extensive visits through Africa – in those days he had seen more than most of the Unknown Continent. More recently, Menzies had approved of the way that Plimsoll, in transiting London, had handled an unexpected meeting with the British Secretary of State for Colonies, Duncan Sandys, at Sandys' request. Sandys had told Plimsoll that the United Kingdom intended to make Rhodesia independent soon. To Sandys' chagrin, Plimsoll had quoted the relevant passage from the United Nations Charter to him and said he doubted that Australia would agree to the grant of independence to a minority government.[3] Menzies had also approved other things Plimsoll had done at the United Nations when unable to get instructions in time.[4] With no other prime minister did Plimsoll enjoy such a close working relationship.

Years later, in 1974, Plimsoll called on Menzies in retirement, days after the announcement of the new governor-general, Sir John Kerr. Menzies said he thought this appointment was a mistake, without saying why. If he had still been in office, he would have recommended Plimsoll for the post – but that is another story.[5]

For nearly 35 years, Jim Plimsoll was one of Australia's leading diplomats. He had an exceptional career. He was secretary of the Department of External Affairs in Canberra from 1965 to 1970. He served as ambassador no less than eight times, all in places of major importance to Australia – Korea, the United Nations in New York, New Delhi, Washington, Moscow, Brussels, London, and Tokyo.

Unlike other dwarfs and mandarins, Plimsoll spent only one-third of his career in Canberra. He was posted abroad for the remainder. He tolerated rather than liked living in Canberra, and bought no real estate. Canberra was all about the job, not a home. It was only the personal persuasion of Dr Evatt, the then minister for External Affairs, that led him to come to Canberra and join the department in the first place in 1948. His ambitions did not lie in power, or management of a large organisation. This was 'not his cup of tea'.[6]

Plimsoll was passionate about the task of representing Australia abroad. He declined offers to take high level posts in the Secretariat of the United Nations, at twice the pay. After reaching the pinnacle, first as secretary then as ambassador in Washington, when he could have gone into other things, he stayed on as a diplomat. Instead, he accepted posts of slightly lower status – indeed, he wanted to be first high commissioner in Papua New Guinea.

---

3   Ibid., 5–6.
4   See Menzies' reply to a parliamentary question from Dr J.F. Cairns on 17 October 1961. *Current Notes on International Affairs*, 32, no. 10 (October 1961), 54–7.
5   Plimsoll in conversation, 377.
6   Sir Garfield Barwick, conversation with author, December 1996.

14. Sir James Plimsoll

Sir James Plimsoll, 1965

Source: National Archives of Australia, A1200, L52865

Plimsoll's upbringing was similar to a number of the other dwarfs and mandarins – attendance at a leading selective state school, and an economics degree as an evening student. But there were some differences. Over the next few years, Plimsoll went through further education and an unusually stimulating on-the-job training in research, analysis, communication and representation. He remained at Sydney University for eight years, during which he added an arts degree, had extensive debating experience in the University Union, and was elected president of the Union. By day he worked in the Research Department of the Bank of New South Wales, the first of its kind in Australia. In order to accomplish all this, he developed an almost monastic approach to living. Work came first, an approach he never lost. His father could have paid for full-time university study, yet with an accountant's caution after the Depression he insisted Plimsoll get a job and study in the evening. During the Second World War, as a captain, he worked with Alf Conlon, a fellow Sydney student politician, in the Directorate of Army Research in Melbourne, with all those often brilliant, eccentric colleagues. In 1945 he went to the United States to attend a school in military government. Out of 350 students, mainly American, British and Canadian officers, he came second. Then, as Major Plimsoll, he was Australia's representative on the Far Eastern Commission in Washington. Other differences were that he remained single, and although the youngest of the dwarfs/mandarins, he died the earliest, except for Crawford – I think due to overwork.

As a diplomat, Plimsoll developed a standing that made key foreigners not only happy to see him, but sometimes want to seek him out to discuss their own problems. In Korea during the Korean War, Plimsoll at age 33, and with very limited experience, had President Syngman Rhee, a much older man, often ask his advice. Plimsoll so impressed the Americans that when he was transferred to Canberra, the Americans, most unusually, requested Australia to send him back, which it did. In Washington in 1973, during a particularly difficult time when the newly elected Whitlam Government's foreign policy approach enraged President Nixon, the Australian Embassy had its normal access to the US Administration frozen. But the US Secretary of State, William Rogers, and his senior people, as well as other members of the Administration, openly flouted this prohibition, such was their desire to maintain communication with Plimsoll. In Moscow in 1977, a group of very senior officials of the Foreign Ministry called Plimsoll in to seek his personal advice about how the Soviet Union should react to Indira Gandhi's shock loss in the Indian elections, which had just occurred. His access to key people enhanced the value of the reports that he sent home – brief, clear, timely. They were closely read at all levels.

It was a great disappointment to Plimsoll that Menzies retired within a year of his becoming secretary in Canberra. Although on good terms with Holt and

14. Sir James Plimsoll

then Gorton, privately he was critical of both. Like others, he was contemptuous of McMahon. With the election of Whitlam, Plimsoll hoped for better things. He had known Whitlam and his wife for some time. His hopes were quickly dashed. It was the immaturity of style in foreign policy; and early on Plimsoll detected Whitlam's ignorance and lack of interest in economic policy. But they remained friends. Plimsoll and Fraser did not know each other well. Fraser was critical of Plimsoll's views about the Soviet Union. When Plimsoll became the first career officer to be high commissioner in London, after only six months Fraser announced that a politician would take his place.

Another way in which Plimsoll differed from the dwarfs and mandarins was in public relations. In those days dwarfs and mandarins were self-effacing, in the background. They rarely if ever uttered a word in public; public relations was up to the minister. Plimsoll was cast in that mould, but with a difference. He was ahead of his time as a public servant who was a confident communicator, who understood the importance of public relations, and was prepared to talk to journalists. When secretary of the department in November 1965 he gave the Norman Smith Memorial lecture on journalism at Melbourne University about Asian issues and the press; he appeared in a television documentary on the department; and, visiting Delhi in 1967, he appeared with his Indian counterpart in a press conference after annual official talks with the Indians. That Paul Hasluck, who as minister was hostile to the very existence of the media section of the department, was prepared to countenance the secretary engaging in these activities underlined his trust in Plimsoll. Plimsoll substantially ghostwrote two books by ministers he served, one by Dr Evatt in 1949, *The Task of Nations*,[7] and one in 1954 by Casey, *Friends and Neighbours*.[8] The first was about the United Nations by Evatt in his capacity as President of the United Nations General Assembly. Plimsoll, based in New York, also conducted negotiations on behalf of Evatt with the US publisher, compiled the index and checked the proofs. The second by Casey emphasised the importance of the Asian region to Australia.

Plimsoll had the usual attributes of a good diplomat, although to this should be added that he worked exceptionally hard, was endlessly curious, had a photographic memory, and was always very well informed on a wide variety of issues. And he had a certain gravitas in his bearing, partly because he looked older than he really was, which was helpful in his thirties and forties when dealing, as he frequently had to, with people who were 20 or more years older. On the other hand he was very private, upright, and socially conservative; and, while approachable, he often had difficulty with small talk. He was somewhat unworldly, and absentminded about details of daily living, such as depositing

---

7   H.V. Evatt, *The Task of Nations* (New York: Duell, Sloan and Pearce, 1949).
8   R.G. Casey, *Friends and Neighbours: Australia and the World* (Melbourne: Cheshire, 1954).

cheques that he received. His monastic, simple way of living, owning neither property nor car, often only one suit, did not change, like his absorption in his work. Plimsoll approved of the following description of John Crawford: 'a very intense man who lived his work day and night, and was always thinking when he was walking around.'[9] The description fits Plimsoll also.

When he had time, Plimsoll's main interests outside work were art, literature and music, in all of which he had considerable knowledge that he was sometimes able to deploy to advantage in his work. In art, while secretary of the department, he served on the interim committee of the National Gallery of Australia. In Moscow, he made a special personal contribution to fostering cultural relations. At Moscow State University he befriended the professor and dean of English and, at her invitation, he delivered a seminar a week for six months to graduate students and faculty members on various kinds of literature – English, Australian, American, other Commonwealth – also on punctuation and grammar. The dean was a strong personality, and she was of sufficient clout in the Communist Party to override objections to a Western ambassador lecturing the cream of Russian students during the Cold War.

Plimsoll was a major figure in what was an early, formative period in Australian foreign policy. He made a major contribution towards a greater realisation of the importance of Asian countries, notably India – about which he was ahead of his time in trying to raise interest. He was a considerable figure in the relationship with the United States. On the other hand, he held considerable reservations about China. Abroad, the post-war period was a time when Australia was a middle ranking country that had only recently found its voice in international affairs, but was little known. Filling this void was a task for many, but Plimsoll contributed significantly because of his stature and that he was so widely respected. Diplomacy was a little known profession in Australia when Plimsoll started during the 1940s. He helped set standards and style. At home he was in the vanguard in making Australian ministers and prime ministers come to realise the value to them of this new professional foreign service.

---

9   Plimsoll in conversation, 16.

www.ingramcontent.com/pod-product-compliance
Lightning Source LLC
Chambersburg PA
CBHW060929170426
43192CB00031B/2870